Business Games Handbook

About the Authors

ROBERT G. GRAHAM is associate professor of organizational behavior in the School of Business and Technology at Oregon State University. He was granted his B.S. from the University of Illinois, his M.B.A. and Ph.D. from The University of Texas.

Before joining the faculty at Oregon State, he was coordinator of the summer conference program and assistant to the director of the executive development program at The University of Texas, and while serving in this capacity he developed his interest in business games. A number of his many articles deal with games as a teaching and training technique. He is currently developing a national business games center on a foundation grant.

In addition to 12 years' industrial experience as sales manager and personnel manager of large national corporations, Dr. Graham is currently president of P.D.M., a consulting and research firm. His professional affiliations include the American Management Association, Academy of Management, Society for Personnel Administration, and Pacific Northwest Personnel Managers Association.

CLIFFORD F. GRAY is an associate professor of business administration at Oregon State University. He received degrees from Millikin University and Indiana University and was granted the D.B.A. from the University of Oregon. His teaching experience includes extensive use of business games in the university and in executive development programs. His research and numerous articles deal with business games as teaching and research devices and with the application of simulation to business problems. His industrial experience includes industrial engineering work with Blaw-Knox and U.S. Steel Corporation; serving as consultant to a wide variety of industrial and business organizations; and, currently, serving as vice president of the consulting firm of Management Research Associates. His professional affiliations include the Academy of Management, American Institute for Decision Sciences, and Association for Systems Management.

BUSINESS GAMES
HANDBOOK

Robert G. Graham

Clifford F. Gray

American Management Association, Inc.

Standard book number: 8144-5183-7

Library of Congress catalog card number: 76-76844

First printing

Preface

THE LITERATURE on business games has become almost as extensive as the number of games. For both teachers and those in the business world, this is a difficult situation. Of the multitude of games in existence, which is most appropriate for a particular purpose, for a particular group, or for a special teaching situation? Which games emphasize a given level of sophistication, or particular models, or mathematical procedures? Which games require computers and which do not? Which ones are best for "openers" and which are most effective in closing training sessions? Where are particular games available? What has been said about their use?

The purpose of this book is to help answer these questions by making readily available to training directors and all others interested in business games an organized listing and description of business games and their sources and to provide a source of sufficient data to help training personnel select games for a particular purpose.

The book developed as a result of a survey conducted by the authors in 1967. Information was sought from training directors and personnel managers of the 500 largest U.S. industrial corporations listed in *The Fortune Directory* of June 15, 1967. One aspect of the information obtained was that there was an apparent need for a source book which would answer, or attempt to answer, some of the questions posed above. We have attempted to address this need by dividing the book into three parts. The first includes readings which have been selected (1) to introduce the concept of the game approach to training, (?) to demonstrate how total enterprise or general purpose games are used by firms, (3) to show how special purpose games are used, and (4) to illustrate how industry games are used for training.

The second part presents abstracts of games currently being used. Each abstract includes a description of the game, the training purpose of the game, the decisions made by the participant, how the game is administered, and the source of our information. The games are grouped in the same manner as the articles: general purpose, special purpose, and industry games. Thus, for example, if a special purpose game seems to be relevant for a training program, the reader can refer to the special purpose readings section for information on how others have used special purpose games.

Part III is a bibliography which includes articles and books pertinent to business games. With few exceptions, articles dealing with operations research and simulation other than in a business game context have been excluded. Many of the articles listed in the bibliography are indexed to the business games in Part II. That is, all articles in the bibliography are numbered. These numbers are placed at the end of the game abstract to indicate which articles contain further information about the game. It is hoped this will further aid those selecting games.

We wish to thank all those who answered our questionnaires and made materials available for our use, and to express a special note of appreciation to the following persons who contributed abstracts.

B. Bruce Bare	Robert Hunstad
Richard F. Barton	Laurence Jacobs
H. N. Broom	Ronald L. Jensen
R. Gene Brown	Andrew M. McCosh
Frances E. Castleberry	Paul D. Miller
Stephen Cotler	Kenneth D. Ramsing
Richard V. Cotter	Erwin Rausch
Robert Fricker	Albert N. Schrieber
Earl I. Fuller	Thomas N. Shaw
John L. Fulmer	Bernard Shorr
R. Wayne Gober	Burnard H. Sord
Paul S. Greenlaw	Sven Sundqvist
Mack Hanan	Robert L. Trewatha
J. L. Heskett	James S. Wehrly
Richard M. Hodgetts	D. Clay Whybark
Peter House	G. F. Wollastan

We hope we have not omitted anyone's name and offer sincere apologies if we have inadvertently done so.

Special thanks are due to Professor Byron Newton of Oregon State University for his time and counsel, to Erwin Rausch and Jeffrey Smith for their valuable contributions, to Mary Gray for editorial advice, and to the many typists who helped in the preparation of this book.

We would especially like to thank Professor Milton Valentine of Oregon State University for his many hours of excellent work on this project.

ROBERT G. GRAHAM
CLIFFORD F. GRAY

Corvallis, Oregon
May 1969

Contents

Industry Games   377

ADVERTISING

AEROSPACE

AGRI-BUSINESS

Introduction

Iꜰ ɪ ᴄᴏᴜʟᴅ just dispose of my experience for half of what it cost me, I'd be rich." Clearly, any device which would allow the acquisition of experience in an inexpensive manner would be popular, to say the least. One of the most durable and widespread answers to the problem of acquiring experience has been the use of games as a teaching-learning tool. From ancient Egypt to the 19th century German *Kriegspiel* and the 20th century Monopoly craze, games have been used, formally and informally, as methods of training. The specific application of games to executive and management development has been a very recent advancement resulting from a number of interacting forces.

With the increasing general recognition of the importance of the management profession has come insistence on better and shorter methods of acquiring management experience—at least vicariously. The force of this demand can be shown by a brief examination of one developmental sequence. The American Management Association generated "Top Management Decision Simulation" in 1956 and used it at Saranac Lake in 1957. Within a year, as Bellman notes,[1]* a number of games modeled after the AMA simulation were used in various universities around the country.[2] Within ten years Klasson[3] and Dale and Klasson[4] surveyed the field and found that more than two-thirds of the 90 responding major collegiate schools of business were experimenting with gaming techniques. In a survey just completed by the authors, 125 deans of schools of business were asked

* All references are listed under "Notes to the Text," which appear at the ends of chapters.

17

for information about the present use of games in their schools. Of 92 replies, all but eight indicated that they were using at least one game, with the majority using more than one.

A second force toward the development of management games has been the emergence of related fields, operations research and the mathematical and statistical developments surrounding the "theory of games" as conceived by von Neumann and Morgenstern[5] and more recently applied and extended by Siegel and Fouraker,[6] among others. Operations research is a quantitative, analytical, experimental means of assessing the implications of alternative courses of action in management decision situations.[7] It began with the techniques developed for determining the location of British radar interception stations during World War II. The relationship between this problem and war gaming is readily apparent. In the field of business gaming, a key concept is simulation. Essentially, simulation involves the development of a description of the organization and its situation which is sufficiently complete and accurate to allow either a computer or a team of judges to provide, within the game, logical outcomes to particular decisions. Once such a description is obtained it can be adjusted, simplified, or extrapolated to provide for sequential decision making in the game context.

A third pressure which has shaped modern gaming has been the educational use of various techniques involving role playing and case studies or both. In one sense all gaming involves role playing since the individual participants are asked to assume the situation assigned; similarly, gaming involves case studies because many games can be traced to individual or collective analyses of particular cases and because the nature of the post-game analysis takes on many of the qualities of a case study. The moderately widespread use of techniques involving role changes—for example, sociodrama or Moreno's psychodrama with the acting out of particular roles in controlled situations—has helped people to accept the notion as something more than children's "let's pretend." Case studies sometimes also involve role playing. For example, a personnel manager may be asked to take action in a particular situation involving, say, discipline, and the effectiveness of his actions is discussed both by observers and by the employee (role player) to be disciplined.

Case studies fall into four general types:
   1. In-basket exercises, designed after Fredericksen's original problem in which the participant is asked to assume the role of a manager and take action on a dozen or more letters, memos, or papers.[8]

2. Critical incident processes, popularized by Paul and Faith Pigors,[9] which call for the selection of a particular course of action on the basis of certain information. The instructor then provides additional information *only on the basis of what is asked*. Typically an arbitration case may be used, with terminal discussion directed toward the reasons participants failed to probe deeply enough for additional information.
3. Case studies tending to be games. For example, unlike the arbitration cases, "Operation Suburbia," which was designed by A. A. Zoll of Boeing, is more nearly a game in that it involves decision making in a competitive situation where five companies with differing goals and assets decide and negotiate, facing problems in decision making and communication both inside and outside their groups.[10]
4. Sequential case studies such as the "Case of the Frightened File Clerks"[11] in which a decision situation involving automation is used and alternate courses of action are open. One of these courses must be selected and the consequences dealt with through three or more decision sequences—each, in turn, involving new developments.

There has been considerable recent discussion about devices to assist teaching and learning: TV, microphotographic film, programmed books, programmed computers; all of these along with games are simply methods of *providing vicarious experience*. Some consideration of learning and vicarious experience, then, should prove of assistance to the training director concerned with selecting and using games.

To begin with, a game or any teaching-learning aid may have any or all of several functions: It may teach a particular model of reality, it may serve as a dramatizing device, or it may serve as a method and inducement for practice and carryover to the "outside reality." Games may simplify or complicate. They may be readily acceptable or productive of resistance and, therefore, they may deal with attitudes as well as specific cognitive materials. For the director faced with selecting a game, two kinds of information are necessary in addition to the description of the game itself: the kind of model on which the game is based (including its logic or mathematics) and the approach to learning which is to be undertaken.

The practical problem of learning will be considered first. Somehow, many of the books discussing games have considered the "laws of learning" as having been canonized in or before 1940. Under most circumstances this approach to learning is almost directly counter to that required for the effective use of the case approach. For the sake of clarity, however, this laws of learning approach provides an easy approach to some more modern developments. Without discussing the underlying theories, "learning-1940"[12] holds that:

1. In order for two events to become associated—for example, "proper performance" and "reward"—the events must occur within a certain time interval (the law of contiguity).
2. The more "satisfying" a result, the more likely that learning will occur (the law of effect). This implies that a "felt need" must be satisfied; a number of educators spend time initiating felt needs so that satisfaction may be developed.
3. The rate of learning increases as the response that the learner makes to the situation or feels in the situation develops (the law of intensity). Presumably, the greater the number of senses involved, the quicker the learning.
4. Learning is more rapid when the material is organized into meaningful relationships (the law of organization).
5. Material previously learned will facilitate the learning of new material if the same responses are used, as in the familiar sequences of organization-known-to-unknown, general-to-specific. Transfer to new situations will be faster and easier when there are identical elements present (the law of facilitation) and more difficult where different responses are required; athletes are sometimes enjoined not to engage in other sports for fear of impairing performance in their specialty (the law of interference).
6. People tend to do what they most recently did; "practice makes perfect" (the law of exercise).

More recent approaches[13] to learning modify or deny the 1940 laws as follows:

1. Time is subjective and humans particularly have the ability to see connections across long periods; in the use of cases or sequential games the recognition and encouragement of this ability is absolutely essential. The participant must see that action taken at Time 1 had no observable consequences at Time 2 but had devastating or highly rewarding consequences at Time 3.

2. Reward or satisfaction is a highly individual (and often not conscious) matter; three subordinates may all say that promotion is one of their goals and believe it—but for one, the promotion will be a positive threat with its

new responsibilities, changed relationships, and new uncertainties; for the second, it will be both a threat and an opportunity; for the third, promotion will indeed be a reward and a satisfaction.

3. That learning occurs under motivation is obvious—but there is clearly an optimum level and type of motivation for each individual. To paraphrase Bruner, under too extreme motivation the consequences of success become too chancy and the consequences of error become too grave with the result that the individual falls back on stereotyped, familiar, and therefore comfortable behavior and does not learn at all. Similarly, "overloading the channel," or using more senses than the individual can simultaneously handle, interferes with learning for many persons. (Most training directors are familiar with the postsession complaint, "Just too much to handle, and it all seemed so academic.")

4. The learning sequence must be meaningful. The problem is, of course, meaningful sequences for whom? The recent work of Bruner and others has clearly indicated that allowing the learner to select his own internal coding produces faster and more durable learning than any superimposed patterns. For example, when required to learn the sequence "chair-tree," some children think "chairs are made of wood which comes from trees," and others, "I sat on a chair under a tree"; each will learn equally rapidly. Some may think cause-effect, some effect-cause, but *if they are forced to adopt a pattern not their own, they will learn very slowly, if at all.* The great advantage of some games in this respect is that they can present the individual with a vicarious reality and allow him to deal with it *in his own terms* without the didactic and artificial interference of an unfamiliar sequence being superimposed from outside the learner. Again, training directors will be familiar with the complaints "I just can't follow it" or "He just doesn't make sense to me" which often come after traditional lecture procedures.

5. Facilitation is a complex problem. In motor or mechanical skills, the idea of identical elements facilitating transfer of learning from one situation to another seems to hold: running for speed in track (particularly for short distances) seems to transfer to, say, football—but only for speed, not to broken-field running. There is, however, a factor recognized by training directors and others which seems to be a general one; *in actually learning, one learns how to learn* and thus becomes more flexible and capable of a wider range of behaviors and adjustments. On the other hand, there is the typical criticism of material presented with no relevance to context: "This game doesn't have anything for me because I'm in transportation and it deals with the Air Force."

6. The law of exercise seemingly needs to be modified in a number of ways. As a start, "practice makes perfect" only if you enjoy the practice; otherwise you may simply avoid the whole situation. For example, witness the child forced to practice the piano who sometimes learns only to hate the piano. One may also learn to avoid something by practicing, consciously, to remember that it is undesirable.[14]

From the management viewpoint, the effects of any training must be considered pragmatically. If games produce better managers, excellent; but the proof of management is observable capability, not reaction to games or training programs. Management skills can be learned. The analysis of learning-1968 suggests that at most levels skills can be best learned through the vicarious experiences provided by games rather than through lectures or similar didactic methods. Games, particularly where the element of competition is accepted and does not become too strong, tend to provide their own motivation. They provide practice in a way that nothing else can. The dilemma created by the teacher's need to dissect the subject into small, highly detailed units and the students' need to see and experience a totality is neatly solved by dividing the game into sections, by providing for commentary and analysis afterward, and by the discussions naturally generated among the participants by the game itself.

These circumstances suggest some conditions for the use and selection of games. First, there must be an atmosphere of permissiveness and exploration if the game is to be used for learning purposes. Second, the structure of the game should coincide with the level of the group—the less sophisticated the participants, the simpler and more didactic should be the games selected. However, the game must not become too consistent, an end in itself. If it is too obvious and consistent it will tend to reinforce that common cause of difficulties, the "gambler's fallacy"—since seven has come up ten times running, it can (or can't) come up again—that is, the tendency to rely too heavily on a naïve and familiar interpretation of past experience. If the game is too highly motivating or too frustrating, the advantages of the game as a learning device may be lost. The observed tendency of some participants, particularly under conditions of difficulty with some machine games, has been to try to beat the machine—that is, to second-guess the program and programmer and to make decisions devoted to doing well in the game while denying that the game *has any reality in and of itself*.

Third, the game should have some rather immediate feedback to the participants. Both hand scoring and machine games sometimes involve delays during which the continuity of experience is lost.

Fourth, the rules of the game need to be stated clearly and be accepted by the participants. The stated rules are both substantive and procedural. A number of games—in order to clarify the situation and simplify the scoring—prohibit major price changes, or forbid the participants to reduce sales forces below certain minimum figures or vary production or expenditures beyond specified amounts.

Finally, the selected game should be just within the capability level of the participants. If it is too easy, it will be dismissed; if it is too difficult, it will most likely be frustrating and depressive.

From the players' point of view, games ought to differentiate clearly, and for easily discernible reasons, between the participating teams. At the outset this helps develop competition, but it introduces some serious dangers. The real purpose of the game is the learning experience. If too much emphasis is placed on winning, then the participants are likely to adopt strategies which are either not exploratory (and therefore produce less learning) or which are directly disruptive. In interactive games, losing teams occasionally attempt to wreck competition by adopting extreme strategies rather than trying to improve their own situation. (There is an element of reality here that can sometimes be used by the game administrators in later discussions.) Winning teams frequently play it close for the duration of the game in order to protect their winning position. Neither group learns as much as it might.

The area of feelings is one of the most important and neglected aspects of the game situation. Although it is not within the scope of this book to consider this aspect of gaming, several general observations may be appropriate. Some preliminary help can be obtained by stressing that learning hurts, and some terminal help can be obtained by reminding the group to refocus on the learning achieved and not on the success in the game. Clearly, the winning team learned less since it knew the answers, etc. Another form of keeping the learning clearly in focus is to include in discussions some indication of how and why key decisions were reached. This allows both winners and losers to gain by derivative insight. ("We nearly made that decision.") The game administrator must remember, too, that the attack on the game, or the reality of the game, is often an avenue for the expression of the frustration and hostility generated in the play itself, and that unless qualified professionals are available to help, it is not always advisable to deal directly with these feelings even though their expression disturbs the illusion of reality which the game seeks to develop.

One of the unstated threads running through the previous paragraphs has been the need for high fidelity simulation. A counter thread has been the need to appropriately simplify and adapt games to the participants. These bring to the fore the problems of simulation itself. What is to be taught? What is to be simulated? And that ultimate question: What is reality? Remembering that the processes of learning are also learned by learning, the designer or selector of a game must keep in mind the fidelity and underlying logic of the game itself. An approach to the problem is to consider the construction of a simple prototype game. Assumption: $Q = f(P)$; that is, quantity is a function of price and of price only. For computational purposes, such a function is usually normalized or made into a smooth curve and a zero point set so that a refrigerator selling at \$750 has a zero demand function and one selling at \$75 has a maximum demand function. The resulting quantity curve would then appear:

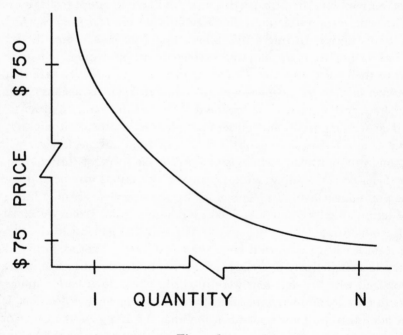

Figure 1

Algebraic manipulation allows the curve to be adjusted to any pricing situation. Similarly, tables of formulae may be devised or derived for the relationships between cost reduction and research and developmental expenditures (Figure 2); maintenance expenditures and breakdown probability (Figure 3);

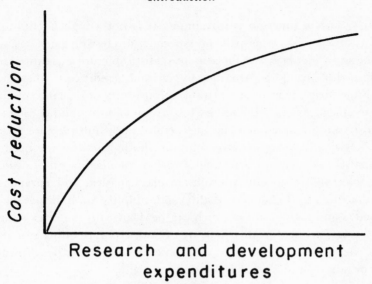

Figure 2

market potential and price versus advertising, sales force size, incentive bonuses, etc. These may be programmed for computer use, translated into tables for manual scoring, or, as a single example, combined into a company decision effectiveness and total market potential formula.[15]

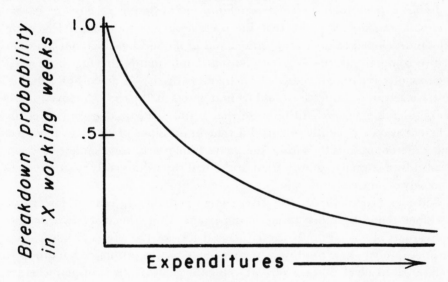

Figure 3

Clearly, such a function is too simple. It is not a high fidelity approach to reality and would not provide an especially interesting game basis. On the other hand, a model based on a more realistic picture of reality could become incredibly complex. Alternate use of funds, credit costs where involved, advertising effects, market attractiveness, continuity of demand, product and company image, availability, service history, and a host of other factors might have to be programmed and the interactions and multiple interactions calculated. Basically, there are two solutions, both based on the need for the participants to experience a feeling of reality: one is to assume a model and use it, selecting a logically appropriate mathematical and parameter complex; the other is to observe reality and simplify it, limiting the game's parameters and logic to those which can be dealt with under existing conditions. Games included in this book are of both types. In either case the game user or designer must examine the consequences of all possible decisions (likely or not) or limit the decisions that are made.[16]

Another problem involving fidelity is likely to plague game designer, trainer, and participant alike. In real life most decisions are made on the basis of incomplete, uncertain, and inaccurate information. Case studies have generally given incomplete but accurate information; machine games, by their nature, tend to operate in terms of accurate rather than inaccurate information. But different games and certainly different educational results can be derived from the same parameters and mathematical models *using differing patterns of supplied information and differing patterns of player group interaction.* Suppose that the oversimplified model for refrigerator sales is developed to include inventory and profit and loss data, but that one of two competing teams is given additional information having to do with the cost of servicing guarantees (which affects profit) on models of differing cost. Clearly, the two teams would be in different ball parks. Moreover, there is considerable research to indicate that teams structured or organized in different ways frequently obtain different impressions of the data provided and different results.[17] Within the game framework, for example, a team headed by a strongly authoritarian leader will react differently from one that is loosely organized.

Consider a competitive, interactive game where the aggregate of forces and decisions made by other teams is important. Even the more experienced individuals often have only a very general idea of the effects of advertising or price. Under these conditions the tendency for the authoritarian group is to respond to a lack of success by attacking the game or the manager, whereas the less organized group has less formal structure to attack and may, over the game period, evolve an efficient leadership. From the game designer's viewpoint this creates a serious problem—should he simplify the model to make it more acceptable and playable, or should he stick with the model with greater verisimilitude? From the viewpoint of the game selector this consideration indicates that he must carefully choose games appropriate both to task and to player group. Basically, the underlying problem is that of fidelity, of creating a game which is at key points isomorphic with reality, but which has been simplified and shortened sufficiently to emphasize the key parameters. This suggests that it is most important for the game selector to examine the underlying logic, mathematics, and assumptions of the game with his particular group of players in mind.

In games where the primary focus is on profits, the situation is different from those in which the focus is on minimizing total costs, and neither of these conditions may in the immediate sense be a direct contribution to the long-range survival of a real company. The games included here indicate a range of ideas, logics, and mathematical approaches; these need not be understood by the players but the selector must understand them.

With the widespread and increasing use of games, it is not surprising to find that there are objectors and dissenters. Again, the reasons center around either the assumptions about teaching-learning or about the reality of the games themselves and about the uses to which games are put—all of these considered against the cost of the game in both time and dollars. Teaching cost is less than executive time cost, and game cost is usually less than either. Apart from the question of whether or not games actually modify managerial behavior, there is a hidden factor in the question of cost effectiveness. In the process of preparing, analyzing, or criticizing a game, the individual is forced to reexamine his own beliefs, assumptions about decision making, and approaches to management. If the goals of gaming include an increase in flexibility and adaptability, the advantages of such forced reexamination must be considered. But how do we know that games actually change behavior in a desirable way when the participants are on the job? The answer—as with other forms of teaching—is "We don't," apart from a kind of clinical observation and intuitive evaluation. What can be said, however, is that in comparison with other forms of teaching-learning, games provide a higher level of involvement, a situation more nearly identical to the job situation, and a more realistic opportunity for both experimentation and evaluation. At the very least, games provide both a stimulating introduction and a transferable closing to a situation acceptable to participants and learning theorists-1940 and learning theorists-1968 alike.

Another criticism of gaming, the question of validity, has been discussed previously at some length. Obviously, there are games with limited fidelity and others with high fidelity; some appropriate for one situation and some for a great many. The problem for the selector is to find the best game for his group. Validity may be limited because the decision area is defined too simply or too narrowly, or the game is too far removed from—or too similar to—the participant's own experience. For example, the participant may believe with deep conviction that advertising is the one best way to promote sales or that advertising has no effect at all. Here careful introduction of the game may be of critical importance so that the participants understand both the source of the game and its presumed validity.

A more serious objection to gaming arises from the fact that most games depend on groups, so that some observers feel that specific needs of an individual may be overlooked or ignored. Moreover, under some circumstances the group reaction may be one of embarrassment for an organization or company when, for example, the sales manager's team does poorly against the team of salesmen, or the company vice president fails to emerge as a team leader. In this case, too, careful planning and preparation and careful selection of the game may avoid difficulty.

The game is a technique, not an end in itself, and it is definitely not a complete training program. With this in mind, the question may be posed, "For what purposes can games be used?" They are as follows:

1. Teaching specific items—the importance of planned and critically timed decisions, PERT, or specific routine items such as Civil Service regulations, or particular decision-assisting tools.
2. Teaching general behavioral factors such as the importance of flexible, organized efforts, the need for inclusion of appropriate persons and factors in decision making, the importance of a balance among managerial functions, the matching of task-person-group, and so on.
3. Teaching the power of the modeling, mathematical, or scientific approaches to business problems.
4. Generating a high degree of involvement as either an introduction or a conclusion to a training program.

This is especially important in generating enthusiasm and involvement if the game is clearly relevant—i.e., if it uses a similar industry, if it is drawn from the immediate context, etc. The additional bonus to such involvement is rapport and a basis for productive discussion. Whenever any of these purposes is involved, a game should be considered. A game is only part of a program; otherwise it is like an engine without an airplane, capable of generating noise and horsepower but without motion or direction. Here, by way of illustration, is the 1957 AMA Executive Decision-Making Course with suggested games which might be used at various points in the program.

Course Outline[18]

THE EXECUTIVE DECISION-MAKING PROCESS

A. Steps in Decision Making—Its Place in the Administrative Process
   1. Definition of problem
   2. Development of solution
      (a) the impact of past decisions and higher level decisions
      (b) practical aspects—errors most frequently made and their correction
   3. Causes and effects of indecisiveness
B. Role of Diagnosis and Creativity in Decision Making
C. Breathing Life into Decisions
D. Ruler or Rogue: The Executive's Own Decision

ORGANIZING FOR EFFECTIVE DECISION MAKING

A. Importance of an Effective Organization: Proper Relationships Between Major Organizational Functions
B. Organizing People for Decision Making
   1. Delegation—assigning duties
      (a) who's on first? solving the riddle of relationships
      (b) decision making as a catalyst for coordination
   2. Communications
      (a) getting the message through
      (b) conveying meanings and motivation
C. Maximizing Contribution to Decision Making from Others

PLANNING—ITS ROLE IN EXECUTIVE DECISION MAKING

A. Determining Objectives and Goals: Long-Range vs. Short-Range Considerations
B. Need for Long-Range Planning to Provide a Framework for Decision Making, to Simplify the Decision-Making Process, to Avoid Possible Overlap and Duplication of Effort in Decision Areas

C. Establishing and Evaluating Plans
   1. Target practice
   2. Means to an end
   3. Milestoning
D. Effect of Company Objectives and Policies on Planning
E. Tools and Techniques Required for Improved Planning
   1. The role of research
   2. How to make theory useful in business practice
   3. Contributions from statistical, mathematical, and computational techniques
      (a) the elusive behavior of average
      (b) rolling the dice
      (c) systems simulation—a laboratory experiment for business
      (d) enter the longhair—mathematics in business
      (e) the electronic computer
 F. Handling Problems of Time and Personnel in Planning
 G. Coordination Between Departments in Overall Planning
 H. Reporting Financial Data for Decision Making
 I. Profit Planning
   1. Objectives
   2. Scope
   3. Limitations

REVIEWING AND REAPPRAISING PAST DECISIONS

A. Reviewing Past Decisions and Resulting Performance
   1. Analyzing variances from planned action and expected results
B. Integrated Data Processing Contributions to More Rapid and Efficient Decision Review and Reappraisal
C. Minimizing Uncertainty, Determining Probability of Outcome, Developing Alternative Solutions Through:
   1. Operations research
   2. Statistical analysis
   3. Other mathematical techniques
D. Revising Decisions

As the outline suggests, games can be effectively integrated with more traditional methods of teaching-learning and the two processes can reinforce each other. A game may reveal a weakness in an area of instruction, suggesting emphasis on that area in following sessions. Interest lacking at a lecture may be stimulated by a game. Preplanning must be considerable but the avenue for spontaneous adjustment must be left open. Time and resources must also be considered. Time for computation is particularly important in manual games, as is availability of the computer in machine-scored games. By scheduling games in the late afternoon and evening, computer time may be more readily available. Also, in some circumstances the time lapse for feedback to the participants is apparently faster since they may have results of their action the following morning with little intervening activity. One of the most effective program positions for a game is as an icebreaker. Carefully selected, the game can provide both a model for later learning and a focus for discussion during subsequent sessions. Teams can be used, compared, broken up.

In integrating the game into the training program the evaluation of results is always of key importance. As has been suggested, the evaluation process may be both formal and informal, but the focus of evaluation is vital. Both the game and evaluation must be combined with a particular teaching-learning situation in which, ultimately, victory in the game is less important than the skills or material to be learned. Evaluation and discussion are best only when all members of each team are present (if possible), so that all of the game players may be heard and participant involvement in both the evaluation process and any ensuing derivative insight may be optimal. Unless the game is obviously being used as a testing device, heavy emphasis on the outcome should be avoided. (And the administrator, particularly, should remember that no game is either participant- or administrator-proof.) Evaluation must strive to be a summarizing link between the program, the game, the participants, and the outside reality. Evaluation often includes the evaluation of the session as a whole. There is a dangerous tendency to be swayed by what people say they like and by player enthusiasm or reports of personality changes. No test other than the practical one can assess what a participant gained; in fact, the very act of testing and evaluating may change the individual. At best, the authors can simply reaffirm their faith in the power of the game technique, remembering that the game may be only as productive as its administration and circumstances allow.

When the training director selects a game, these steps should be followed:

1. Define the characteristics of the course, the participant group and the administrative staff, the situation in terms of goals and desired behaviors.

2. Select materials, including the game(s), with those considerations in mind, allowing for time, finances, and computing facilities (if needed).
3. Allow several alternate routes and choices if possible, and in general select no game that the administrator has not participated in or at least observed.
4. Schedule the game(s) for maximum dramatic impact and utility, with general and complex games usually at the beginning or end and single-purpose games typically in the middle of the program.

The problem of dramatic impact seems to involve five aspects of a game: (1) verisimilitude, (2) involvement, (3) interaction, (4) instructions, and (5) capability for significance or generalization.[19] The ideal game has sufficient resemblance to the participants' own circumstances for them to recognize parallels and sufficient distance for them to be able to learn without being under too much threat. As a general rule, if the material appears threatening and if the idea of reality can be preserved, it is better to select a game (and training circumstances) removed from the daily life of the participants.

Next in importance is involvement. This should be at a feeling level, not only at the intellectual level. This means that the individual participant must somehow be induced to commit his ego to doing well in the game. Competition is often useful in this, but, as has been indicated, the competitive aspects rather than the learning aspects may become the focus of the game. Sometimes out-of-the-group competition can be used. For example, the administrator might say, "Most other groups solve this problem in twenty minutes" or "Most groups double company assets." This aspect of competition, too, often causes an undesirable focus of attention on "How did we do?" in comparison, rather than on "What did *we* do?"

Both involvement and verisimilitude depend on subjective probability. This, of course, involves the element of chance which, in learning, presents another serious problem, since the game focus may be on doing well by allowing for chance factors and playing probabilistic strategies rather than on making sound decisions or following appropriate and high-quality management decisions. The problem is the appropriate inclusion of random factors: If they are entirely excluded the game will lack reality; if they are included too frequently the game will not allow the participants to focus on quality decisions.

To some extent factors such as the part played by chance, the relative reality of the simulation, and the individual participant's role relative to the game can be controlled in the instructions. One suggestion which is sometimes made is that the game is a kind of "self-administered evaluation" of personal or habitual management style. (This must be said carefully, if at all, for some groups will feel that the whole process is a selection device and therefore they will operate under considerable threat.) Unless the point of the game is variation in management style, the patterns of interaction should be as realistic as possible. The end product is presumably different, reinforced, or improved behavior for participants. Hence the need for identical elements.

On the other hand, a high probability, high significance game is likely to become a defensive guessing game with participant concerns focused on *defense* of self, position, or previous beliefs. A low probability, low significance game is not defensible for any reason and should be avoided. A high probability, low significance game will result in little significant learning and frequent, usually trivial, often unrelated output. Also, a high probability, low significance game produces a situation in which learning or latent learning may occur, but in which the participants will not find or express prolonged interest. Low probability, high significance games are likely to focus undue attention on individual personality patterns to the exclusion of generalized principles. For example, in a five-company, competitive game, played over more than a dozen periods, one company may obtain a one-sided advantage which not only is unrealistic but which also makes it most difficult for the trainer to abstract principles of wide usefulness since the idiosyncratic behavior of the "winning" team may easily be seen as the correct approach.

The games selected for this book were chosen on the basis of five criteria: First, the game should be readily available for use. A number of outstanding games have limited circulation either because proprietary rights have been maintained or because special professional knowledge or skill is required in their administration. Second, games were chosen for their usability, impact, dramatizing value, participant interest, and efficiency as vicarious learning tools. Third, games were chosen for their appropriateness to a wide variety of business and management circumstances—*The Crisis Game*[20] and similar military and war games were excluded. Fourth, games were chosen on the basis of timeliness and the general currency of their important concepts. Finally, games were chosen to provide a meaningful variety, a sampling of both content and style, so that the reader might have readily available a number of different models and approaches.

For ready use the games have been grouped into two major classifications: total enterprise games and special purpose games. In addition, games associated only with specific industries have been identified in a third classification. The articles included in this book were selected by the authors as contemporary and of special interest to those who are directly concerned with training, rather than to those who are more directly concerned with the constructs of operations research, game theory, and simulation. The underlying approach has been practical rather than, hopefully, professional.

The available literature shows a heavy stress on theoretical articles, mostly published in the early to mid-1960's. These dates have sometimes been interpreted as demonstrating a decline in interest in games. Actually, this decline is more apparent than real. It results from the end of the honeymoon period as well as delegation of game development and administration to universities or to training consultants and their companies. The demonstration of the usefulness of games, however, is no longer a question. As vicarious experience, a game must be simplified and compacted reality—but a limited reality which can be manipulated, analyzed, and discussed, and for which the results are not permanent except as learning. The present phase is one of testing through use and application. In the opinion of the authors, Robbins' statement from the ASTD *Journal* stands: "Most people [attending] . . . agreed that within a couple of years simulation probably will be the most widely used tool of management training."[21]

NOTES TO THE TEXT

[1] Richard Bellman, "Top Management Decisions and Simulation Processes," *The Journal of Industrial Engineering*, Vol. IX, No. 5 (September-October 1958), p. 464.

[2] One of the problems with the general literature dealing with games and simulations is the inconsistent use of terms. Some writers use "simulation" to mean only the formal mathematical models which have been tested or derived from reality; others use "games" and "simulations" (and sometimes even "models") interchangeably. In some discussions nonmachine games are identified as "games" and computer-based games as "simulations" whether or not they have been checked with "reality." The practice in this book has been to use "games" as the generic term, covering all types of formal interaction in vicarious situations, and "simulations" to identify the more formal, developed, checked, and mathematically explicit interactions.

[3] Charles R. Klasson, "Business Gaming—A Progress Report," *Academy of Management Journal*, Vol. VII, No. 3 (September 1964), pp. 175-176.

[4] A. G. Dale and C. R. Klasson, *Business Gaming—A Survey of American Collegiate Schools of Business* (Austin, Texas: University of Texas Bureau of Business Research, 1964), p. 2.

[5] J. Von Neumann and O. Morgenstern, *Theory of Games and Economic Behavior* (Princeton, New Jersey: Princeton University Press, 1944).

[6] S. Siegel and L. E. Fouraker, *Bargaining and Group Decision Making* (New York: McGraw-Hill Book Company, 1960).

[7] C. West Churchman, Russell L. Ackoff, and E. Leonard Arnoff, *Introduction to Operations Research* (New York: John Wiley & Sons, 1957), pp. 1-56.

[8] Norman Fredericksen, D. R. Saunders, and Barbara Wand, "The In-Basket Test,"

Psychological Monographs: General and Applied (American Psychological Corporation, Vol. LXXI, No. 9).

9 Faith Pigors and Paul Pigors, *Case Method in Human Relations: The Incident Process* (New York: McGraw-Hill Book Company, 1961), pp. 32-35.

10 Allen A. Zoll, *Dynamic Management Education* (Seattle, Washington: Management Education Associates, 1966).

11 C. Goetzinger and M. Valentine, "The Case of the Frightened File Clerks" (Boulder, Colorado: Institute of Behavioral Science, Division of Communication Research, University of Colorado, 1963).

12 E. R. Hilgard, *Theories of Learning* (New York: Appleton-Century-Crofts).

13 Jerome Bruner, *et al.*, *Studies in Cognitive Growth* (New York: John Wiley & Sons, 1966).

14 K. Dunlap, *Habits: Their Making and Unmaking* (New York: Liveright, 1932), pp. 194-231.

15 Detailed discussions of simulation can be found in P. S. Greenlaw, L. W. Herron, and R. H. Rawdon, *Business Simulation in Industrial and University Education* (Englewood Cliffs, New Jersey: Prentice-Hall, Inc., 1962); J. M. Kibbee, C. J. Craft, and Burt Nanus, *Management Games, a New Technique for Executive Development* (New York: Reinhold Book Corporation, 1961); and C. W. Churchman, R. L. Ackoff, and E. L. Arnoff, *Introduction to Operations Research* (New York: John Wiley & Sons, 1957).

16 There is a third solution provided by some of the very early war games but not generally included in the games listed in this book; it is the provision of a referee or team of judges presumably familiar with both reality and the logic and mathematical parameters of the game being played. This allows for greater flexibility and greater dissatisfaction on the part of the participants. Somehow the glamour of the machine outweighs for most people the flexibility of the judges.

17 N. Domenico, J. Winterton, J. Paciko, *An Integrated Study of Communication in Variously Structured Task Oriented Groups* (unpublished M.A. Thesis, Department of Speech, University of Colorado, 1963).

18 J. M. Kibbee, C. J. Craft, and B. Nanus, *Management Games: A New Technique for Executive Development*, p. 57. Reproduced by permission of Reinhold Book Corporation, a subsidiary of Chapman-Reinhold, Inc., New York, 1961.

19 C. Goetzinger and M. Valentine, "Business and Professional Communicators Training Programs," *Today's Speech*, Vol. XI, No. 4 (November 1963), pp. 10-11.

20 Sidney F. Griffin, *The Crisis Game* (Garden City, New York: Doubleday & Co., Inc., 1965).

21 Robert Robbins, "Decision Making Simulation Through Business Games," *Journal of the American Society of Training Directors*, Vol. XIII, No. 8 (September 1959), pp. 12-19.

Part I

A

Introductory Readings

Business Games: A Technique for Teaching Decision-Making

John R. Carson

WHAT ARE business games? They have been variously defined as follows:

Business games are simplified mathematical abstractions of a situation related to the business world. The game participants, either individually or in groups, manage a whole firm or an aspect of it, by making business decisions for successive periods.[1]

A business simulation or game may be defined as a sequential decision-making exercise structured around a model of a business operation, in which participants assume the role of managing the simulated operation.[2]

The key words in these two definitions are "successive periods" and "sequential." *Business games are case studies with feedback and a time dimension added.*

One of the major criticisms of the case study method has always been that the student could never measure the effect of his decisions. He has only the

At the time this article was published, JOHN R. CARSON was Plant Controller, Hunt-Wesson Foods, Inc., Bayonne, N.J.

Reprinted with permission from *Management Accounting*, October 1967.

subjective, qualitative judgment of the instructor and his fellow students to measure the correctness of his answers to problems. In a business game the student sees the impact his decisions have upon future events in the reports fed back to him by the game process. He can react to these effects and make new decisions in light of the altered circumstances. Thus, just as in the real business world, business simulation decision-making is a continuing process with later decisions tempered by the effects of those that went before. In these games the results of decisions can be measured quantitatively; bad decisions lead to bad results which can usually be measured numerically. In fact, one of the criticisms raised against games is that they exclude qualitative factors; there is no subjectivity.

Types of Business Games

Business games generally fall into two classifications: general management or total enterprise games and functional games.

The *general management games* are designed to teach decision-making at the top management level where all major functional areas of the total enterprise are involved in achieving fundamental organizational objectives, such as maximum profit, return on investment, or attainment of certain sales levels or a certain share of the market. In one general management game, the players are divided into teams of four or five players each. Each team represents one company engaged in the manufacturing of up to three different products. The teams (companies) are in competition with one another.

The periods of play are quarter years for which the players must make various decisions—for the firm as a whole and for each product of the firm. After making these decisions, each team receives a set of reports on results for that quarter: for the firm as a whole, for each product of the firm and for the industry. With these results in hand, a new series of decisions for the next quarter is then made.

Generalized games of this type are designed to teach objective decision-making through experimentation, evaluation, and modification.

Functional games are intended to teach specific skills in a particular management area such as marketing, production, inventory control, finance, or some other. They are aimed at teaching better decision-making at the middle and lower levels of management.

In these games, instead of trying to maximize attainment of some organizational goal, the players are usually working to minimize costs through efficient operation. This type of game is most useful in teaching the value of a specific set of decision rules such as the EOQ in inventory control. Teams normally do not compete with one another in a market, but try to get the highest possible score relative to a perfect operation.

OTHER CHARACTERISTICS OF BUSINESS GAMES

Some other characteristics of business games which should be noted are: interactive or non-interactive, individual or group, simple or complex.

A game is interactive if the decisions of one group affect the results achieved by other groups. Their decisions interact and they are competing with one another. The total industry games are usually of this type while functional games are more often non-interactive.

All games can be played by individuals, but the general management type is usually played by groups while functional games are more often designed for teaching the individual.

Games can be quite simple and still be used to illustrate management principles. The more complex games are played with electronic computers. The decision parameters of the game are programmed into the computer, and it analyzes the decisions made and feeds back results.

Many of the more simple games can be scored by hand. Many that can be scored by hand are still scored by computer where one is available because of the speed with which it produces results, less chance for errors, and neater reports.

WHAT DO MANAGEMENT GAMES TEACH?

What if anything do these games teach? First, they teach the importance of planning and timely decision-making. This is done through three types of time variation: time compression, time lag and time cumulation.

Through use of computers it is possible to simulate years of business experience in a matter of hours. This compression of time makes it possible for the player to see the long-run, as well as the immediate, results of his decisions.

Many games have time lags built into them so that decisions must be made in one time period in order for their results to be achieved several periods later in answer to problems expected to arise then. This teaches the need for future planning in management.

Time cumulation lets the game player see how his decisions build on one another and hence should be based on long-run policies and objectives.

The interpersonal forces at work within the gaming group serve to teach the art of working through and with people. The team itself becomes a miniature human relations laboratory in which the members must learn how to get along with one another and to be able to organize to reach decisions acceptable to the whole group.

Simulation demonstrates that decision-assisting tools provided by the management accountant can be of aid to managers in solving problems. The need for designing, then reviewing and modifying tools such as break-even charts, financial statements, forecasts and budgets is graphically demonstrated in a dynamic game. Here we find the importance of the control function being taught. Without control devices for measuring performance, the game player, like the real business manager, soon loses all hold over his operation.

The elements of risk and uncertainty are introduced here. If they did not exist, control would not be necessary. But they do exist in the real world, and they are introduced into business simulations through inclusion of some chance elements in the results fed back at the end of a decision cycle.

BENEFITS FROM BUSINESS GAMES

Business games can be used to reintegrate specialized functions by demonstrating the need for reaching a dynamic balance between various interacting managerial functions. Games can make generalists out of specialists. Executives who have become overly concerned with their own specialties soon learn to have proper appreciation of overall company operations when the interaction between men, money and materials is demonstrated in a simulation. By changing game requirements or altering decision parameters, it is possible to point a game toward demonstrating the value of a particular functional area if that should be desired.

In computer games different portions of the underlying mathematical model can be brought into play to increase the number of functional areas involved, or to change emphasis between them. If the game is played on a computer, managers who have previously been skeptical of the value of these electronic beasts can be made aware of their speed, accuracy and flexibility in computing results of inputs.

The games can be an end in themselves, used to teach managers simulation. Simulation can be a very powerful tool in solving problems when it is used to gain experience which otherwise could not be acquired because of cost or technical factors. For example, a proposed policy change could be fed into a management game to measure its effect upon team members and also upon competitors. This is operations research.

One interesting aspect of business games, unfortunately one not often tried, is the possibility of calling back a decision which has turned out poorly. Experimentation with different alternatives becomes possible when using simulation. It becomes possible to return to a previous point in the game and proceed again, making a different set of decisions to determine their advantages and disadvantages in comparison with those previously tried. How often a player will say, "If only we could go back; we see now we should never have cut our price but should have put more money into marketing." With computers it is possible for them to go back and play that decision over again and see how the results arrived at differ.

To sum up: Business games through their simulation of years of experience in a very brief time give managers a chance to study the long and short term results of their decisions side-by-side. This leads to balance between these, at times, conflicting considerations. They also teach the manager to balance the various specialized managerial functions, and they do really teach the basic functions of planning, organizing, directing and controlling.

LIMITATIONS OF BUSINESS GAMES

One criticism quite often raised against games is that the players become too preoccupied with "playing the game." They are so busy trying to win that they have no time to learn. Experience is still the best teacher, and the more involved a player becomes in the game, the more real the experience becomes, so the better he will learn.

Business games are expensive. They are costly in terms of time, space and money. If a game is being played by a fairly large group of middle and top level executives, the cost of their time, during the period of play, would be staggering if totaled. The initial cost of developing a game is very high, but once developed it can be modified and used for various purposes. Games already developed by others are available at low cost. Computer time for the more complex games can cost a great deal, but there are simpler hand-scored games which can be used to fill many training uses. When one weighs the advantages of the lessons and experience gained from making mistakes in the simulated environment against the possible cost to a business if these same mistakes were to occur in the real world, the arguments about how expensive games are do not appear so strong.

It is said that business games are too quantitatively oriented. They ignore such qualitative factors as product style, leadership, labor relations, morale, political and international climate, et cetera. For example, most games will give an automatic increase in sales if there is an increased expenditure on advertising, although the law of diminishing returns is applied. There is no consideration of the fact that the quality of a marketing campaign will affect its success or failure as much as the total dollar sum spent. This criticism cannot be denied. However, attempts are being made to remedy this situation. Games do not claim to recreate reality; they only create the illusion of reality.

How Effective Are Business Games?

Critics say the teaching efficacy of business simulation has never been validated. It has never been proven by "before" and "after" tests that games actually teach what they are intended to teach. But then there have been very few validation studies successfully made of any other management development techniques.

A possible danger is that of erroneous transfer. A specific game lesson is carried literally back to the real world when this happens.

One student reported he had learned from the game that price is the most important factor in competition; another said he had learned that advertising influences sales more than price does; a third concluded that every business should have an electronic computer.[3]

This danger can be minimized by having a critique at the end of the game in which the participants are made aware of what they should have gained out of the play. Also, making the game just one tool, or part of an overall training program can help the student keep in proper perspective the lessons learned from the game.

It is said that games are unrealistic, that their mathematical models are based upon the assumptions of classical economics and that in practice these assumptions are not always valid. It is also claimed that business games discourage innovation and originality in problem solutions. To discourage extreme strategies most games have built into them penalties for radical changes in behavior. While in most cases this encouragement of safe, sane, conservative decision-making is desirable, nevertheless, it cannot be denied that occasionally it is the radical innovation in solving an old problem which wins the prize.

Some people have criticized games because they are fun to play. There is no reason why learning should be drudgery. On the contrary, this aspect of enjoyment is one of the strongest arguments in favor of business simulation as a training technique.

OTHER POSSIBLE USES OF GAMES

Some attempts have been made to use business games in employee selection and testing. As a testing device they would seem, at least for the present because of lack of validation, to have only limited application.

The questions arise as to what is being tested and what constitutes bad performance in playing a game. If the purpose of a game is to teach, the point could be made that the student who has made many mistakes and corrected his errors has learned more than the one whose decisions have been consistently good.

More promising is the prospect of using management games as a research tool. As such, they have several advantages. Simulation is very versatile in handling a large number of problems involving probabilistic elements. Formulating models is conceptually easy. And there is ease of communication of results to the potential user of the results. As a research tool, the business game can act as a model of the company itself and be used as a direct aid in decision-making. If a new problem arises, feed it into the game and then experiment with various possible solutions to test their results.

Finally, simulation techniques present the psychologist with an opportunity to study the ways in which people make decisions. The game becomes a little laboratory for use in human research. This aspect becomes especially appealing when the possibility of using real, live executives as guinea pigs is considered. It might be possible to train scientific observers through having them observe games in action.

FUTURE OF BUSINESS GAMES

To sum up what has been said, and to make some estimates as to the future of business games, a word of caution or emphasis is in order. It must be remembered that the game is only as good a teacher as those who administer it, and succeeds in imparting knowledge only as part of a greater educational context.

All the physical sciences make much use of the laboratory to demonstrate to students their principles and to give these students practice in exercising their methodology. As business management becomes less and less of a social science and more of an exact science, it is business simulation which will serve as its laboratory. Through business games students will experience the principles of management. These games will be the laboratory in which business research takes place which will further refine and define the exactness of these principles.

NOTES TO THE TEXT

[1] John Whedon Acer, *Business Games: A Simulation Technique,* State University of Iowa, Iowa City, Iowa, 1960, p. 7.

[2] Paul S. Greenlaw, Lowell W. Herron, and Richard H. Rawdon, *Business Simulation,* Prentice-Hall, Englewood Cliffs, N.J., 1962, p. 5.

[3] *Simulation and Gaming: A Symposium,* Management Report 55, American Management Association, New York, 1961, p. 24.

What's Wrong with Business Games?

Arthur L. Roberts

Mᴜᴄʜ ᴏғ ᴛʜᴇ literature which has been published recently in the area of business games has been highly favorable, with the more extreme enthusiasts proclaiming that business gaming will soon become one of the major methods of training personnel in business concepts and in the performance of specific managerial tasks. Definite proof of these claims, however, is lacking, and as the usage of games has increased, a note of skepticism and caution can be detected in recent evaluations.

Let it be admitted that business games have made many fine contributions to the general area of business training and education. However, before all aspects of these games are wholeheartedly endorsed, a review of their weaknesses and shortcomings is in order.

Weaknesses and shortcomings which were once hidden by the novelty of business games are continually being discovered and identified.

At the time this article was published, ARTHUR L. ROBERTS was Chairman, Department of Personnel and Production Management, San Fernando Valley State College.

Reprinted, with permission, from *The Journal of Industrial Engineering,* November-December 1962.

REALITY IN BUSINESS GAMES

Reality appears to be one of the key factors around which the value of business games is hinged, but too much reality in the game makes it more desirable to use on-the-job training in its place, so that the firm will attain some benefit, at least, from the normal productivity of the trainee. Training costs resulting from the use of business games can be high when the cost of the original game development, the out-of-pocket costs of running the game, and the lost productivity costs of the trainee are considered. Wikstrom, in his discussion of the decision making process, warns of excessive game realism.[4] He indicates that too much realism permits the trainees to perform on the basis of their normal operating procedures which they have developed on the job, instead of forcing recognition of the importance of constant analysis, and gaining experience in the decision making process. These are the real benefits to game participants. Thus Wikstrom believes that players should be forced to make decisions about business situations which are at least partially unfamiliar to the trainees.

On the other hand, when there is too little reality, participants are literally playing games for fun, whereas learning, not recreation, is the purpose of using games, even though many admit that business games are fun to play.

Who can say how a person trained by the business game method will react to similar problems in the real business world situation, when all of the participants and competitors are using "live ammunition" instead of "blanks"? Realistic decision making experience is difficult, if not impossible, to obtain in a game environment which has no real system of rewards or penalties to insure realistic play. Nearly everyone who has played poker for matches or for fun has immediately recognized how such "fun" play reduced the personal involvement and interest to a point where such a game lost all resemblance to real poker. The play money feature of business games, likewise, does not provide an effective substitute for training personnel who normally deal with real money. This aspect of business games is comparable to military field maneuvers, a training method which is felt to be inadequate by military experts because of the lack of emotional reality.[3] The lack of the most essential element of realism, fear, greatly reduces the value of such war games, and it is felt that business games lack this same essential ingredient—fear of making a mistake or wrong decision—resulting normally in reprimand or discharge. On the other hand, successful conduct of one's job in business usually results in reward, while in the game situation, the personal satisfaction of winning is the most tangible feature that the participants can grasp. Business games are not intended to be "won," yet many participants play only to win.

It has been found that participants frequently will not expend sufficient effort to play realistically, whether the game is realistic or not. This lack of effort has been attributed generally to the resentment of business personnel who are busy with on-the-job problems and duties. Their antagonism stems from the additional time and effort required to play a business game, which is conducted for their supposed benefit, unless they are relieved of some of their regular duties and responsibilities.

Information requirements for business game play, though limited, may come too easily to participants, in contrast to the difficulty, effort, and cost of obtaining similar information in reality.[1] In some instances, experienced employees may be reluctant to reveal their ignorance of information or its significance in an artificial situation created during the play of a business game. Such threat situations are not realistic, and destroy the learning environment.

Ability of Game Administrator

A second key factor that affects the success of using business games as a training technique is the umpire or game administrator's ability. The umpire, admittedly, has a heavy responsibility for the success or failure of gaming sessions. His knowledge regarding the detailed operation of the game, and in the creation of an atmosphere in which the greatest enthusiasm and benefit to the participants will be attained, is of primary concern. Psychologists point out that observation and retention of information increase with interest, and that game players must remain interested for maximum benefit. Players must forget external distractions, whether play is carried on over a few long continuous sessions, or as a series of short sessions. It has been observed, however, that interest in the business concepts which games are reported to teach best falls off rapidly if play is continued for an excessive period of time. Excessive business game usage has been found to have a negative effect on interest and learning, a condition requiring a highly qualified administrator to detect, understand and correct.

The umpire's role includes not only the important responsibility of holding the interest of players, but also that of effectively conducting the pregame briefing of players, of being familiar with the game abstraction itself, direct-ing the play of the game, revealing in his postgame critique the significance of the abstraction, and evaluating how effectively participants may have worked to attain the goals established by or for each team. The magnitude of the umpire's duties and responsibilities has become so great that few in-dividuals are truly qualified as game administrators.

It is the contention of Greenlaw and Kight that if gaming is to be success-fully used as a change inducing training medium, a trained observer, in addi-tion to the traditional umpire, must be placed with each team of participants during the decision making periods.[2] This observer provides a semicon-tinuous critique by utilizing the time between decision making periods to explain the human dynamics of the group at work and the interpersonal skills displayed by the individual team members. This type of critique is felt to be superior to the usual "one shot" critique provided by the umpire at the conclusion of the gaming session, since it permits the participants to try out new patterns relating to the group environment. A further example of the qualifications required of a successful observer is International Business Machines' use of a trained qualified psychologist to observe the players dur-ing the interactions of the playing phase.[4] During the critique he points out how the relationships of the players either assist or impede them in trying to reach their objectives.

In summarizing the umpire's duties and responsibilities, it can safely be said that he must be a mathematician, a psychologist, an accountant, an experienced business executive, and a teacher. He must be able to create and to hold interest and enthusiasm for the game, and to understand the game's mathematical basis, as well as the organizational aspects of the model. He must also be familiar with all of the functional areas of business, that is, production, finance, and distribution; and the planning, organizing, direct-ing, and control functions of management. He should be acquainted with the cost and effect of advertising, research and development, depreciation and obsolescence, inventory control, accounting practice, and a multitude of other supportive functions and techniques. A thorough knowledge of all of the generally accepted management principles is another requirement.

In short, where can a really qualified umpire be found? The obvious an-swer is that there are relatively few who possess an adequate background, or who have received sufficient training to carry out properly the responsibility of the umpire role. All too many who have entered the field as business game experts or umpires have done so in order to exploit business' continual search for an effective, low cost, training technique, and have failed to possess even the minimum background of a qualified umpire. Such abuses of the umpire's or administrator's role have already tarnished the reputation of business games, and left many a firm and its trainees with nothing but disappointment to show for large expenditures of time and money.

CONCLUSION

In conclusion, business games are not effective as training devices in a great many situations. This will continue to be the case until a realistic system of rewards and penalties is devised which will eliminate the "play money" feature. No other feature of realism is as important or meaningful to business game success.

The present group of game experts, umpires and administrators may someday be likened to the "efficiency experts" of yesterday, self-trained experts who perform part of the administrator's tasks well, but who are not actually prepared to perform a real service to the organization as a whole. Many of them lack the qualifications to perform a professional training job that incorporates the use of business games.

Until these two weaknesses of business gaming are corrected, its contribution to the business world will be highly questionable.

NOTES TO THE TEXT

[1] Cohen, Kalman J., and Rhenman, Eric, "The Role of Management Games in Education and Research," *Management Science*, Vol. VII, No. 2, January 1961, pp. 151-152.

[2] Greenlaw, Paul S., and Kight, S. S., "The Human Factor in Business Games," *Business Horizons*, Vol. III, No. 3, Fall 1960, pp. 60-61.

[3] Marshall, S. L. A., *Men Against Fire*, Washington, D. C.: Combat Forces Press, and New York: William Morrow and Company, 1947, p. 71.

[4] Wikstrom, Walter S., "The Serious Business of Business Games," *Management Record*, Vol. XXII, No. 2, February 1960, p. 8.

Management Games:
An Answer to Critics

Burt Nanus

I<small>N</small> T<small>HE</small> five years since their introduction as an educational device, management games have gained wide acceptance in business schools and industrial management development programs. More than 100 games are now available and many thousands of students and executives have participated in them.

The growing use of the technique has been accompanied by controversy and, strangely enough, the past year has seen both the greatest progress in the use of games and the greatest criticism by its opponents. The purpose of this article is to review and comment upon some of the criticisms heard and suggest some work for the future.

S<small>OME</small> C<small>LAIMS</small>

Let us start positively and list some conservative claims for the use of management games for which there seem to be general agreement:

At the time this article was published, BURT NANUS was Director, Western Systems Training Center, Operations Research Incorporated.

Reprinted, with permission, from *The Journal of Industrial Engineering*, November-December 1962.

1. A good management game can provide a degree of involvement of participants in the learning situation which exceeds that usually attained by other teaching techniques in the field of business management and this, according to current learning theory concepts, is desirable.
2. Games can be used to demonstrate principles of management relating to the interaction of decision areas over time better than static techniques such as lecture or case study.
3. Games provide an effective means for demonstrating some of the decision making problems associated with a specific functional area (for example, marketing) to those experienced in other areas (for example, manufacturing or finance) and thus helps to clarify organizational relationships.
4. Properly designed and administered games can provide extremely effective demonstrations of the application of certain time related management tools such as budgets, forecasts or mathematical inventory control models and the capabilities of electronic computers in rapid data analysis and report preparation.
5. Games are useful as simulated task situations for certain types of organizational research relating to communications, leadership, group structure, decision making and related.concepts.
6. The process of building a game often provides useful insights into the relationships existing in the business being simulated.

LIMITATIONS

Serious educators are also aware of some limitations of the games technique. The most obvious of these is cost; games should certainly not be used if some other technique can attain the same objectives for less money. But there are many factors to consider in determining relative costs. One must not forget the value of the time of the participants when they are middle or top executives. If a game can achieve in one day the objectives of part of an executive program normally requiring two or three days, this may well justify the expenditure of several thousand dollars. Also, one must remember that the largest costs of games are in the development and testing of the model and it may be possible to use one of the many existing games, perhaps with a slight modification, at a very low cost.

A second legitimate limitation often recognized is that certain games require the use of a computer, and the scheduling of facilities becomes a problem. One solution is to use one or several manual games. However, even where a manual game cannot be used, it is sometimes possible to avoid this problem entirely by conducting "discontinuous" plays. That is, one can schedule a single set of decisions per week over several weeks so that reports can be generated on second or third shifts, or at a facility geographically far removed from the participants.

One other limitation clearly recognized is the possibility of the participants carrying away from the game situation incorrect ideas or unwarranted conclusions. For example, a marketing professor would not want his students to conclude that advertising is *always* a better means for increasing sales than lowering price or increasing salesmen's motivation just because this worked best over ten periods of a game play. On the other hand, he *would* want them to retain the methods of analysis they used in reaching this conclusion. Insuring that the correct lessons are learned is one obligation of the instructor which can be achieved only by careful preparation of the exercise and effective guidance of the critique discussions.

Other claims and limitations have been advanced and are well documented elsewhere.[2] Let us now turn to some of the less justified criticisms which have recently been levied against management games.

CRITICISMS

A typical argument is that games are not useful because they are not realistic enough to help solve management problems.[1] This is a case of confusing management games, which are used primarily for education or certain types of research, with simulations, which are built for problem-solving purposes. Anyone who builds more realism into a management game model than is necessary to achieve his educational or research objectives is either wasting his time or building a model with the hope of later finding an application for it. It is true that verisimilitude, the illusion of reality, is a desirable quality in a game to achieve involvement and provide a lifelike framework for analysis. However, this is quite another thing and it may or may not involve a more precise duplication of the "real-life" mathematical relationships. For example, a simple straight line price demand relationship may be quite sufficient for an educational exercise despite its obvious artificiality.

A second frequently heard criticism is that games lack validation. This is true, and research is currently being conducted at several universities to see if games really do teach the lessons they are intended to teach and whether, in fact, they *can* influence management behavior on the job. It is really no defense to point out that more evidence is being demanded to prove the effectiveness of games in education than was ever contemplated for the case study, role playing, or any other technique, however true this situation is. Games should be judged in relation to other available teaching techniques and measured by the same standards, but these standards certainly could profit from a more precise definition.

A third type of criticism levied against certain games is that they are too easy to "beat," or too complex, or too difficult to run, or allow too little time for decision making, or are too much dependent upon random elements, etc. These are simply the results of poor game design or administration and deserve to be criticized, but they do not justify a condemnation of the entire field. Frequently these comments come from people whose exposure to games has been extremely limited—perhaps to one or two game plays—and their generalizations are unjustified, inaccurate and detrimental to the efforts of serious educators. Such comments could be useful if they were aimed at cautioning people in the use of games rather than condemning the technique itself.

A final commonly heard complaint, even among serious educators, is that games are too quantitative and do not include the many important qualitative areas of business. This is true, and considerable work is being done to overcome this shortcoming. But is this really a cause for not using games? No tool can do all jobs for all people; we don't throw away screwdrivers because they can't be used to hammer nails. If games are useful for teaching and research in quantitative aspects of sequential decision making, then they should be used for this purpose. If they cannot teach about labor negotiations and personnel policy, then other methods such as case study or role playing should be used for those areas until more effective techniques come along.

Abuses of Management Games

That these general criticisms do not seem justified is not to say that abuses of the use of the tool have not appeared. They have, and the following are among the most flagrant:

1. Using games strictly for entertainment or publicity without clearly warning the participants that the training value of a game, which

is not part of a larger, carefully planned educational context, will be very small. Much of the criticism levied against games has come from participants who had unhappy experiences in one or two of these carelessly run exercises.

2. Using a game for a course before its parameters have been thoroughly tested. Too many games used today can be "beaten" by unreasonable strategies.

3. Designing a game before its objectives have been clearly defined. This was a particularly common problem in the early days of game design, but even now games are being built by mathematicians and operations research specialists with insufficient guidance by educators. The result is games which are more "sophisticated" than necessary or too difficult to handle administratively.

4. Permitting a game to be used before complete documentation of its model and computed program is available.

SUGGESTIONS FOR THE FUTURE

Turning to the future, what can be done? There are many feasible research projects in the field of management games which would significantly advance the state of the art. For example, games can be developed for industries or functions which have lagged in the application of operations research techniques as a means for arousing interest in mathematical model building. Such games could be built to simulate the controllership function, hospital or library management, or even university administration.

Another useful project would be a controlled experiment to study the extent to which people react to game situations as they do to real-life situations. Such studies will help determine whether games can be used as testing devices.

Management games can be used to study the effects of forms design and information flow upon management decision making. For example, if the same information is presented in different ways, can this lead to different courses of action? What are the best ways to organize and present data?

Finally, games should be used to study the economic behavior of management. Existing games can help to explore the reaction of experienced managers to competitive price fluctuations, the effects of increased or decreased taxes, and the influence of union pressures. In particular, it would be interesting to see just how much executive decisions tend toward maximizing profits.

It is clear that there have been abuses in the use of games, but these do not justify a lack of faith in the approach. Much of the criticism of management games as "fads" or "toys" seems to come from misinformed sources. This article has offered a rebuttal to some of this criticism and suggestions for improvements in the use of the technique.

NOTES TO THE TEXT

[1] Christian, William, "Don't Bet on Business Games," *Business Automation,* July 1961, p. 22.

[2] Kibbee, Joel M., Craft, Clifford J., and Nanus, Burt, *Management Games,* New York: Reinhold Book Corporation, 1961, pp. 41-48.

General Motors Institute
Experiences with Business Gaming

Using a Non-Complex Business Exercise
for Middle Management Training

Adair Smith, Thomas B. Scobel, and Ronald J. Le Frois

THE PLANT Management Training Department of General Motors Institute offers a broad variety of management development services to the divisions and plants of the General Motors Corporation. Among these services is the development of new materials and techniques in the area of formalized training. Thus, in 1959, we too became interested in the possibilities inherent in the training technique known as the Business Game, and we developed a Business Exercise of our own.

At the time this article was published, the authors were with the General Motors Institute. ADAIR SMITH was Manager of the Management Development Research Staff; THOMAS B. SCOBEL was with the Management Training Department; and RONALD J. LE FROIS was on the Research and Development Staff.

Reprinted by special permission from the April 1961 issue of the *Journal of the American Society of Training Directors*. Copyright 1961 by the American Society for Training and Development.

We tested our first Business Exercise in a one-week Intensive Program attended by Manufacturing Superintendents. It was then revised, tested with another similar group, and after the second revision, used in five training programs, each of one week duration with superintendent to staff level personnel of our Canadian subsidiaries. We are now experimenting with its usage in inplant training on a one-hour per week schedule with plant staff level people.

We are not experts on Business Gaming. We are merely training people who have developed a Business Exercise and used it in an industrial training situation. We have, we think, learned a few things from this experience, and we would like to share this with you.

Our experience with Business Exercise, including the development and use of one, has led us to believe that . . .

1. It is essentially a decision-making exercise, but it is unique;
2. It can be used to show relationships between facts and principles in both a specific and a broad general way;
3. It is not an end in itself, but, as with any other training technique, a means to an end.

Let's examine each of these points:

1. In most Business Exercises, the conferees are given certain facts, and/or they deduce facts from a mass of data, and use these facts to make decisions, analyze them, and attempt to improve them. This process of making and correcting decisions is repeated again and again in the exercise.

The atmosphere that surrounds the usual Business Exercise is also unique. Companies, conferee teams, are competing for sales; enthusiasm runs high; results are eagerly awaited. In this type of simulation approach, if properly used and conducted, participation and involvement are impressive. It is not a game but a serious matter. In this type of environment, the conferee is willing and able to sweat his way to learning.

2. Regarding the second point, the Business Exercise can be used in an almost infinite variety of ways. It can be likened to a case study in that what will come out of a case depends upon what has been written into it. So with the Exercise, what the conferees will learn depends upon what has been planned for and built into it.

Almost any aspect of business operation that is measurable to a degree can be developed into a Business Exercise or a part of a Business Exercise. Wherever management is provided with a report in figures that can be analyzed and compared with past experience and upon which decisions can be based, there is data that can be developed into an Exercise. Some areas are more easily handled than others, of course.

By careful construction of the Exercise, the important factors upon which decisions in each specific area are based must be built in to be used by the conferees to make decisions. Poor decisions should be indicative of improper handling of these factors and of failure to deduce relationships, and this should be fed back to the participants in terms of poor results.

We have also been able to use our Business Exercise with another specific purpose in mind. Several of the forms we use are based upon General Motors reports. Because these forms are used to convey information regarding the operation of the business, the conferees examine these reports and become more adept at analyzing them.

But the Business Exercise can be much broader than merely illustrating specific relationships within a given decision area. It can include many decision areas. A current G.M. model includes these decision areas: units to be produced, man-hours to be scheduled, size and distribution of the work force, maintenance, quality, price, advertising and selling, research and development, dividends, and annual budget.

By providing the conferees with information necessary to make decisions in all of these areas, we are able to show that relationships exist among all of these specific decision areas. Thus, the Exercise is complex and many factors in different areas must be considered before making even one decision.

The more areas that are built into the Exercise, or the more decisions that the conferees must make, the broader becomes the experience until the point is reached that to arrive at decisions requires long-range planning, the establishment of broad company objectives, annual and quarterly objectives, and rather specific policies. This type of Exercise can give a real feeling of what it is like to be the top operating executives of a business. In addition, the conferees can test their objectives and policies against the results they are achieving during the course of the exercise. In this way, they can more easily recognize the importance of long-range planning, meaningful objectives, the weighing of decisions in terms of immediate and more distant goals.

3. Lastly, we have learned that the Business Exercise is not an end in itself but, as with any training technique, a means to an end.

We have always felt that the first step in planning a training program is to establish the training needs of the organization. It is then necessary to develop the specifications for the content of the program, and lastly to decide upon the best techniques, that is, best in terms of sound principles of learning, of getting the content across to the participants. There is a temptation to ignore this precept with the Business Exercise because of the unusual characteristics of the technique.

Since we feel that the results of a training program should lead rather immediately to improved job performance, changed attitudes, new perspectives, or new skills, we feel that training techniques must be developed and used to further these ends. Thus, we have learned that the exercise should be constructed so that it is tied closely to what the training program is to accomplish.

We decided to develop a Business Exercise because we were looking for a means that would, among other things, assist middle-management conferees to:

1. Improve the quality of their decision-making ability.
2. Broaden their understanding of Business Management.
3. Familiarize themselves with G.M. accounting principles.

We felt that a Business Exercise could be used as one of the training techniques that would assist in the accomplishment of these objectives. A model of the Exercise is now being designed as a part of an in-plant training program with similar objectives. To be more certain that the results of the technique would accomplish these objectives, we took great pains to tie the exercise closely to General Motors' experience and practices. We emphasized manufacturing, cost control, and inventory control, because these areas were the most pertinent to the specifications of the training program we were developing.

We have learned, too, that the Business Exercise must be part of a training program that contains other elements, techniques, and content. The Business Exercise, at best, is a technique that reflects the world of reality only in a small way. Certainly, there are many more decisions that the managers must make in the operation of a business than are built into an Exercise. Even in those areas where decisions must be made in the Business Exercise, the facts the manager must consider before arriving at a decision are much more extensive than can be built into the Exercise. In addition, these relationships most likely do not precisely parallel the relationships in the plant. For example, it is unlikely that the variable costs in a plant's operation rise and fall with volume exactly as they do in a specific model of the G.M. Business Exercise. Therefore, it is essential that some other training activity be coupled with the Exercise, not only to be certain that the relationships which are built in are being recognized, but also to bridge the gap between the restricted world of the Business Exercise and the real job of the manager. Thus, we feel the Business Exercise is similar to the case study, the incident process, the in-basket, and other techniques in that it is not a training program; it is merely another very versatile tool.

GAME OPERATION

We would like to get more specific regarding the operation of one of our programs using the Business Exercise. At the outset, a presentation or conference is held. This conference is entitled "Setting Objectives for the Operation of a Business." The conferees are encouraged to examine certain environmental variables before setting their own company objectives. For example, it is pointed out that a company must examine its market, competition, resources, capacity, and manpower in order to set realistic goals.

The participants are then grouped into teams to participate as competing companies. Ideally, a team is made up of four men, each with a different background and experience.

Before proceeding with the simulated exercise, certain background information must be given to the companies. We furnish the data in two ways. First, a manual is used which consists of information about the company and its products. Second, the background information is furnished by having the simulated business already in progress. Thus, a budget for the first year has already been prepared, the balance sheet for the previous year is on hand, plant reports illustrating the department efficiencies are completed for the first and second quarter of the current year, and accordingly, the quarterly profit is shown. Therefore, when the team makes its first set of decisions, they will be doing so for the third quarter.

The Exercise proceeds with third quarter decisions being made; these are then processed, and the results returned to the teams who analyze and use them to make better decisions in the next quarter. This is a continuous cycle which, in our opinion, reaches a point of diminishing return around the end of ten sets of decisions.

The first of the quarterly decisions made by each team is the number of units to be produced. Here a firm must refer back to its broad and specific objectives as to the market penetration desired. The team must then think of efficiency. In planning production, consideration based on experience must be given to anticipated losses due to scrap and machine down time.

The next decision is balancing the number of plant hours required with the size of the work force, with overtime and night shift premiums. In making this decision, a firm must be concerned with the most effective use of labor to minimize cost in addition to considering their overall or broad policies which might call for stable employment.

The next decision pertains to manufacturing expenditures. It is important that the firms discover for themselves that manufacturing costs in each department do not vary in direct proportion to the volume of production. The teams must also discover that the cost-volume relationship differs in each department.

A second consideration centers about the analysis of the plant report. If a team's labor and burden efficiency is below standard, they must try to analyze past expenditures to determine why this has happened.

The next decisions pertain to marketing strategy. Here the team must establish prices for its products and determine expenditures for advertising and selling. The total marketing strategy involves much more than these two decisions. In effect, it goes back to the sales objective established and to the sales income forecast in the annual budget. Marketing strategy must be related to the overall operating policies.

The last of the quarterly decisions is the expenditure for research and development. This decision reflects the long-range plans of the company. It must consider the entire economy. Research and development expenditure, in proportion to the profits of a company, to the nature of its business, and to the status of its competitors, is of utmost importance if the objective of a company is to grow and expand.

At the beginning of the year, each firm must draw up an annual budget. This budget, in the simulated business as well as in an actual plant, is intended to serve as a guide to management in the execution of its management functions. The budget, in effect, requires a firm to set annual objectives. In doing this, a firm considers its long-range objectives; it examines its past performance in all areas such as manufacturing, sales, commercial expenses, and even dividends paid out. And, the alert team will use economic forecasts as very influential.

RELATED ACTIVITY

In the operation of the Business Exercise, it is important that all conferees weigh the long-range effects of their decisions. Based upon the experience and background of the participants, we have found it advisable to use additional stimuli.

The conferees attend management conferences during the exercise. These conferences are conducted by members of the class, other plant personnel, or university professors. A conference consists of a 30- to 45-minute presentation on some phase of business operation. The management of each firm is then advised to hold its own company management meeting to make application to its own situation.

Some of the typical conferences are: Financial Management, Determining Inventory Policies, and Preparation of Annual Budgets.

Another alternative for introducing stimuli is to make use of reading materials related to each of the decision areas of the exercise.

GAME CRITIQUE

At the end of the Business Exercise, we have a critique. At a Board of Directors meeting each firm makes a comprehensive report to the Board and to the Stockholders. Preparation of this report causes a team to analyze its operation in respect to many financial criteria, such as return on investment, dividends as a per cent of net worth, changes in operating capital, changes in net worth, net profit, and profit as a per cent of sales. In handling this report, we again try to develop an appreciation for other points of view. Consequently, we ask some of the conferees to role-play the part of the board and others to take the role of stockholders. A vote as to whether the management of the firm should be retained adds a humorous touch to the conclusion.

GAME CONSTRUCTION

From our experience with this development project, three points about game construction should be mentioned.

First, the aspects of computer or non-computer games have been expressed in every article written on this subject. There are advantages and disadvantages of both. We have constructed a non-computer exercise for these reasons: one, it gives us greater flexibility in its use; two, having forms worked out by hand gives the participants an appreciation of the rationale of the accounting procedures; three, because we are attempting to teach principles and relationships, accuracy is of secondary importance. The use of slide rules or hand calculators is quite acceptable.

Our second point about game construction is this: if the objective is to demonstrate relationships as they actually occur in the plant, then extensive research is needed in order to develop realistic models. This is an extreme. If the objective is one of demonstrating principles of how relationships are detected and analyzed, then reality need not be so closely simulated. In our development, we went to General Motors plants in the Flint area. We found two products whose characteristics we later adapted as the products in our exercise. Working with these plant organizations, we established the formulas which are applied in our exercise.

In constructing a business exercise, the planning of the decision variables and relationships that are to be employed and the development of the formulas is, no doubt, the most difficult task.

The last point in construction is this: we found that such a development takes a good deal of trial and error testing. In our testing of this technique, which started some six months ago, we have learned many things. For example, just because participants are busy, perhaps deeply involved or engrossed in their work, does not mean that time is being used most productively in the training situation. Effective coaching, the use of additional material, presentations, texts, or articles to which we have previously referred, and the minimizing of repetitious paper work are all aimed in this direction.

So much for our experience. We have come a long way in exploring this tool in our training situations, but there remain many variations and many aspects into which we have not yet delved.

Part I

B

General Purpose Games Readings

Decision Making Versus Strategy Determination: A Gaming and Heuristic Approach

Robert C. Meier

Since the introduction of business games about ten years ago, they have become a widely used tool for business education and management development. A large variety of games have been developed with different emphases as to complexity, functional areas included, and degree of competitive interaction.

Regardless of the specific structure, games normally have been formulated to operate on a period-by-period basis. That is, the participants or players in the game make decisions, these decisions are evaluated or scored under the rules of the game (in many cases using a computer because of the complexities and volume of calculations), and the results for one period of operation of the game are returned to the participants. In most games competitive elements are present so that the decisions of the participants interact in determining the results, and there also may be random elements included which affect the results. Following the receipt of the results for one period,

At the time this article was published, **ROBERT C. MEIER** was an Associate Professor in the Graduate School of Business Administration, University of Washington.

Reprinted, with permission, from *Business Review*, April-June 1966.

the participants evaluate their positions, make a new set of decisions, and the cycle is repeated.

I. A Game Focusing on Long-Run Strategy

The focus in the play of business games is on the immediate problem of making a decision for the following period. Long-run strategy over a larger number of future periods is, of course, a consideration, but not one which need be made explicit by the participants.

A properly constructed business game, however, can provide a vehicle for explicit consideration of long-range strategy determination rather than immediate, short-run decision making. To do this, we have developed a computerized business game in which the participants write game-playing subroutines which play the game repetitively period after period *without* intervention of the participants each period.[1] In this way emphasis is shifted from the immediate *decision* for one period to a consideration of strategies which will be effective over a larger number of periods. Structures of this general type have been used before in computerized checker-playing programs[2] and for military games,[3] but there has been little application of the concept to business games. The differences in play between a normal computerized business game and the game which we have developed are shown schematically in Figure I.

The game is a simple one, since the complexities of writing game-playing subroutines even for a limited number of decision variables are great. The hypothetical environment of the game is a competitive market for a single product whose price is in the $5.00 per unit range. The market is structured so that the total market available to the teams is a function of an economic index, the industry marketing expenditures, and industry average price. The total market behaves in a conventional way—rising with increases in the economic index, or increased marketing expenditures, or decreased average price, and falling conversely. Company market shares are determined by the company price level and marketing expenditures relative to those of competitors. Both the total market behavior and behavior of the company market shares are determined by functions in the computer program which are set to yield realistic results.

II. Playing the Game

The game was developed and tested using manual scoring and by playing it in the conventional way as shown in Figure I (a).[4] Using the structure shown in Figure I (a), the players make five decisions each period:

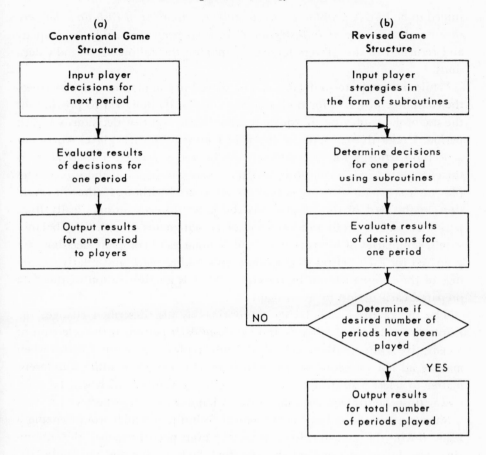

Figure 1

1. Price per unit
2. Marketing expenditures
3. Production rate
4. Additional plant and equipment purchases
5. Loan repayments

The first step in the scoring after the decisions are made is to determine whether the scheduled production rate is consistent with plant capacity; if not, production rate is reduced to plant capacity. The total market and each company's share is then determined together with the ability of the company to fill its demand from inventory and production. If the company cannot fill its share of market demand, any shortage is distributed to the other companies unless they cannot fill this demand, in which case the demand is assumed to be lost. A *profit and loss statement, statement of cash flow, balance sheet,* and *summary of industry data* are then prepared for each company and returned to the players for use in making the following period's decisions.

While the computerized game can be played in the manner just described, the computer program for the game was specifically designed to provide for the use of game-playing subroutines rather than input of decisions for each period. Under this concept, as shown in Figure I (b), each player works out a decision *strategy* for each of the five decision variables. This strategy is then converted into a computer program, a subroutine, and the subroutines play each other for as many periods as are desired without further intervention on the part of the players.[5] As the play proceeds automatically from period to period, profit and loss statements, statements of cash flow, balance sheets, summaries of industry data, and summaries of company decisions are prepared for each period so that the events taking place and relative standings of the companies can be traced. Table 1 is an illustration of the data prepared each period for each team.

The use of the game-playing subroutines as just described changes the emphasis in the game from *decision making* each period to the selection of an effective *strategy*. While it is not difficult to play a game such as this when making ad hoc decisions on a period-by-period basis, it is quite a different matter to select a strategy for each of the five variables which will be effective against the strategies of competitors, whatever these may be.[6]

Since we have found no mathematical techniques which would enable a team to win[7] the game (or, for that matter, even play the game), the subroutines which we have devised thus far for playing the game fall under the broad class of techniques known as heuristic methods.[8] That is, player strategies as programmed in the game-playing subroutines are heuristic in that they involve selection of values for the decision variables from a very large number of possibilities in somewhat the same way that a human decision maker might make the selection. This use of heuristic methods is different from the use of analytical methods such as game theory, linear programming, or calculus optimization models, none of which appear to be directly useful in playing the game.

Our experimentation with this form of game structure is in its earliest stages, and only the simplest game-playing subroutines have been devised thus far. These have, to date, been principally of the type that look at the data from the last period only and make decisions on that basis. Other obvious possibilities would be to employ data from a number of previous peri-

Company 4 Period 5

Profit and Loss Statement

Sales – 50,000 units at $5.32 per unit		$266,000.00
Less – cost of goods sold	$150,000.00	
depreciation	17,600.00	
marketing expenditures	23,000.00	
administrative expense	42,000.00	
interest paid	1,000.00	
Total current expenses		233,600.00
Net income before federal income taxes		32,400.00
Federal income taxes		16,200.00
Net income after federal income taxes		16,200.00

Statement of Cash Flow

Sales	$266,000.00	
New bank loan	0.00	
Total cash provided		$266,000.00
Less – material and labor	150,000.00	
marketing expenditures	23,000.00	
administrative expense	42,000.00	
interest paid	1,000.00	
federal income taxes	16,200.00	
additional plant, equipment	0.00	
loan repayment	0.00	
Total cash outlay		232,200.00
Net cash flow		33,800.00

Balance Sheet

Assets

Current assets –		
Cash	$408,391.00	
Inventory	0.00	
Total current assets		$408,391.00
Fixed assets –		
Plant and equipment	880,000.00	
Less – depreciation	268,000.00	
Total fixed assets		612,000.00
Total assets		1,020,391.00

Liabilities

Current liabilities –		
Total liabilities	$ 50,000.00	
Long term liabilities	50,000.00	
Loans outstanding		$100,000.00

Net Worth

Capital stock	320,000.00	
Retained earnings	600,391.00	
Total net worth		920,391.00
Total liabilities and net worth		1,020,391.00

Industry Data

	Previous period	This period
Economic index	105.00	107.0
Industry weighted average price	$5.07	$5.07
Industry marketing expenditure	$73,000.00	$76,000.00
Total market (units)	220,000	224,000
Company average profit after taxes	$17,658.12	$18,373.87

Company decisions

Price per unit	$5.32
Marketing expenditures	$23,000.00
Production rate	50,000
Additional plant, equipment	$0.00
Loan repayment	$0.00

Other data

Sales lost (units)	15,090

Table 1

ods and incorporate learning in the selection of decision procedures within the subroutines, both of which would make greater use of the power of the computer. However, it is difficult enough to conceive of sensible strategies when the game is viewed in the most elementary fashion, and we have not yet advanced to the point of experimenting with truly sophisticated game-playing subroutines.

III. Strategy Determination

Before we move on to more sophisticated subroutines of this nature it is necessary to gain some experience with and understanding of some of the simpler possibilities, and this alone is a substantial task.

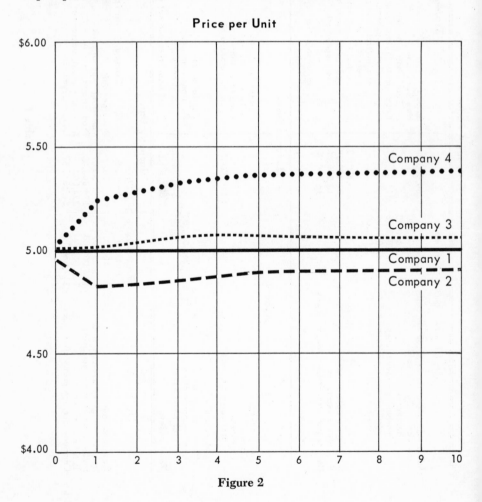

Figure 2

PRICE STRATEGIES

To illustrate, for one of the five decision variables, price, it is not difficult to conceive of a substantial number of possible (and reasonably sensible) decision strategies. Among the most elementary are:

1. Hold price constant at some value.
2. Set price at the previous industry average.
3. Set price at some multiple or fraction of the previous industry average.
4. Select price at random from a specified distribution.

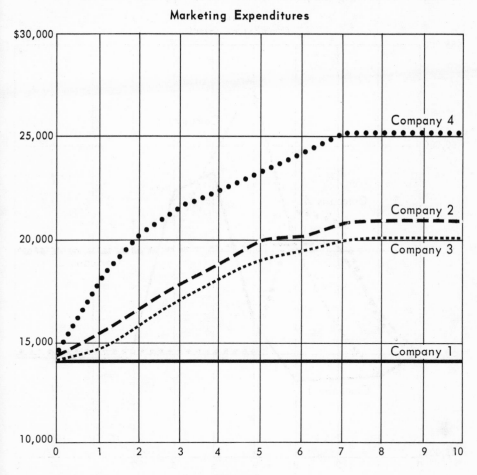

Marketing Expenditures

Figure 3

5. Increase the price if sales are above the last period industry average, and decrease it if sales are below.

These and many others are eligible candidates for strategies for just the one decision variable, price, and their effectiveness must be weighed in conjunction with the specific selection of strategies for the other four decision variables.

LACK OF THEORY OF STRATEGY DETERMINATION

As we have begun to work with this problem of selecting a set of decision strategies for playing the game, it has become apparent that there is a lack

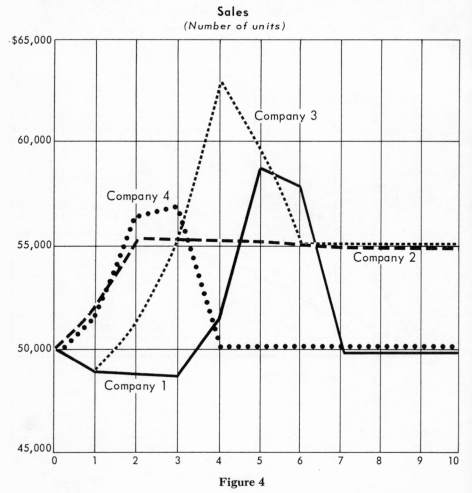

Figure 4

of adequate theory to use as a guide and that available techniques are inappropriate or inadequate. However, the absence of theories, or even suggested approaches, is probably only indicative of the fact that the problem has not been made explicit before since neither the real business world nor previously developed models provide the proper sort of controlled environment in which concepts of competitive strategy determination in a dynamic situation can be evolved and tested. The business game just described provides a useful vehicle for exploring this question of *strategy determination* as opposed to *decision making* and is a significant extension and elaboration of the gaming technique. In addition, the unique structure of the game permits the exploration of certain aspects of the question of automated managerial decision making, a subject which is gaining increasing importance with the

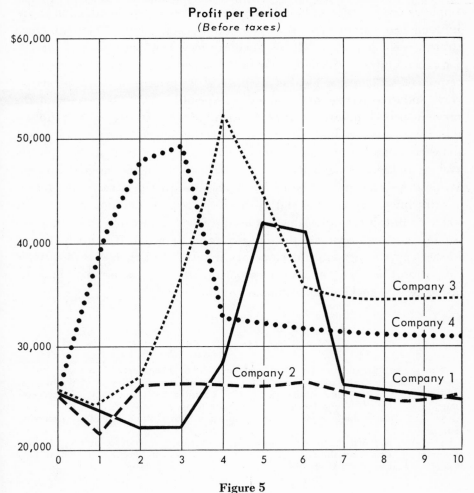

Figure 5

advent of the computer age. It also affords the opportunity for investigating questions of competitive equilibrium and market strategy in a dynamic fashion which was not possible using previously available tools of analysis.

IV. Conclusions

Because our results and experience to date are quite limited, the purpose of this article is not to draw conclusions about the relative merits of various strategies. However, to demonstrate the operation of the game, we include in Figures 2 through 5 summaries of a portion of the results from a trial run of the game with four companies playing for 10 periods. In this run the major emphasis was on price and marketing strategies while the production capacity remained constant and equal for the four companies. Company One's strategy was essentially a "do nothing" strategy in which price and marketing expenditures were held constant at $5.00 per unit and $14,000 per period respectively. Company Two set its price at 97 percent of the previous period's industry average and marketing expenditures at 105 percent of the previous period industry average. Company Three's strategy was to "follow the crowd" and set both price and marketing expenditures equal to the industry average. Company Four set price at 105 percent of the industry average and marketing expenditures at 125 percent of the industry average. While these strategies are both elementary and extremely naive, the results are still interesting. By the end of the 10 periods, a condition of relatively stable equilibrium in the game has been reached, a situation which is somewhat unexpected in view of the four divergent strategies. We anticipate that further experiments with the game in the future will enable us to increase considerably our understanding of problems of strategy determination, automated decision making, and competitive equilibrium.

NOTES TO THE TEXT

[1] The general structure of the game was designed by the writer. H. Richard Burson wrote the computer program as part of his master's work at the University of Washington.

[2] See A. L. Samuel, "Some Studies in Machine Learning Using the Game of Checkers," *IBM Journal of Research and Development* (July 1959), pp. 211-229.

[3] See E. S. Quade, *Analysis for Military Decisions,* Chicago: Rand McNally & Company, 1964, p. 78.

[4] The game was first tested with a group of executives in attendance at the Advanced Management Seminar of the Concrete Products Association of Washington held at Lake Wilderness Lodge, March 21-25, 1965.

⁵ In actuality, the number of periods is determined by the number of values of the economic index which are given to the program as input data.

⁶ One strategy which we have ruled out is that of industrial espionage. Since all data concerning the industry and companies are available in common storage in the computer memory, it would be possible to obtain perfect information about the other companies. Although it is doubtful that even this information would permit a company to select overwhelmingly successful strategies, we have established the ground rule that a company will use only its own company data and general industry data as shown in Table I.

⁷ "Winning" in the context of this game is in itself an ambiguous concept since the criteria for evaluating success are not as clear-cut as in games such as checkers or chess.

⁸ For a discussion of heuristic methods, see Herbert A. Simon, *The New Science of Management Decision*, New York: Harper & Row, 1960, pp. 21-34.

Management Training
Using Business Games

An Eastman Kodak Report on
a Profit Management Program

Robert W. Dobles and Robert F. Zimmerman

At the Kodak Park Works of the Eastman Kodak Company, we have made what we believe is a unique application of business games to our newest supervisory training program entitled "Your Part In Profit Management." This program has the following objectives:

1. Remind the individual supervisor of his stake in, and responsibility for, Company profits.

At the time this article was published, **ROBERT W. DOBLES** was Staff Assistant, Training Department, Kodak Park Works, Eastman Kodak Company, Rochester, New York; and **ROBERT F. ZIMMERMAN** was a member of the Kodak Park Training staff.

Reprinted by special permission from the June 1966 issue of the *Training and Development Journal.* Copyright 1966 by the American Society for Training and Development.

2. Develop a more comprehensive understanding of the total management job in operating a business in a competitive economy.
3. Familiarize the participant with the functions of specialized units that can assist him in meeting his goals.

Previous and current participants have been very enthusiastic in their reception of this program. In fact, it has been more enthusiastically received than any previous effort of this type. The reasons for this directly result from the two principal characteristics of the program: First, the basic structure of the program which combines business exercises with presentations by top-level experts about the subject-variables of the exercise and second, the interdependent and coordinated development of all the meetings in the program.

The first of these is unique. The second, while essentially a good training program development principle, has contributed no less than the first to the overall success of the program.

We are particularly pleased with this success since there has been a previous history of conferee negativism toward cost and profit-oriented programs. No matter how talented, polished, or expert the speaker, we have been unable to stimulate the participants to the degree required to get the utmost benefit from these presentations. In this new program, participation and interest have continued at an extremely high level.

Another interesting aspect of conferee approval is their response to the question, "What did you find most interesting about the program?" Previously, we could predict that accounting, finance, etc. would be found to be the least interesting. Now these are reported among the most interesting topics. Since we are interested in achieving a favorable response toward this subject matter, this change in attitude is very gratifying.

BASIC STRUCTURE

There are a total of 17 weekly meetings in the complete program. These average 2½ hours per meeting, yet are variable in length. Some are as short as 1 hour, and some as long as 4 hours. One should be certain to note the interlaced design which results in a dispersion of the Camera Kit Business Exercise Meetings throughout the topic meetings. This is evident in the Meeting Topics listed below. There is a mutual interdependence here since the decisions in the exercise support and engender an interest in the topic material.

Meeting Topic

1. Andlinger Business Exercise
2. Critique and Program Introduction
3. Camera Kit Business Exercise—1
4. Camera Kit Business Exercise—2
5. Forecasting, Planning & Scheduling
6. Camera Kit Business Exercise—3
7. Marketing
8. Camera Kit Business Exercise—4
9. Research and Development
10. Engineering
11. Finance & Accounting, Camera Kit—5
12. Finance & Accounting, Camera Kit—6
13. Finance & Accounting, Camera Kit—7
14. Industrial Engineering, Camera Kit—8
15. Camera Kit—9, Pricing
16. Management Systems Development
17. Camera Kit—10, Program Summary

The group members are involved immediately in management simulation exercises. Sometimes referred to as a "management game," this kind of activity provides a vehicle for teams of participants to grapple with difficult management problems in a competitive pressure situation. The competitive nature of the situation obliges each man to participate fully.

Published by G. R. Andlinger, Harvard, 1958, the Andlinger Business Exercise is the "starter" for the total program. This was one of the earliest exercises developed for schools and industry. We have found that Andlinger, a relatively simple exercise, offers worthwhile lessons to the participants in both the fundamentals of business economics and business-gaming. We have had excellent success using this exercise.

The Camera Kit Exercise, a different exercise from Andlinger, provides a supporting frame-work for the rest of the course. In this environment, participants lean on their past experiences and draw from new information on business theories brought to their attention in the topic presentations.

Decision making takes place in such areas as:

Planning man hours to meet production requirements
Meeting standard labor costs

Quality and maintenance control to insure proper level of production and profit
Budgeting funds for research and development
Budgeting funds for advertising
Establishing selling prices
Establishing inventory levels

Teams of participants plan and carry out strategies intended to return a suitable profit over a three-year simulated operating experience.

In a conference of 15 people there are three teams or companies of five people each. These groups organize, give themselves names such as the Fearless Camera Co. and the Constamatic Camera Co., and very enthusiastically compete with one another. Time limits are established for the decision periods in order to add reality and urgency to the situation.

The basic logic of the exercise is predicated upon sound business judgment. The game administrator can control any given situation by introducing a crisis of some sort should the situation demand. Participants are expected to establish objectives such as budgets for costs and sales, sales forecast figures, etc., on an annual basis.

In the critique session, at the close of the exercise, each company discusses its successes and failures regarding original objectives.

TOPICAL MEETINGS

In addition to the business exercises, there are 11 topical meetings, each about 2½ hours long which cover the functions listed below. Also shown are the speakers for these meetings. Session presentations and discussions are conducted by this faculty of top level management. Presentation emphasis is placed on what service can be extended to the supervisor rather than on who does it. Discussions provide participants the opportunity to learn from each others' experiences. Outside reading assignments and home work problems are required for most of these meetings.

Topic	*Speaker*
Program Introduction	Asst. Vice President, E. K. Co., and Asst. General Manager, Kodak Park Works Asst. to the General Manager, Kodak Park Works

Production Planning and Forecasting	Director, Production Planning Div.
	Supervisor, Master Data Section, Production Planning Div.
	Supervisor, Paper Planning Dept. Production Planning Div.
Finance and Accounting	General Supervisor, Kodak Park Accounting
	Asst. General Supervisor, Kodak Park Accounting
Marketing	Asst. Vice President, E. K. Co., and Director of Marketing, Consumer Markets Div.
	Advertising Manager, Consumer Markets Div.
	Sales Manager, Consumer Markets Div.
	Staff Asst. to the Sales Manager, Consumer Markets Div.
Industrial Engineering	Director, Industrial Engineering Div., Kodak Park Works
	Supervising Engineer, Industrial Engineering Div., Kodak Park Works
Management Systems	Director, MSDD, Kodak Park Works
	Section Supervisor, MSDD, Kodak Park Works
Pricing	Staff Asst. to Vice President, Eastman Kodak Co.
Engineering	Director of Engineering, Kodak Park Works
	Asst. Director of Engineering, Kodak Park Works
	Superintendent of Shops, Kodak Park Works
Research and Development	Asst. Director of Research,
	Technical Asst. to the General Manager, Kodak Park Works

COORDINATED DEVELOPMENT

The second basic characteristic of the program is inherent in the topical presentations themselves as well as in their original development. As noted previously, each topic is presented by the top management of the function. These men are experts in their fields. Also, the development of each of these presentations was closely coordinated. As a part of the development procedure, each speaker reviewed an outline of his planned presentation at a meeting of all other speakers. After this effort, each speaker gave his speech to the other speakers for the sole purpose of practice, coordination, and criticism. Needless to say, at this high level, much give and take resulted.

The outgrowth of this developmental coordination led to two important results. First, in the light of the future meetings, the left-hand knew what the right-hand was doing. This permitted and encouraged the speakers to refer to one another as the program progressed. The attending conferees realized that each speaker knew what the other was to say. Secondly, and of equal importance, from this give and take development, the speakers developed an identification with the program which is apparent in the enthusiasm with which they make their presentations. The conferees fully recognize the sincere effort each speaker gives to make the topical material interesting, informative and meaningful. These men have, as one, and as a group, succeeded in achieving the objectives of the program by relating their function to profit, to the conferee, and to company management. Their success has been outstanding.

EVALUATION

For this program, an evaluation questionnaire was developed in cooperation with our E. K. Company Psychological Services. Professional trainers, not associated with the program, after proper training, interviewed the original participants in the program. Some of the actual responses are listed below.

Favorable Responses:

1. "The presentation by the Assistant General Manager was thought provoking—a re-evaluation of the picture especially valuable because it was right up-to-the-minute."
2. "Very impressive series of meetings. The Assistant General Manager's introduction was very good because he recognized the group as management and spoke accordingly. Other presentations were also extremely good because the individuals concerned, all high level people, tied in their material with the business exercises and by references indicated their familiarity with the rest of the program."
3. ". . . Got two major things of value: (a) better concept of decisions management must make (b) better concept of tools they (mgmt.) must use in reaching these decisions. Business Exercise gave added incentive of forcing you to make decisions."
4. "The most valuable thing was not a part but the whole. The game

pointed out problems which were then elaborated upon in the talks. The result was a better understanding of the entire management picture."

5. "Finance and Accounting presentation was most valuable. Sales presentation very illuminating because I had little previous job contact with this function."

6. "The Forecasting, Planning and Scheduling portion was most valuable—some of my men could use this."

Unfavorable Responses:

1. "— Accounting went over some ground more than once. This presentation could have been shortened up."

2. "Some of the lectures were longer than necessary. I think most of the lectures could have helped the program more by tying more directly to the Camera Kit Exercise."

3. "More emphasis in the sales and advertising presentation on *how* things are done, i.e., forecasting, money spent, organization and less on the advertising pitch . . ."

The criticisms of the participants were analyzed. Where possible and appropriate, changes were made in the original presentations to correct the problems. Subsequent evaluations will result in other changes. One should remember, however, that these changes and criticisms were made and offered in an effort to make a good program better.

The Game

Bob Nicholson

THE TRIP OUT to Detroit on United's jet mainliner took just 70 minutes from New York's Idlewild Airport. The bus-ride into town from Willow Run took nearly 60 minutes.

Somehow the contrast took on symbolic significance. I and several other fairly normal human beings were going to utilize a wondrously advanced electronic computer to measure, almost instantly, the effects of our ponderously made decisions. The Burroughs Corp. was staging a management decision game.

Snow clouds rolled in from the north, giving the evening sky a grey-flannel cast. A pelting, sleeting rain slicked the streets. Bill Grimshaw, Burroughs' promotion director, and I trotted, coat collars up, from the parking lot to the front door of company headquarters. I was to meet the other "players" at 7 p.m. We were right on time.

The Burroughs plant has a small sixth-floor penthouse which features a pocket-size auditorium (wonderfully comfortable chairs) and a machine-

At the time this article was published, **BOB NICHOLSON** was Executive Editor of *Sales Management* and was invited by the Burroughs Corporation to participate in a "total enterprise management decision game." This is his personal play-by-play report.

crammed display and demonstration room. It was here that we were briefed by John de Jong, a personable and bright Burroughs staffer.

A management decision game, he told us, is simply an attempt to simulate a business and market environment in which several "companies," made up of players, compete in a close-to-realistic situation.

An electronic computer, in this case a Burroughs 205, is not actually a part of the game, but serves as a useful computational tool. It is programmed with a set of mathematical formulas representing the relationships of specific and combined actions. Within minutes after each company makes its decision for a given quarter, it comes up with a printed report showing the results of those decisions.

Thus, the individual player experiences in a few minutes the whole range of emotional reactions involved in executive decision-making. He must think; he must plan; he must calculate. He must work as part of a team. He must analyze data, organize it and make a decision, all within a far-too-short time period. He experiences the pain of selecting alternatives. He uses his judgment skills. And, since he never has all the information he would like, he sticks out his neck, takes a risk, a gamble. Maybe he wins, maybe not.

Then he gets his quarterly statement and here, as his eye moves down the ordered columns of figures, he experiences the thrill of having been wise in his judgment and in his perception, or the despair of noting a loss, with the inevitable sag in his ego. But, as he plays each quarter he learns. He learns about the market, pricing, production, the economy, his competitor—and he learns about decision-making.

The other men assembled at Burroughs that night were all corporate executives from the Detroit area. They were quiet and intense as rules were explained.

There were to be four companies, each having 25% of the market. Each with the same capital, same inventory, same past-quarter performance. The group was broken up into three management teams, which were to guide the destiny of three of the corporations. The fourth corporation was a dummy. It would continue to follow the same pattern of operation as before, but its success, or lack of it, would be affected by the three "newly staffed" companies.

The companies are engaged in the manufacture and marketing of a moderately priced consumer item, sold nationally to distributors. It is a non-staple item; demand fluctuates with economic prosperity, price, innovation, sales (and advertising) effort. We were not told to what degree each of these had a bearing. Play was to run for eight consecutive quarters.

We were given the following guides, taken from the experience of the old company.

SELLING PRICE

Price affects consumer demand. Prices of similar products made by the competing companies affect volume. An unusually high price, approaching $10 an item, will cause a drastic reduction in a firm's market. Low prices tend to increase market. High prices tend to decrease it.

PRODUCTION VOLUME

Rated production capacity of plant is based on net book value. Production below capacity allows unit production at a fixed cost. Cost per unit rises sharply if production exceeds capacity. Unit production time is short and items are available for sale within same quarter.

ADVERTISING EXPENDITURES

Competitive nature of market makes advertising an important consideration. Ad expenditures affect total market and also demand for firm's own product. Advertising has greatest effect in quarter in which it is placed.

RESEARCH EXPENDITURES

Product must undergo continual modification and refinement in order to remain competitive in a volatile market. Because of similarity of competing products, minor improvements affect consumer demand. Money spent for research and development has an immediate effect upon consumption in the quarter in which it is allocated, *but its maximum impact is not felt until the quarter following.*

CAPITAL INVESTMENT

Plant depreciates quarterly and capacity decreases in proportion. New capital investment must be made to maintain or increase rated capacity. Investment planning is required, since increases in productive capacity due to capital investment *do not become effective until the quarter following the quarter in which expenditure was made.*

DIVIDENDS

Old company never paid a dividend, hence effect on market is unknown.

There were other details regarding administrative costs, inventory storage costs, income taxes, etc.

Play Begins

It was a lot to absorb. There weren't many questions, but the participants all looked a little unsure. The names of members of the respective management teams were read and work rooms were assigned. We were to make our decisions for the first quarter that night and reconvene at 8:30 the next morning.

I was put on a management team with three sales executives: Fred Wehle, Jr., branch manager, The E. F. Hauserman Co.; Jack R. King, sales manager, general products and systems group, Burroughs Corp.; and J. M. Tenney, assistant general sales manager, Kelvinator Division of American Motors.

We were given a "last quarter's statement" (Fig. 2) and decision sheet with six places for unit and dollar decisions (Fig. 1). The four of us, all strangers a few minutes before, stared at the two sheets of paper and smiled weakly at each other. None of us knew just where or how to start and we were a little embarrassed by our apparent quandary.

Quarter 1

"The first thing we have to decide is a selling price," Wehle proffered. "Can't do that until we decide production," said King. Tenney and I mumbled something about hitting hard with advertising from the start. Actually, each of us was simply trying to fill up the uncomfortable and awkward confusion with words. None of us had a real plan. We proved that we weren't entirely incapable of decision by taking time to elect a president. Then, we were back with the problem once more. Perhaps 15 minutes had passed. We had decided nothing. At this point a monitor came in and shocked us by saying, "All decisions due in five minutes."

ACTIONS AND RESULTS—

At the start of each "quarter," teams were supplied with a blank Decision Sheet (Fig. 1) on which they were to record their desired actions. This was then handed in. A few minutes later, the computer spit out the results (Fig. 2) of these actions after having interrelated all the actions taken by the competing companies.

NOTE: All figures are fictitious.

BURROUGHS ECONOMIC SIMULATOR
QUARTERLY DECISION SHEET

Decisions for Quarter No. 4	
Firm Number	3
Selling Price per Unit	$ 7 2 5 0 0
Production Volume in Units	1 7 5 0 0 0
Advertising Expenditures	$ 1 5 0 0 0 0
Research Expenditures	$ 1 0 0 0 0 0
Capital Investment in Plant	$ 0
Dividends Declared	$ 0

ESTIMATE OF SOURCE AND APPLICATION OF FUNDS FOR THIS PERIOD

SOURCES
SALES REVENUE (Estimated) $1,600,000
NET CASH ASSETS (Present) 427,990
TOTAL SOURCES $2,027,990

APPLICATIONS
MANUFACTURING COSTS (Estimated) $525,000
ADMIN. & SELLING (Estimated) 350,000
ADVERTISING 150,000
RESEARCH & DEVELOPMENT 100,000
MISCELLANEOUS (Estimated) 30,000
TOTAL CASH EXPENSE $1,155,000
ADDITION TO INCOME TAX FUND (Estimated) 0
DIVIDENDS PAID 0
INVESTMENT IN PLANT 0
TOTAL APPLICATIONS $1,155,000

Figure 1

OPERATING STATEMENT

FIRM 3   PERIOD 6

SALES VOLUME   231990
PERCENT SHARE OF INDUSTRY SALES   42.21
CURRENT INVENTORY QUANTITY   115051
PRODUCTION CPY. NEXT QUARTER   217709

PROFIT AND LOSS

INCOME, SALES REVENUE $1681933.

EXPENSE
MANUFACTURING COSTS $ 631413.
REDUCTION IN INVENTORY VALUE   64559.
ADMINISTRATION AND SELLING   352396.
ADVERTISING   200000.
RESEARCH AND DEVELOPMENT   200000.
DEPRECIATION   305235.
MISCELLANEOUS   17257.
                                              $1570862.

PROFIT BEFORE INCOME TAX $ 111070.
ADDITION TO INCOME TAX FUND $ 57756.
NET PROFIT, AFTER INCOME TAX $ 53313.

DIVIDENDS PAID $ 0.
ADDITION TO OWNERS EQUITY $ 53313.

RECEIPTS AND DISBURSEMENTS

RECEIPTS, SALES REVENUE $1681933.

DISBURSEMENTS
CASH EXPENSE $1401067.
ADDITION TO INCOME TAX FUND   57756.
DIVIDENDS PAID   0.
INVESTMENT IN PLANT   250000.
ADDITION TO CASH ASSETS $1706624.
                                              $ -26891.

FINANCIAL CONDITION

ASSETS
NET CASH ASSETS $1080452.
INVENTORY VALUE $ 345155.
PLANT, NET BOOK VALUE $4354198.
OWNERS EQUITY $5779806.

Figure 2

We made our decisions very quickly and very unscientifically.

- We cut the old price of $7.50 down to $7.00, to get rid of a rather high inventory.
- We raised research expenditures from $50,000 to $250,000 on the hunch that we'd benefit by having a more greatly improved product than our competitors.
- We jumped advertising from $50,000 to $150,000 after a heated argument. Our 4-man team seemed to split two-to-two on the wisdom of heavy advertising. We justified this on the basis that we wanted to further implement reduction of inventory.
- We cut production from 200,000 units to 150,000, again to cut inventory.

After the monitor collected our decision sheet, we all stood around discussing how we'd play the seven following quarters the next day, but we were still groping. We broke up about 10 p.m.

"Mack" Tenney drove me to my hotel. We talked strategy all the way. He came up to the room, and, over several drinks during the next two hours, we worked out a tentative long-range plan which called for heavy advertising, heavy R&D, a high price, and high capital investment to meet terrific anticipated demand.

King and Wehle had done some thinking, too, because when we met the next morning, they argued us out of our high unit price, suggested delaying capital investment for a while, and when we finally submitted our decisions for Quarter 2, Tenney and I could hardly recognize our plan. After that we worked as a 4-man team—arguing, persuading, baiting and debating, but coming up with something close to a mutually agreeable decision each time.

Our second-quarter decisions were affected somewhat by the operating statement that recorded our first-quarter performance. We had captured 33.43% of the market. Our sales had risen 35,000 units, but even at that our inventory had increased. Our cash position was off $40,000. We had captured a bigger share of the market, but we had no profits to show for it. Of course, our R&D investment in Quarter 1 wouldn't pay off for six months yet.

Quarter 2

We decided to repeat our first-quarter decisions, with some modifications, since we still had no indication of what power each factor had. We kept the price at $7.00. Cut R&D $50,000. Raised advertising $50,000. And, anticipating more unit sales with our bigger market share, we raised production 50,000 units.

Results of Quarter 2 showed another jump in sales, up another 24,000 units. Our share of market rose slightly. We were dismayed to see our inventory leap up another 29,000 units and our cash position fall off $76,000. Jack King spent a lot of time at one of the Burroughs calculators that surrounded us. At the rate we were going, he figured, we'd capture the market about the same time that we went bankrupt.

Quarter 3

Earlier we had voiced a long-range plan to double sales and capture 50% of market. These were laudable goals, but we were becoming more and more divided on how to achieve them. Our first-quarter investment in R&D was to take effect this quarter and maybe we'd find out how important a factor this was. Meanwhile, we were still wondering what effect all the other variables had. We hadn't really tested anything. We decided to experiment with price and advertising.

We boosted unit price to $7.50 from $7.00. We raised advertising another $50,000 to $250,000. To save money, we cut R&D $50,000, down to $150,000.

Quarter 3 results were sensational! We won 36.02% of the market, sold 205,000 units—up 29,000. R&D definitely paid off. We finally had an absolute. We made a profit, raised our cash position $130,000 and actually reduced inventory 5,000 units.

Quarter 4

The four of us argued hot and heavy as we prepared to make our decisions for the fourth quarter. We were still showing a loss for the year and we wanted a good annual report. The plan was to slash all expenses—production, R&D, and advertising—as well as our price, and thus make a profit on existing inventory.

The big argument concerned advertising. It was costly, running $250,000 the quarter before. We had no proof that it was effective. Here, the four of us split down the middle. Two argued that we could "save" money if we'd cut it to the bone. Two argued that we couldn't sell without it. Time was running out and the factions were still at loggerheads. Finally, the pro-advertising side gave in. It said that we'd cut advertising $100,000 to $150,000 with the understanding that this was just a test.

So, we cut advertising $100,000, cut R&D another $50,000, saved $75,000 by reducing production, cut price to $7.25 and crossed our fingers.

The results of the fourth quarter and the annual report were not due until after lunch. We went down to the cafeteria. There we lied to our "competitors" about our respective strategies, joked a lot, but ate rather hastily and went back upstairs to see results.

Quarter 5

King, Wehle, Tenney and I were quite jubilant when we received our fourth quarter report. Sales volume was up to $248,000, more than double what we had started with. Our share of market was 40.54%. Inventory was down a wonderful 73,000 units. Profits were way up and we had $913,000 in cash, more than double what we had started with.

Of course, our plant value was down $460,000, since we hadn't invested in it at all. And, it seemed that our reduction in advertising hadn't hurt. The "conservative advertisers" grinned and asked for another reduction in advertising "costs." A cut of $50,000 was OK'd.

We felt more product improvement was needed, especially since it paid off so well, and we raised our investment in this from $100,000 to $200,000. We kept the price stable at $7.25.

Quarter 6

The somewhat smug team on which I was playing got a sharp shock when fifth-quarter results came through. We had lost volume. We had lost share of market. We had reduced inventory only slightly. Our profits were cut in half. There was only one possible conclusion. Our price had been the same. Our R&D three quarters before had been high. Only our advertising had been cut. This we figured was the reason for our shellacking.

Consequently, in Quarter 6 we upped advertising to $200,000. Manufactured at our capacity. We also decided to build up the plant and poured $250,000 into this investment.

Quarter 7

Apparently, we were doing most things right. Our volume went up to 232,000. Our share of market jumped to 42.21%. We made a $53,000 profit.

Now, on our decision sheet for Quarter 7, we began thinking about maximizing our profit for the end of the game, the end of our second year.

We were all fond of advertising by this time, so we kicked it up to $250,-000. We cut R&D down $150,000 to a mere $50,000. We manufactured at capacity. And, wanting to end up with a healthier plant than we inherited, we put $500,000 into plant investment. We also paid out $50,000 in dividends to see whether it had any effect on market. (It didn't!)

Quarter 8

We were pleased to see that our sales volume in Quarter 7 held up nicely. In fact, units increased 7,000. Share of industry hit a high of 43.91%. Inventory was cut to 94,000 units and profits were good.

Thus, in our final quarter of life, we put $300,000 into advertising. Just $50,000 into R&D. We produced at capacity, which now was some 241,000 units. We put $200,000 into plant and paid another dividend.

Final Report

When the report came through for 8th Quarter operations, it showed that we had achieved one goal. We had more than doubled sales volume, from 112,000 units to 250,000 units. We fell short on share of industry with 42.87.%

Our profits after taxes for the quarter were $73,000 and we had, in our two years of operation, increased the net worth of our company $114,000, while paying out $100,000 in dividends.

Competitor No. 1 lost $449,000.

Competitor No. 2 lost $614,000. The old company, still operating under its old policies, lost more than any other, $818,000.

*　　*　　*

The game closely simulates actual business life, and it points out even more clearly than life itself that most of the problems with business stem from human frailties in the art of making good, sound executive decisions.

Management Decision Tester:
Computer Used to Simulate
Operations of Small Business

Alfred G. Dale

EXISTING COMPUTERIZED BUSINESS GAMES generally pose problems in a simulated environment to be designed to represent large-scale enterprises. The decision inputs required from participants in such games are usually on a grandiose scale and represent the allocation of very large expenditures at a top policy making level. The competitive environment is typically that of a closed oligopoly, in which participants may manipulate aggregate demand for their hypothetical products, as well as the allocation of demand within the industry. Whether or not such games adequately mirror the view from the board room of a large corporation, they clearly do not convey the flavor of managerial decision-making in smaller companies. Both

At the time this article was published, ALFRED G. DALE was with the Bureau of Business Research, College of Business Administration, University of Texas, Austin, Texas.

Reprinted, with permission, from *Computers and Automation,* October 1962, © 1962 by and published by Berkeley Enterprises, Inc., 815 Washington Street, Newtonville, Massachusetts 02160.

have in common the requirement of resource allocation, but to the executive of a small company, the question of means is as important as the question of ends. His span of direct control over, and intervention in, the microprocesses of the enterprise is necessarily broader and deeper than that of his counterpart in the large company. He must be both strategist and tactician. He cannot, in general, avoid the administrative consequences of his major strategic decisions.

SMALL BUSINESS GAME

The Texas Small Business Game[1] is an attempt to construct an environment in which analogues of typical small business problems will be generated, and in which some of the skills necessary for their resolution can be illustrated.

CHARACTERISTICS OF THE MODEL

The model permits competitive interaction among a maximum of ten competing companies operating manufacturing enterprises with initial assets of $250,000, and with 25-30 employees. They are producing a homogeneous (in the economic sense) small metal fitting used in building construction, and selling to construction contractors in a fairly well defined regional area. Aggregate demand for the product is externally determined. The small companies are also competing in the market with a number of much larger concerns who may unilaterally modify marketing procedures to the disadvantage of the small companies, with little fear of reprisal. In brief, the initial environmental situation is one in which the small companies occupy an essentially static and defensive position.

Internally, the scale of production facilities is nonoptimal, inventories are relatively high, and the working capital situation is tight.

TRIALS OF SMALL BUSINESS

These environmental and internal characteristics of the companies in the initial stage of the simulation typify the conditions under which many, perhaps most, small manufacturers live, and to which too many also succumb.

In the long run, the success and viability of the small enterprise depend on how it adapts to its market environment, and how its internal operational procedures are organized. The small firm operating in a restrictive competitive environment must seek to create or find a new set of conditions over which it can assert a greater measure of control, and within which it can reassume market initiative. Internally, because the firm does not possess the resources to cushion the consequences of poor decisions (a small company cannot launch an Edsel and survive its foundering), its information collection, analysis, and planning procedures should provide an adequate basis for necessary routine control over operations, and for rational risk-taking under conditions of uncertainty.

THE STRATEGY SPACE

The Small Business Game permits solutions to the problem of initial environment via new product development and new geographic market penetration. An interesting and, in some respects, the key feature of the simulation is that while participants are given an elaborate scenario prior to play, describing the history and current conditions of the industry, the range of permissible strategies is not revealed. Participants are advised that they may request information of any type they desire, that is not included in their manual, or contained in the periodic feedback from the computer runs. They are also advised of the possibility of proposing changes in their method of operation. This open-end feature of the game has proved most successful. Psychologically, it leads participants to invest their mythical operations with a sort of auto-created reality. Pedagogically, it allows us to encourage players to recognize the existence of restraints, to seek relevant information in a specific type of problem context, and to propose solutions. The game administrator has an extensive pre-prepared information bank consisting of reports and data that cover most of the information typically requested during the course of a game. An inventive administrator can also produce relevant *ad hoc* information to supplement the prepackaged material at his disposal. We recognize, of course, that the market solutions permitted within the game are not necessarily relevant for all small companies under actual conditions. In post-game discussions with players we consider the solutions available within the model simply as particular instances of the general necessity for a small company to attempt to gain control over some of its environmental parameters.

Thirty-Five Decision Variables

Operationally, the players are required to set values on up to 35 routine decision variables at each decision sequence, covering elements such as pricing, deployment and support of salesmen, production scheduling, short-term financing, and hiring and layoff of personnel. This relatively large number of inputs to the model, and the feedback in terms of manufacturing cost, financial status, and sales reports, puts a premium on adequate processing and analysis of internal accounting and other data.

Use of Computer

A group will take an average of one and a half hours to prepare a routine decision input. If nonroutine decisions are also in process, the time might be much longer. For this reason, we have never considered the game suitable for continuous sessions with rapid decision sequences. Data processing and keypunching take about thirty minutes. Running time on the 1604, exclusive of printing time, is less than three minutes when all sections of the model are being utilized. The model consists of three interlinked programs written in FORTRAN, one containing the demand model for the original geographic market area, together with all production and accounting models for all companies, one comprising the demand model for an additional market area, and a printing program to generate output for the companies and the administrator. The largest program uses about 12,000 words in the 1604, including arrays, although it has been compiled with modifications on a 7070 with 10K core.

The time requirements for the decision process, computer requirements, and the problems involved in small business in releasing managerial personnel for several days at a time, combined to suggest that use of the game by small business management would have to be incorporated in some type of discontinuous program organized so as to make minimal extra calls on executive time.

Experience with the Game

The gaming session plan adopted for a series of games initiated in September, last year, required participating groups to make decisions on their own time at 10-14 day intervals, mailing decisions to the University computer center for processing and running with a 2-3 day elapsed time between dispatch of the decisions and receipt of the results. Gaming sessions were organized in seven different cities, involving about 220 participants from 53 companies. Each gaming team consisted of officers from the same firm, an arrangement that permitted participants to organize decision-making sessions to suit their own convenience. After an initial briefing session, held as a joint meeting with all participants present, each team operated quite independently, subject only to the requirement that decisions be mailed in on designated dates. Each gaming session had a project representative in the locality for local liaison, but administration was centralized.

RESULTS OF GAMING

The sessions extended from September, 1961, to February, 1962, permitting play through twelve decision periods in most games. Aspects of a couple of the games are illustrated in the accompanying charts. The first shows the pricing patterns that developed in Game 1, with a steady initial decline in the average price of the original product to the $22 level, a period of stability in the middle game, and renewed competition in the closing periods. The thin bars show the price ranges on the substitute new product, introduced in this game in the fourth quarter of play.

Contrast the pattern of Game 1 with that of Game 5. Again, there is an initial downward movement with a period of midgame stability, with prices tending to be somewhat lower than Game 1 for the original product. But aggressive price competition for the new product was characteristic almost from the outset, and the final stages of the game witnessed ruinous price cutting across the board among a group of companies laboring under chronic overcapacity.

The net income figures for Game 5 illustrate the dangerous state of the companies towards the end. The corporate histories in Game 1 tended to be more satisfactory, largely because the industry as a whole had not built an unsustainable capacity.

ADVANTAGES OF THE SMALL BUSINESS GAME

Experience with the gaming sessions suggests that the technique we followed can be successfully applied in small business executive development

Game 1
PRICES, PRODUCTS A AND B

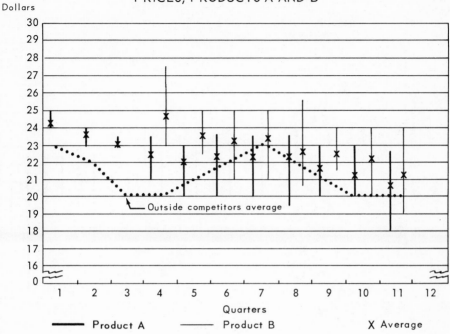

Product A   Product B   X Average

Game 1
QUARTERLY NET INCOME (ROUNDED TO NEAREST DOLLAR)
Company

Quarter	Co.1	Co.2	Co.3	Co.4	Co.5	Co.6	Co.7	Co.8	Co.9
1	4,897	5,167	4,677	5,519	5,900	5,382	5,336	3,830	5,103
2	3,433	4,160	3,803	4,704	4,531	2,966	4,831	5,009	5,899
3	− 490	4,693	− 884	2,962	5,624	4,561	2,932	3,757	2,576
4	− 2,580	−1,210	− 544	52	2,270	2,192	1,334	− 1,656	−10,329
5	− 794	45	− 4,363	−1,118	8,210	4,994	− 695	5,955	− 9,189
6	1,643	2,462	4,646	− 6	9,629	5,904	4,499	8,900	− 6,695
7	965	4,892	3,366	1,625	11,455	5,035	6,125	5,032	− 2,061
8	− 3,977	3,630	3,811	965	9,645	1,358	3,596	13,129	− 3,596
9	− 6,008	5,571	8,699	251	19,992	−13,364	9,426	17,652	−13,345
10	− 8,790	4,759	8,241	− 8,858	15,804	− 8,402	7,924	11,816	−18,494
11	− 8,905	3,170	6,457	− 9,822	3,385	809	4,586	6,573	−22,883
12									

Game 5
PRICES, PRODUCTS A AND B

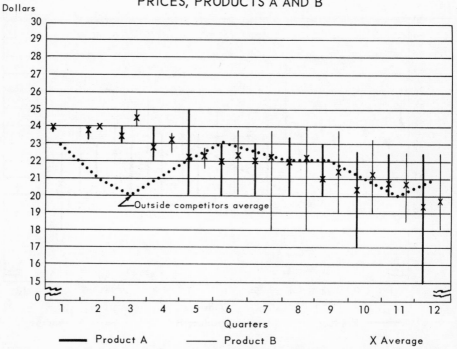

Product A ———　Product B ———　X Average

Game 5
QUARTERLY NET INCOME (ROUNDED TO NEAREST DOLLAR)
Company

Quarter	Co. 1	Co. 2	Co. 3	Co. 4	Co. 5	Co. 6	Co. 7
1	4,587	5,582	3,678	4,721	5,099	5,179	4,481
2	4,292	4,528	3,123	135	4,301	1,071	4,051
3	2,246	− 531	1,551	1,157	5,628	6,700	358
4	− 713	− 4,424	6,141	− 2,266	2,187	− 394	770
5	− 2,614	− 44,430	− 2,266	1,564	− 5,640	− 8,277	472
6	− 35,736	− 3,652	5,182	814	− 480	− 8.847	− 1,356
7	− 7,518	1,671	2,946	6,190	4,541	997	5,899
8	− 5,745	− 13,720	− 1,871	5,147	421	− 4,458	5,016
9	− 28,013	− 16,068	6,770	3,420	1,458	− 1,649	8,226
10	− 11,596	1,998	5,489	− 2,523	2,406	− 13,075	1,385
11	− 9,226	4,875	− 30,733	− 7,909	− 3,428	− 16,023	4,171
12	− 29,235	− 9,450	− 22,572	− 8,958	− 1,424	− 8,596	− 6,601

programs. The two great advantages are, first, the possibility of efficiently and flexibly integrating program activity with other demands on participants' time, and, second, the high motivation and interest of participants in the problems generated by the simulation. Even though the gaming sessions extended over five months, we observed no significant diminution of interest.

SUMMARY

In summary, we feel we have created a system suitable for middle-management training in larger small businesses and for top-management training in the smallest companies, that has been adequately debugged, and that can be used by interested organizations after minimal familiarization and set-up time.

It appears to have particular training value in the following areas:

1. Use and analysis of internal accounting data for control and planning purposes.
2. Use and analysis of environmental information as a basis for planning.
3. Appreciation of the functional relationships existing within the total enterprise.
4. Emphasizing the need for evaluating information specific to a particular environment and acting upon it, rather than upon preconceived notions of what correct behavior may be.

Finally, the simulation illustrates the importance of certain principles crucial to the survival of the firm. For example, unbalanced inventory positions tend to cumulate rapidly in the simulation, and it is most difficult for players to recover from any severe erosion of their working capital position. Such principles may be clichés: but one thing a businessman, and particularly an unsuccessful one, learns, both in the game and in the real world, is never to underestimate the value of a cliché.

NOTE TO THE TEXT

[1] The development and testing of the Texas Small Business Game was supported by research grants from the Small Business Administration.

Part I

C

Special Purpose and Functional Games Readings

These Men Are Playing . . .
Maintenance Management Games

G. W. Bechberger, W. F. Keleher, and F. L. Hunziker

No COMPUTERS, no blue-sky theory, and no special costs are involved with this management game. A few homemade charts and a handful of straight pins are about all you need. These and some managers who want to improve fast. This game helps teach managers to look at their decisions the way the front office does—in terms of total impact on the profit-and-loss statement.

Like all management games, this technique is a form of simulation. But it's not off in the clouds somewhere. It gives the players some realistic experience in a very short time. Best of all, it lets young managers learn by making mistakes—but the mistakes are all on paper. They don't cost you anything.

It's cheap in other ways, too. This is a sort of classroom deal. You can play it in an office, in a conference room, almost anywhere you can find a table and some chairs where you won't be interrupted. Now, don't let that

At the time this article was published, G. W. BECHBERGER, W. F. KELEHER, and F. L. HUNZIKER were with Allied Chemical Corporation, New York.

Reprinted by permission from McGraw-Hill in an article in the February 1961 *Factory*, now *Modern Manufacturing* Magazine.

word "play" fool you. The men playing this game are working—at a furious pace.

The game really consists of imitating, or dummying up, the paperwork involved in managing a typical maintenance operation. The better the imitation—the closer it is to the real facts of life in your plant—the more the men will get out of it.

STAGE SETTING

The basic idea is to have young managers pretend they've just been put in charge of maintenance at a plant where costs and downtime have got out of hand. They try to whip things into shape by deciding how best to use the men, money, and facilities available. Emphasis is on scheduling, but the men also learn a bit about the fine art of spending money in order to save it.

The players know what product their plant is making, and how many maintenance men—with which skills—they have. They also know the average number of work orders and emergencies they can expect in a week. Finally, they know the average labor hours and lost production associated with each type of maintenance job.

The players don't know how many maintenance personnel will be absent at any time. They don't know which machines will break down, or how long the repairs will actually take. They don't know exactly how many or what kind of work orders they'll get each week, what emergencies will show up, or which jobs will be held up because of material shortages. Finally, they can't tell in advance (without a study) what benefits—if any—will result from the adoption of certain management techniques.

REALISTIC GROUND RULES

The more true to life the ground rules are, the better the results will be. So each company has to design its own game, to reflect actual conditions. Each should choose appropriate average numbers, to correspond with its actual experience, for the following variables: number of scheduled work orders per week; percentage of emergency work orders per week; time per job; production loss per job. This way, the experience gained will really count back in the shop. Decision results are fed back promptly, so you can easily cram several "months" of operations into a two-day game.

At Allied Chemical, we divide our players into teams of four to six men (larger groups slow up the decisions). Each team has a "referee" who provides the operating data on which the team makes its decisions. The teams don't compete against each other—directly. Instead, each team tries to cope with the economic facts of life. It's a learn-by-doing situation. So there are no losers in this game. The real winners are the men who get the most out of it.

The method of play is to have the men make out weekly schedules for maintenance, in an attempt to get minimum costs and minimum downtime. Each team works at its own pace, and declares a "week" to be over as soon as it has finished its planning. Later on—after the players have learned how to control costs by better scheduling—the game gets more involved. The players are permitted to adopt various management tools, such as work sampling, materials control, and preventive maintenance. Costs and benefits have to be weighed carefully.

SEQUENCE OF PLAY

To begin, each team gets a bundle of assorted work orders for the following "week." They have to schedule these realistically, taking into account crew sizes, time and skills needed, priorities, downtime, and the backlog of work that they "inherited" from the previous management. Overdue jobs are realistically penalized—they cost more, take longer, and cause more lost production.

When the week's completed schedule is given to the referee, he posts to each work order the "actual" (as opposed to scheduled) time the job took, and the production lost while the machine was down. The referee selects these figures from a chart of random numbers shown in the figure. Also, he flags those jobs that could not be completed because of material shortages. These, too, are taken from the random number chart. Finally, the referee adds the pre-set number of emergency work orders, and returns the whole bundle to his team of players.

Emergency orders get priority. The players first have to deduct the manpower that was needed on these jobs—and record the production loss suffered. With the emergencies out of the way, the team figures out how many of its scheduled jobs were finished with the time and skills remaining. If the total time needed was *less* than that scheduled, some workers were idle, and the extra time is just lost. But it's also likely that the time needed to

HERE'S HOW THEY WORK:

The real heart of this game is the random number charts from which the referees pick off the "actual" times and lost production of the scheduled and emergency jobs. You can set up these charts on pegboards, computers, or what have you, but we get fine results with a sheet of paper and a couple of straight pins.

The key is the actual historical averages (labor hours and lost production) of typical maintenance jobs in your own company. With each of these as a base, you can develop a table of random numbers that have the same averages as the actual job (or group of similar jobs). To keep our game under control, we at Allied selected a dozen "jobs," each with different crew sizes, skills, number of labor hours, and lost production.

For each of these jobs, we generated 20 random numbers for labor hours and 20 for amount of lost production.

In each case, the average of all 20 numbers of each type is given to the players, so they'll have some basis for planning and scheduling these jobs.

Using the chart is simple. The referee sticks a pin into any pair of numbers aligned with each job. When a work order for a job shows up in a schedule, the referee posts the numbers under its pin onto the work order. These numbers tell the team how long the job took and how much production was lost while the machine was down. The referee then moves pin to the next pair of numbers.

Our charts (sample at right), with 20 random numbers for each job, are very convenient. For example, at the start of the game, we want the players to suffer material shortages 10% of the time. So we just put a strip of black plastic tape over any two of the 20 columns. This blots out two pairs of numbers for each job. When the pin hits a blacked-out column, the job goes back to the team as "held up for materials." Later, if a team installs material controls, we can slash stockouts 50% by just pulling off one of the black tapes.

In the same way, we put red tape over two columns when a team puts in preventive maintenance. When a pin is on a red column, and that job comes in on a schedule, the referee marks it complete with 0 hours and 0 lost production. Result: PM has cut the work load and emergencies by 10%. If you want a 5% change, of course, you place a tape over only one column.

Switching charts adds versatility. When a team adopts a management technique that will bring about improved worker performance—rather than fewer jobs—we switch to another table of random numbers. This table has lower averages per job, which has the effect of getting the jobs done sooner with less production loss. At Allied, players can boost performance two ways: first, by using a combination of standard data, work sampling, and added supervision; second, by using an incentive system. Here again, there is a definite expense involved with each technique. Of course, you can vary the game with other types of improvements and their corresponding random number charts. But the only way to keep things realistic is to decide how big an improvement would likely result if such programs were actually started in your company.

Types of Jobs	Preventive Maintenance			Preventive Maintenance	Stock Out
M Labor Hours →	8	4	3	4	7
Units Lost →	8	4	3	4	7
N	7	11	5	8	6
	35	55	25	40	30
O	11	13	8	4	6
	11	13	8	4	6
P	20	16	14	12	16
	40	32	28	24	32
Q	18	16	14	18	16
	27	24	21	27	24
R	28	34	36	36	30
	7	8	8	8	7
S	34	28	26	38	34
	51	42	39	56	51
T	70	72	60	60	62
	105	110	90	90	93
U	70	58	58	64	62
	8	7	7	8	7
V	58	56	48	8	60
	17	14	12	12	15
W	150	120	130	120	120
	18	15	16	15	15
X	160	156	166	150	160
	80	78	83	75	80

complete all the work was *more* than the amount scheduled. In this case, the team has to decide whether the extra work orders should carry over into the next week, be done on overtime (at a 50% premium in labor cost), or be contracted out (at double the normal labor cost).

The team then calculates its total maintenance and downtime costs for the week, and checks the impact of these costs on operating profit. In this game—as in business itself—the "score sheet" is the profit-or-loss statement. One purpose of the game is to show the players how maintenance costs affect profits. So each team calculates the effect of its weekly maintenance costs on total manufacturing cost. They also figure the sales dollars lost as a result of lost production while equipment was down for maintenance. For simplicity, dollars per unit of production are kept constant. We also assume that weekly sales costs are constant, and that salesmen can peddle all we produce. Each team tries to get maximum production at the lowest possible maintenance cost.

After the team calculates its profit for the current "week," it picks up another bundle of work orders and the cycle is repeated. For the first few "weeks," the game is restricted to working down the backlog of orders, coping with emergency jobs and material shortages, and adjusting schedules for variations in "actual" job time.

MANAGEMENT CONTROLS

As the new management gains experience, the game gets more realistic. After the players have mastered scheduling (this will take several "weeks"), the team can consider adopting better maintenance controls—decentralized shops, materials control, standard data, and so on.

Some "improvements" may not be economically justified, because of the size of the plant, type of operation, etc. (In all aspects of the game each company should try to dummy up situations that are as close as possible to actual conditions, or the training will be less effective.) The teams are told what it will cost to set up and operate a new program, but without a study they don't know what benefits to expect. They can buy a study from "staff services" to find out what the probable results will be.

At our company, for example, a team can pay a thousand dollars and the referee will report that "preventive maintenance will reduce average work orders and emergencies per week by 10%." The team then has to decide whether or not to spend the money to set up and maintain PM. Mistakes hit profits hard, so the teams learn to look at all the angles, and to balance care-fully costs and benefits for long-run improvement.

REHASH SESSIONS

Although the teams don't compete directly, we've found that setting aside about an hour for a good rehash session after the game pays big dividends. The men are interested in hearing about each other's solutions, and learn from them.

We've been using this maintenance management game at Allied Chemical for over a year. It teaches faster than anything else we've tried. The players go back to their plants with some concentrated experience, and a much better idea of how to manage the maintenance function efficiently.

A Collective Bargaining Game

Simulation Technique in
Industrial Relations from BNA

Dr. Wendell L. French

Does business "gaming" have application for industrial and labor relations seminars and classes? Can collective bargaining be taught by the game method? Can collective bargaining be simulated in the laboratory situation, thus providing opportunity for the development and examination of skills, approaches, and philosophy? A recent innovation provides at least partial answers to these questions.

Union officials, professors of personnel and labor relations courses, and executives concerned with management development will be interested in

At the time this article was published, DR. WENDELL L. FRENCH was Associate Professor of Policy, Personnel Relations, and Production in the College of Business Administration, University of Washington, Seattle.

Reprinted by special permission from the January 1961 issue of the *Journal of the American Society of Training Directors.* © 1961 by the American Society for Training and Development.

a "Collective Bargaining Game" developed by The Bureau of National Affairs, Inc. BNA, a publisher of a number of informational services to businessmen, developed the game as a service to business and labor clients. One game was developed in 1959, and another game was developed in 1960. The idea was essentially that of Fred Joiner, Director, Training and Development Services of the staff of BNA, and the case materials were developed by John D. Stewart, Executive Editor and Vice President of the same organization.

The content of the collective bargaining game includes instructions to the participants as to procedure, case materials describing a fictional company and a union, and past history of the two organizations, including a history of the collective bargaining relationship. In addition, copies of the most recent contract between the company and the union, and the most recent issues of the company newspaper and the union newspaper are included.

MATERIALS FROM ACTUAL CASES

In the case of the BNA game, the materials are not completely fictional, since the case materials are composites drawn from a number of actual situations, lending a great deal of authenticity to the game. In the 1960 BNA game, presented in Washington, D. C. and in San Francisco, the authors of the material called the company "The Cooley Container Corporation," and the union the "United Metal Product Workers." The company paper was called "The Clarion," and the union paper "The UMP News."

The game was introduced as a part of BNA's annual Briefing Sessions on Collective Bargaining in 1959. A new game, containing some modifications and an entirely new factual situation, was used in BNA's 1960 Briefing Sessions.

Participants in the BNA sessions were all "real-life" management or union officials, many of them highly-placed industrial relations officers from the country's largest companies, or officers of larger unions. They represented many diverse backgrounds—industrial, type of union dealt with, bargaining strategy used, etc. Attendance was limited to 20 participants at each session to insure free and full discussion. The primary purpose of the collective bargaining game, for this group, was to provide an opportunity for sharing of advice and experience on realistic bargaining problems.

The San Francisco session, which the author attended, utilized the first of two days for collective bargaining briefing sessions. "The Economic Climate for Bargaining in 1960," "Management and Union Approaches to Bargaining in 1960," "Trends in Wages and Fringe Benefits," and "Legislation Round-Up" were subjects discussed by members of the editorial staff of The Bureau of National Affairs.

THE GAME

The second of the two days was devoted to the game. At 9:00 A.M. all participants gathered to hear a general briefing on the rules. All were expected to have studied the case materials carefully prior to the session. Half the participants were then assigned to "union" bargaining teams and the other half assigned to "management" bargaining teams. Choices of participants were considered in assigning team members. It was interesting that a number of the company officials desired to participate on the union teams and that union officers desired to participate on the management teams—people apparently wanted to gain perspective on bargaining approaches of the other side.

At 9:30 all members of "management" teams and all members of "union" teams had separate meetings to frame the bargaining objectives for their respective sides. They were told that they would be evaluated in terms of the extent to which they achieved their objectives. Agreement was then reached by the participants of each side as to what contract changes they were going to try to obtain, including objectives as to fringe benefits, length of the contract, and the wage settlement.

From 10:30 until 11:30, each of the three individual bargaining teams on each side caucused to develop strategy and to draft specific contract proposals. At 11:30 each small bargaining team met with its respective opposing group, and commenced bargaining. Negotiations were resumed after lunch, and continued until 3:30. It was to be assumed that a number of weeks had passed during lunch, and that the expiration of the contract date was almost at hand. At any time after 2:15, the union was free to seek authorization from the "international" to strike. (A member of the BNA staff served as a representative of the international.) If the parties requested, a BNA observer would mediate a dispute. If there was a strike and a deadlock, the BNA observer might intervene as a mediator without invitation.

At 3:30, the teams met jointly to compare their bargaining successes and experiences, and to hear an evaluation by BNA observers. Trophies were awarded to the members of the team on each side which came closest to meeting the objectives developed by the respective side. The evaluation took into account not only success in meeting objectives, but the extent to which the teams negotiated clauses which would avoid serious problems for the future.

In the game, one of the basic problems presented to negotiators was a company desire to modify a contract clause which restricted management's right to modernize the plant. The Cooley Container Company had recently been taken over by the nationwide Consolidated Can Company, and the new management was moving unmistakably in the direction of modernization, if not outright automation. The stumbling block to these plans was Section II-B in the old Cooley contract which required "mutual agreement" to any changes in "departmental working conditions" and, in case of failure to agree, final and binding arbitration of such changes. Each management group in the "game" set itself the task of eliminating or modifying this clause on the best terms it could get.

Dangers of Hasty Actions

The negotiations on this and other problems, and the final settlements arrived at, provided much exercise for ingenuity and much food for thought on the part of both union and management negotiators. Several participants, who thought they had achieved a signal "victory" in their solutions, were ruefully forced to concede that they hadn't considered all the ramifications of the contract terms they had agreed to. If nothing else, the game provided a lesson in the dangers of proposing or accepting proposals in the heat of negotiations which have not been clearly thought through.

For example, one management negotiating team won elimination of the arbitration features of the clause, but in return gave an unconditional guarantee of no layoffs and no reduction in pay for any employee during the course of a two-year agreement. Another team took a two-week strike, and gave the union a substantial wage and SUB package, in exchange for a clause giving management the right to determine crew size on old and new equipment. One group of company negotiators offered the union 10 cents an hour to use in any way it wanted. The union applied the whole amount to an exotic fringe benefit, leaving the company's wage rate 10 cents below the going rate and presumably forcing the company later to grant a wage rate increase to bring it into line.

I mention these examples, not in any sense of criticism of the negotiators, but rather to give the reader an idea of the extent to which simulation in a problem of this type can give the participant valuable experience for future "real life" negotiations. Fortunately, mistakes of judgment made in a simulation exercise do not have costly repercussions.

Aside from the actual "experience" which such games can give to participants, the principal benefit comes from the frank and full discussion of the "settlements" in a round-table evaluation session following the negotiations. Here I was pleased to find "real-life" union negotiators giving frank and candid advice to "real-life" management negotiators (and vice versa) regarding the future implications of their settlements.

A number of innovations could readily be made in the game procedure, for example, the game could continue longer and could involve more time in bargaining sessions. In the college situation, the game might very well be played over a period of weeks. Furthermore, the collective bargaining game might be dovetailed into a broader management decision game, with the results of bargaining in an industrial relations class being incorporated into the gaming in a policy course.

COMPUTER NOT NEEDED

The collective bargaining game does not seem to readily lend itself to much quantification, and therefore, the need for machine accounting assistance or high speed computation is minimal. However, the game does depend upon calculations of costs of various fringe items, and either the class or the instructor, or both, must spend considerable time in calculating costs. This in itself, of course, would be an important educational experience for the participant.

LIMITATIONS

There were two limitations in the effectiveness of the technique. Some participants seem to have a tendency to "act out" a role—to try to act in a way they thought bargainers should behave, rather than "playing it straight" and bargaining the best they themselves knew how to do. The result was some "put-on" emotionalism which may not necessarily be constructive. This can be corrected or avoided by proper explanation of the game before the bargaining starts.

A second limitation of the game is the tendency of the participants, because of the stringent time limitation, to agree to clauses in the contract without exploring all of the facets, as noted above, thus leading to poorly worded or ambiguous agreements. This limitation can be offset by lengthening the time in which the game is played and by proper structuring. Of course, all negotiations work against time limitations, and finding out the consequences of hasty agreements can be an educational experience in itself.

In conclusion, it appears that The Bureau of National Affairs, Inc., has developed a very significant teaching and management development tool in the field of industrial relations—a tool which can have considerable value in workshop, seminar, and classroom situations. We can expect to see a number of interesting innovations by management development executives, union officials, and by professors, building upon BNA's very constructive venture in the development of a collective bargaining game.

Who Picks Up
the Marketing Marbles?

Mack Hanan

GENTLEMEN, GENTLEMEN. May I re-state the problem? No one is suggesting that we ignore the decisions of our competitors. It's a question of how we react to them. If we simply follow them, how can we ever hope to lead the market?"

"But it isn't just a question of competition. It's a question of what we do with our own experience. We must have learned *something* worth while all these years. Why don't we apply it—competition, research and all the rest be damned."

These are the voices of industrial marketing men simulating an annual marketing campaign. You are one of them. It began at nine o'clock this morning. An envelope from the office of the Chairman of the Board was on each man's desk. "Welcome," the letter inside read, "to the marketing management of our company."

"As you know," the Chairman's letter continued, "we manufacture and

MACK HANAN is managing partner of Hanan & Son, New York management consultants.

Reprinted, with permission, from *Industrial Marketing*, May 1965, pp. 108-119. © 1965 by Advertising Publications Inc., 740 Rush Street, Chicago, Illinois 60611.

market two aluminum products: household foil, sold to consumers, and containers which are sold to industry. It will be your immediate assignment to help us plan a national marketing campaign for one of these products, *containers*. Media advertising is our primary marketing tool for containers. Nonetheless, you will quickly become involved in many other decision-making areas of marketing as well, including collateral advertising and sales promotion, pricing, production, product naming and theming and marketing research. We will also be choosing a new advertising agency.

"We market containers in fixed lots of 2,000 units. Only this single size lot is marketed. Approximately 600,000 lots were sold last calendar year, January through December. Of this total, 50,000 lots were sold during the last quarter of last year. Now, at the outset of the first quarter of this new year, our sales price is still the same as it was then: $100 per lot. You can see how we distributed this income in our last quarter Operating Statement, which I am attaching." (Figure 1)

Operating Statement
Fourth Quarter—Last Year

Sales   50,000 units @ $100 = $5,000,000
Less
Cost of Sales 50,000 units @ $ 60 = $3,000,000
                    Gross Margin = $2,000,000

Less
   Advertising & Research $100,000
   Other Marketing   400,000
   Inventory & Distribution   200,000
   Corporate Overhead   300,000

TOTAL OTHER EXPENSES = $1,000,000
           NET PROFIT = $1,000,000
    ACCUMULATED
        NET PROFIT = $X X X X

STOCK REPORT
On Hand Opening 50,000
Sales   50,000
From Production   50,000
On Hand Closing 50,000
Orders Received   50,000

Figure 1

"Containers are purchased primarily by producers and packagers of all sorts of containable products such as soft drinks, beer, soup, canned fruits and vegetables, waxes and polishes, automobile oil and other commodities formerly or still packaged primarily in 'tin cans.' Plastic, paper, cardboard and even foil containers also are used to some extent by these producers and packagers who represent a key market for us. So do consumers, the ultimate end-users of containable products. And so may retail and wholesale distributors who buy from the producers and packagers and then sell to the end-users.

"The market has a choice of three brands to select from: our own brand or the brands of our two competitors. Each competitor is, like us, a national manufacturer and marketer of a product almost identical to our own, selling at exactly the same price and promoting approximately the same user benefits. Each competitor possesses a current inventory and production capability which parallels our own. It is therefore not surprising that each of our three companies enjoys an equal share of market and that all of us are, at this moment, equally profitable.

"We are calling on you to help break the three-way deadlock in our industry this year by helping us *to maximize our accumulated net profit over the next 12 months.*"

The Chairman's letter concluded with the reminder that your company's accumulated net profit will depend on the interaction of your own decisions with those of your nine fellow members of the marketing plans board plus, of course, how all of you together influence and are influenced by your competitors.

Where will you begin? What will you plan first, second, third? How will you harmonize the specific requirements of advertising, sales promotion, pricing, production and marketing research into a total marketing plan? How will you balance day-to-day needs on a short-term quarterly basis and then balance quarterly needs over an annual basis? These are the questions posed by Adplan. After reading their copies of the Chairman's letter, members of each 10-man Adplan team locked themselves into their company's plans board room. Maximum security prevailed. There are three such teams, all with similar directives from their chairman to guide them. Now, at exactly 10 o'clock, a buzzer sounds. The first quarter of Adplan's campaign year is under way.

ORGANIZING FOR MARKETING

The ten members of Company A take their places around the conference table. Their president, the senior marketing man among them, sits at the head of the table. You, in your role as consultant, sit in a comfortable convertible chair at the president's left. This is where the action is. From this position you will be able to advise him softly yet with authority.

"Gentlemen," the president begins. "The most essential duty each one of us has is to agree upon our over-all objective and to keep it fixed in the bullseye of our thinking every minute of today. Our objective is simple: to maximize our accumulated net profit. I would like to see us achieve this objective by playing a steady ball game, getting off to a good start consistently, not trying to put the other guys out of business in the first inning. We have four quarters to play. The key words in our objective are *accumulated profit*. Let us accumulate consistently, gaining at as steady a rate as possible quarter by quarter. No matter what our competitors do, I want no panic. Unless the roof shows signs of falling in, I want us to create a basic plan and to stick to it through thick and thin. Any questions?"

There are none. "All right, then, let us accumulate."

The president hands sheets of paper to his colleagues. "Put your name at the top. Then, one-two-three, list in descending order the functional areas of marketing in which you feel most competent. Don't expand on them— just itemize them. Remember, the clock is running."

The president scans each page. Then he organizes his company. Calling off names in pairs, he assigns two men to each of five marketing functions:

1. Marketing Management, including pricing and production decisions.
2. Marketing Research Management, including all decisions for or against all forms of research.
3. Creative Management, including all decisions in the areas of product naming and theming.
4. Media Advertising Management, including all print and electronic media decisions.
5. Collateral Advertising Management, including all non-media advertising decisions.

"I may have done one or two of you an injustice," the president apologizes. "But let's get started. We can always reorganize as we go." Then he remembers. "Just one last word: Let's try to make the right decision the first time. If we go wrong, we're stuck with a bad decision throughout an entire quarter."

A quick glance at the clock. It is now after 10:30. Haste and caution must somehow be harmonized. For a few moments there is cautious silence. Then the need for haste prevails. One of the two men assigned to pricing and production decisions raises his hand. The president acknowledges him, calling him by his functional title:

"Yes, Mr. Marketing?"

"Well, let's start at the beginning. The operating statement shows we sold 50,000 units last quarter. That was October, November, December. Now, we've inherited 50,000 units for this current quarter from our predecessors. As I see it, we have two basic decisions to make. What price shall we set to get rid of these 50,000 units? Then, number two, how many new units shall we schedule for this current quarter? And let's be careful about this. There's a carrying charge for all goods unsold at the end of every quarter. And if we under-schedule, those orders are lost to us forever. So let's avoid stockouts. There's no way we can make them up."

"Well," the president intervenes, "what do you recommend?"

Before Mr. Marketing can reply, Mr. Marketing Research raises his hand insistently.

"Yes, Mr. Research?" the president says.

"Hadn't we better be realistic?" Mr. Research asks. "How can we set production schedules or even plan pricing until we evaluate market demand? How about investing in some market research?"

"Let's be careful how we spend our money," Mr. Marketing warns. "I have nothing against research, you understand. But experience is the best market research. What do you think this operating statement is—it's a market research report, nothing else. And it's all bought and paid for. Why don't we apply its lessons first, before we go off ordering more information?"

"The operating statement's all very well and good as far as it goes," Mr. Research replies. "But it stops on last December 31st. I, for one, am not going to assume that what was true in the last quarter of last year is necessarily projectable into the first quarter of this year. What about market growth, for instance? What about seasonal factors? We don't even know if there are any. What about the economic cycle? Is it going up or down? All of these things are important to know before we start planning. And we can't learn any of them from the operating statement."

"While you're at it," Mr. Creative Management interrupts, "don't forget the variable effect of creativity on demand. It's my job to give us a sales theme that will motivate the market in a way it's never been motivated before.

"But I don't know what motivates them. I'm going to need some motivation research. And some copy research, too. Do we have them available?"

"Yes, they're available. Here's the availability list. All in all, we can choose from ten types of research." (Figure 2)

CHOOSING AN ADVERTISING AGENCY

As Marketing, Research and Creative put their heads together, the president turns to you and whispers in your ear. "There's nothing like having a genius for organization. I've put everybody to work. But I forgot one very important decision area entirely. We have to select an advertising agency, don't we? Well, since I didn't give that as an assignment to anybody, let's you and I make the decision. What do we have to choose from?"

RESEARCH					
Markets	5	10	25	50	100
Media	5	10	25	50	100
Message	5	10	25	50	100
Motivation	5	10	25	50	100
Product	5	10	25	50	100
Packaging	5	10	25	50	100
Pricing	5	10	25	50	100
Production	5	10	25	50	100
Distribution	5	10	25	50	100
Economics Trend	5	10	25	50	100

Figure 2

This is a reproduction of an actual tool used in the marketing game. Figures represent the types of research available (in thousands of dollars).

You shuffle through the papers on your lap and come up with a sheet titled "Advertising Agency Profiles." Five types of agency are tersely described on it. (Figure 3) They include an old established agency, a new, young agency, a long-established industrial agency, a small diversified agency and a house agency. "A five-horned dilemma," the president mutters.

"Let's take them from the top," the president suggests. "The bottom's easier," you answer. "We ought to rule out a 'House Agency' right off the bat, I'd say. Then, a small, diversified agency. Nothing wrong with its size.

Advertising Agency Profiles

Advertising Agency "A"

Old, established agency. Five branch offices throughout U.S., ten branch and affiliated offices in Europe, South America and Asia. Annual billings exceed $200 million, divided 3 to 1 between "consumer" and "industrial" accounts. Reputation: broadly experienced, highly detail-minded and staffed in creative and administrative depth. Experienced in selling through all types of retail outlets.

Advertising Agency "B"

New, young agency. No branch offices. Annual billings have grown rapidly within two years to $20 million based on widespread reputation for unusual creativity. Diversified accounts oriented toward consumer goods. Largest single account bills $2 million. Three principals, each in mid-'30s, concentrate supervision and planning within themselves.

Advertising Agency "C"

Long-established industrial agency. Three branch offices within continental U.S. and two affiliates overseas. Annual billings average $40 million. Reputation: solid, business-minded organization creatively serving many of the same clients for over a generation. Last year began to diversify into consumer product accounts, making successful yet limited penetration. Committee management composed of former top-level business executives.

Advertising Agency "D"

Small, diversified agency. Ten years old this year. Presided over by founder, a man of acknowledged advertising genius now in his mid-50's. Some consumer, some industrial accounts. No single account dominates agency. Reputation: capable of unusual creative approaches to difficult problems, forceful decision-making, centralized responsibility. No branch offices but willing to establish branches if needed.

Advertising Agency "E"

"House agency" to be set up as wholly-owned subsidiary, functioning as extension of company advertising department. Budget allows staffing by creatively-skilled practitioners in copy, art and media. President of house agency to become member of company board of directors. Sufficient number of minor accounts assured to guarantee media recognition.

Figure 3

It's just that I'm suspicious of men of genius." The president looks at you inquiringly over the rims of his eyeglasses. Have you alienated him? "Unless they're authentic," you add quickly. "Well, where does that leave us?" he asks.

He answers the question himself. "I'd like an old established agency. It's the kind I've had the most experience with myself. But I'm afraid we'd be a small frog in a mighty big pond. What do they bill: $200 million? And what did we spend last quarter: $100 thousand? Let's choose between the new, young agency and the long-established industrial agency. How do you vote?"

This is a tough one. The industrial agency is long-established. That's in its favor. It's also industrial. Two of our three market segments are industrial, too, as the Chairman of the Board outlined in his letter. The third segment is clearly consumer. But this agency is beginning to diversify into consumer products. It looks like a safe choice. That may be the only thing wrong with it.

The president looks up and smiles. "May I read your mind?" he asks. "You figure, just as I do, that the long-established industrial agency is the obvious choice. But we have a new product to sell. Every new idea, every innovation will be a necessity to us, not a luxury. Therefore, we must shun the obvious. That means we must choose the new, young agency."

"That's the way we go, then," you say.

THE RESEARCH PLAN

By now, Marketing, Research and Creative have reached agreement. Mr. Research proposes a four-point research program. "Mr. President, I am going to recommend that, before we do another thing, we invest immediately in research in four, possibly five, vital areas. I understand that the one way in which this simulation exercise departs from reality is the availability of 'instant research.' We get the research reports as soon as we order them."

"Yes, I know," the president agrees. "But we mustn't let that go to our heads. Remember, there are penalties for wrong choices, as well as for either underspending or overspending."

"I haven't forgotten," Mr. Research assures him. "I've tried to adhere to reasonable norms. Here, let me present my recommendations: I'm suggesting $40,000 for market research. I know that sounds like a lot. But we have no basic market information at all. And $40,000 is just a drop in the bucket over the course of an annual campaign. Then, if you agree to that, I'd like to suggest we support our copy and media people with $20,000 worth of message research, including pre-testing of basic sales points, product names and themes; $10,000 worth of motivation research to buttress our copy recommendations; and another $10,000 worth of media research divided about equally between print and electronic media. That's $80,000 so far. I'd dearly love to buy some economics trend research at $10,000, to see if we're going to have to be counter-cyclical in our total marketing effort or if we can coast a bit on riding the crest of a prosperity wave. But I'm willing to let that go until the second quarter if you'll approve the rest of my program."

The president leans back in his chair, his eyes closed. "Forty thousand for market research seems a bit high," he says slowly. "Can't you do with less?" "Maybe," Mr. Research answers. "But I'd rather overspend in this one area than run the risk of underspending. What I'm really overbuying is, at the most, $10,000 or $20,000 worth of time." He taps his watch meaningfully.

"On that basis," the president says, "go ahead."

THE CREATIVE PLAN

Once the research reports are in, the campaign recommendations come thick and fast. "Mr. Creative," the president calls. "What do you propose?"

"On the basis of our motivation and message research," Mr. Creative announces, "I'm prepared to recommend the three most salient sales features. We're only allowed three out of the ten on the list, you know." (Figure 4)

"That's two more than many successful products ever enjoy," the president says. "But go ahead."

"Well, in rank order, I recommend that 'strength' be our prime copy claim. Before I go any further, how does that strike you?"

"A glancing blow," the president replies. "I thought sure you'd go with 'lightweight.' How come?"

"That's precisely the point: Our message research says that everyone ex-

---

SALES FEATURES FOR CONTAINERS

1. Economical	6. Disposable
2. Non-Toxic	7. All Sizes
3. Lightweight	8. Natural Finish
4. Rustproof	9. Leakproof
5. Strong	10. Reputation

Figure 4

pects aluminum to be lightweight. That's practically aluminum's other name. So why advertise it first? On the other hand, what isn't so well known is that even though it's lightweight, aluminum is strong. So, by choosing 'strength' as our prime copy claim, I want to tell our markets first-off what they don't know. At the same time, I want to reassure them. If they buy aluminum cans, the contents won't spill or leak. By saying 'strong,' we also say 'leakproof' without actually saying it. That way, I sneak in what really amounts to a fourth copy claim. Okay? Finally, I want to wrap up our copy story by saying that we're 'economical,' too. The reason for that is that 'aluminum' means 'expensive' to many of our prospective customers, according to our motivation research. So I want to tell them that our aluminum isn't."

The president has been nodding agreement. Now he stops. "Strong, lightweight, economical. Strong, lightweight, economical. All right, I'll buy that. Now, what kind of a basic theme does that add up to? And what about product name? That's got to be related to our sales points too, doesn't it," he says, rather than asks.

Mr. Creative now explains that his first choice for a basic theme would go "something like this: 'So Strong—So Light—Yet the Price is Right.' " The president wrinkles his nose. "What's your second choice?" he asks. "Well, I anticipated your reaction, if you'll forgive my saying so. I really presented my second choice first. My first choice is the most simple statement it's possible to make with our three copy claims. As a matter of fact, I've modeled it after the classical Ivory Soap theme 'Pure-White-Floating'. This is how it goes: 'Strong-Light-Economical'. Could anything be simpler? Or more to the point?"

"Save your persuasiveness for the market," the president rejoins. "What about a name for our Ivory Soap? Or do you want to borrow their name, too?"

Mr. Creative says, "I'd like to call the product 'Aluminall'. That gets the aluminum in there. We're not a tin can, we're aluminum. The 'all' ties back to the all-advantage, all-purpose trinity of our copy claims. If you want a strong container, get 'Aluminall'. If you want a lightweight container, get 'Aluminall'. If you want an economical container, get 'Aluminall'. And if you want all three, strong, light and economical, get 'Aluminall'. We get them coming and going."

The president looks at the group, then at his watch. There are no dissenters. "One question. Two l's or one in 'Aluminall'?"

"Two. It's *'all'* on the end."

"Approved."

THE MEDIA PLAN

"Now," says the president, "How will we distribute our product name and message? What is our media plan?"

Mr. Media and Mr. Collateral are finishing their last-minute calculations. Mr. Media holds up a forefinger, still writing with the other hand. Then the media plan is ready. "We were given three market segments. Creative is going to have the job of adapting the basic product theme to as many of them as we plan to reach. For the first quarter, at least, we would like to address ourselves directly only to two of the three segments, omitting the middleman: the retail and wholesale distributors. Instead, we recommend that we concentrate our media impressions against the market segment composed of producers and packagers of containable products, number one, and, number two, consumers, the ultimate users of containable products. I'll have the total number of impressions figured out in a few minutes. Meanwhile, here's how it works out:

"In newspapers we recommend general daily newspapers, two Sunday supplement insertions, and a trade weekly schedule. In magazines, we'd like to use a supermarket monthly and one trade book each in the food, beverage and petroleum fields, plus a packaging and purchasing monthly. We have our schedule practically complete. One thing worth mentioning right now, though. We're recommending nothing less than full-page units, to stress the newness and importance of the product. And we're going with black-and-white throughout, as Creative prefers. We'll make up in size whatever attention value we might sacrifice without color."

The president is making notes furiously. So are you. Mr. Media pauses just long enough to let you catch up. "Our total print budget, both newspaper and magazine, to reach producers, packagers and consumers, will run about $350,000 for the first quarter. Yes, I know that's a considerable jump from the last quarter of last year. But I'm not through yet. Market research shows the market for our product should be expanding. So I'd like to supplement our print investment with a television campaign of 20-second spots, just to see what the combination of print and TV can do for us. This will run us another $120,000 or so, using prime time when we have the best chance of catching both the producer-packager in a relaxed environment plus Mrs. Housewife herself. Finally—well, I'd better let Collateral speak for himself."

COLLATERAL ADVERTISING

Samples	10	25	50	100	250	500
Coupons	10	25	50	100	250	500
Premiums	10	25	50	100	250	500
Contests	10	25	50	100	250	500
Direct Mail	10	25	50	100	250	500
Outdoor	10	25	50	100	250	500
Point-of-Sale	10	25	50	100	250	500
Transit	10	25	50	100	250	500
Catalogs	10	25	50	100	250	500
Trade Shows	10	25	50	100	250	500
Motion Pictures	10	25	50	100	250	500
Dealer PM's	10	25	50	100	250	500
Trade Directory	10	25	50	100	250	500
Mobile Displays	10	25	50	100	250	500

Figure 5

Choices and amounts (in thousands of dollars) for the various kinds of collateral advertising in this aid used in the game.

"Well, coming on top of a $470,000 media request, I'll be short and sweet. While we have a lot to choose from (Figure 5), both of us—Media and I, that is—feel strongly that we ought to invest in one or two traveling displays at $20,000 each, to get our message to the producers and packagers where they live, so to speak. If we run into budget trouble on this recommendation, I'd like to counter with a $20,000 expenditure for a motion picture of our product's manufacture and user benefits. That's all for now. As we go on, I may want to come back to you for some retail point-of-purchase tie-ins with our users . . . assuming we convert some."

The president leans toward you. "I've put checks against my approvals and crosses against my disapprovals for each media recommendation," he says quietly. "Compare your thinking with mine." When you do, you find that while you both are in agreement on over-all strategy, he has been more disapproving of individual recommendations than you might have guessed. Finally, you agree on a master media mix. The print campaign remains almost as proposed, except for a $50 thousand slash. "You'll note that the purchasing magazine covers comes out of there," the president says. "This type of purchase decision isn't yet in a purchasing agent's hands. We're talking higher up." The television campaign is cut to 10-second spots, resulting in approximately another $50 thousand saving in production and time costs. The traveling displays are shelved but the motion picture is approved.

The president is sitting back in his chair again, eyes closed as before. As if to the ceiling, he says, "So much for our outputs. Now, what can we hope to get back from this creative and media expenditure? Mr. Marketing, now that you know how much we plan to spend, how much product do we have to make and how much do we have to charge for it to take in more than we put out?" Leaning forward now, he says, "Let me re-ask that question in a more marketing-oriented way. How *little* product can we get away with making and how *high* a price can we dare charge for it?"

Do We Have an Objective?

Mr. Marketing looks unhappy. All the while the others have been making their recommendations, he has been busily taking the operating statement apart, trying to isolate its variables and project the group's recommendations into them. But all the while, he has also been smarting under what he has now come to regard as an unwise inversion of roles.

"Look here," he says, "I don't want to be disruptive or anything. I know we don't have time for ego-involvements. But I've been learning something. You said it yourself, Mr. President: we need first of all to agree on our objective. If that's true, then we should have set it first and all of us could then plan how to reach it as the logical second step. We've gone about it backwards. You're making the achievement of an objective come as a *result* of a certain creative and media plan. I say that an objective should be the *cause* of the creative and media plan. They should be subservient to it, not the other way around. The way I see it, first of all, you should give me a quarterly profit objective. Then, I should be able to get some pricing research to go along with the market research we're already agreed on. Then I ought to come to you with a profit forecast: at such and such a price, we can sell so many units. This will return us so many dollars, out of which we will be able to take so much profit, thereby meeting our objective. But you haven't given me an objective. And the reason you haven't is that nobody's given you a demand forecast."

Now it is you who leans toward the president. You show him a note you scrawled after one of his earliest comments. "Objective cannot be stated merely to maximize accumulated net profit. Must be quantified. How much profit? Per quarter?" The president purses his lips. "So we haven't had an objective after all?" he asks himself. "Mr. Marketing. Sit down as quickly as possible with Mr. Research. Get him to order your pricing research for you. Then pool your thinking and come up with a demand forecast. This will be a top-secret figure, to be shared only among the three of us. Then, when you have estimated total demand, estimate what our fair share of it will be: how much we could reasonably expect to obtain as one supplier in a three-supplier situation on a minimum, average and maximum basis."

The president turns to you once more. "I think I see the problem a bit more clearly now. We don't really have a new product, do we? What we have is only a new way of doing something—containing things—that's been done another way for a long time. Our way is called aluminum. The other way is called tin. We're really a switch-brand, that's what we are. We're trying to switch tin-can users to aluminum. Our market right now is a piece of their market. The size of the piece we get determines our profit. Let's call it our market-acceptance objective; that comes first. Then comes our profit objective, based on it."

Isn't that what everyone said, in one way or another, at the beginning of our planning session? It sounded that way. Where did we go off the track, you wonder? But it is almost 11:30 now. Post-mortems will have to wait.

PRICING AND PRODUCTION

Mr. Marketing looks relieved. "All right. Here goes my neck. I'm going to recommend a first-quarter net profit objective of approximately $3 million. If we project this ahead on a consistent four-quarter basis—and neither I nor Mr. Research can see any reason why, if we're successful at all, it shouldn't be consistent—that leaves us with a $12 million to $15 million accumulated net profit over the year.

"Now for the variables. To achieve our profit objective, we need to multiply our sales income by two and our advertising and research expenditures by—let's see—well, two would be close to ideal. But I know that three will probably be more like it. We can live with that, I guess. But all this presupposes that the price stays the same. If we lower price, there goes the income we need to sustain our increased advertising. Besides, I don't think we're going to penetrate this market on a price basis at this point. We have to offer benefits that are at least equal in all respects to tin and superior in some, don't you agree? Now, let's look over our copy and media strategy in the light of how well they can help us achieve our profit objective."

"I've been thinking about that while you've been speaking," says Mr. Creative. "You've probably heard Media and me whispering together these last few minutes. Fortunately—maybe I should say 'intuitively' in this case—we're still in good shape. Our original plan fits our objective to a T. We recommend full speed ahead with no changes."

It is a good thing. Just then there is a knock on the board room door. "Time, gentlemen," says the scorer as she enters. "May I have your first-quarter decisions, please?" It is exactly 12 noon. Oh, if only we had gotten organized faster; spent more time on the heart of things. Over the shuffle of papers and the scraping of chairs, the president is heard telling Mr. Research to be sure to order competitive information on both competitors for the quarter "so that we don't end up playing blindfolded."

You look at the campaign year timetable. The three remaining quarters will be only 40 minutes each in length, with 20-minute intermissions in between. By 4 o'clock, the final results will be in. Thank goodness there is a full hour for lunch from 1 to 2 p.m.

"We'll have a lot to hash over tonight," the president says to you. "And for many another night, too," you add. "Well, we might as well keep busy while we're waiting," he says. "Let's chart all our decisions. Then, when we get our competitive information, we'll add that to our own on a master audit. Meanwhile, we might begin thinking of alternate strategies to adopt, depending on how we're doing when the scores come in." You find yourself sketching out a master audit for the first quarter and, just as you finish, your results and the competitive results are brought in. (Figure 6)

You take a long, careful look. "Well, this is a fine kettle of fish," you hear yourself say as you examine the audit. "We multiplied our sales income by two, all right. But our net profit is way below what we'll need to reach our fourth quarter objective. What did we figure on? A $12 million to $15 million accumulated net profit over the year? That means—let's see, four times 2,590,000 equals 10,360,000—we'll be more than a million and a half under our minimum objective. Where are we off? Are we overspending on advertising? Or are our spending decisions wrong in some ways? Creatively speaking, did we interpret the research in some incorrect way? What about pricing—can we step up volume if we drop price? Or is our objective unrealistic in the first place? Maybe the market just isn't as absorbent right now as we would like. What do you think?"

Master Audit—First Quarter

Marketing Decisions:	Company A	Company B	Company C
Name	"Aluminall"	"Lite Wate"	"Tuf-Can"
Sales Features	Strong Lightweight Economical	Lightweight Strong All Sizes	Strong Disposable Economical
Sales Theme	"Strong-Lightweight-Economical"	"The Lightweight Container That's Strong on Versatility"	"The Can-Do Can—At a Can-Afford Price"
Price ($)	100	99	101
Sales (units)	100,000	90,000	75,000
Research (add 000)	Market Research ($40) Message Research (20) Motivation Research (10) Media Research (10) Pricing Research	Market Research ($10) Message Research (10) Pricing Research (10)	Market Research ($20) Production Methods (10) Distribution Methods (10) Economic Trends (10)
Advertising Agency	New, Young Agency	Long-Established Industrial Agency	Small, Diversified Agency

Media Decisions:	Company A		Company B		Company C	
Collateral Advertising (add 000)	Motion Picture	($20)	Direct Mail Trade Shows Traveling Displays	($60)	Trade Shows Catalogs Co-op Advertising Trade Weekly	($50) ($30)
Newspapers (add 000)	General Sunday Supplements Trade Weekly	($75)				
Magazines (add 000)	Supermarket Monthly Food Trade Beverage Trade Petroleum Trade Packaging Trade	($225)	Food Trade Beverage Trade Petroleum Trade Packaging Trade	($30)	Food Trade Beverage Trade Petroleum Trade Packaging Trade	($90)
Television (add 000)	10-Sec. Spots	($70)				

Profit:	Company A	Company B	Company C
Net Profit	$2,590,000	$2,460,000	$1,925,000
Accumulated Net Profit	$2,590,000	$2,460,000	$1,925,000

Figure 6

You look up at the group. They have been only half-listening. Each is immersed in competitive evaluations in the area of his own decision-making responsibility. You try to get their attention. "Gentlemen, I know that, competitively speaking, we're in the lead. But it's only by a hair. We still have our own race to run." You aren't getting anywhere. So you decide to listen.

"Look at Company B," Mr. Marketing is saying. "They lowered their price $1 a unit. Advertised only $90,000 worth. Yet they came within 10,000 units of us. This is a price-sensitive market, all right."

"Why not look at it the other way around?" Mr. Research asks. "We maintained price. That's advertising's responsibility: to maintain price. Through our advertising, we outsold them even at a higher price. Instead of saying that this is a price-sensitive market, why not call it an advertising-sensitive market? We advertised—and we got results without tampering with price."

"What gets me about B," Mr. Creative says, "is their nearly identical list of copy claims. Yet I think they fell for the light-weight trap."

"I agree," Mr. Media says. "And look at their media list. They're entirely trade. No consumer at all. Maybe they think that trying to influence the consumer right now is premature. That it will take too long to set up any significant consumer back-pressure against the producers and packagers. Maybe they're right, at least over the short run. But I still think our pincers strategy is best over the long run. And remember, we have three quarters yet to go."

"What about C?" the president asks. "We can't write them off. To look at it pessimistically, they're only $600,000 behind us. They spent $170,000, too. So they're not afraid to spend. At their higher price—if they maintain it, that is—they can afford to sell fewer units. If they can find a balance between their proper advertising expenditure and their sales income, they may be more of a challenge than B. And isn't it interesting," he adds almost as an afterthought, "how all three companies chose different types of agencies?"

"I wish we could get B's traveling displays away from them," murmurs Mr. Collateral. "Remember how I recommended them originally?" "I'd like Company C's economic trends research," Mr. Research interrupts.

The soul-searching ends abruptly as the president clears his throat. "Gentlemen," he says tightly, "the second quarter has begun. May I have your recommendations, please?"

*   *   *   *   *

SUMMING UP

In Adplan, as in the actual market, one company generally "wins." The act of winning itself, however, is transient. Of far more permanent value is acquiring knowledge in the art of winning. What are the marketing methods we can learn from observing marketing men make Adplan decisions? This exercise teaches us that marketing men who make successful decisions methodically follow five basic principles:

1. They set *objectives.*
2. They acquire a well-researched *fact base* about their product, its markets and their competition to help them rationalize their objectives.
3. They *plan* to reach their objectives, using their fact base as the foundation for their planning.
4. They build into their plan a periodic *self-administering audit* which helps them validate the plan's effect while it is still in progress and allows them to know when corrective action is necessary, what action to take and how effectively it is working.
5. On the basis of the audit's findings, they *reevaluate* and *renovate* their plan so that it is always current and consistent with market fact.

This is the method of marketing leadership, the ideal answer to the question "How Industrial Marketing Men Make Decisions." It is an answer which can apply to all business, new or old, large or small. It is independent of product type, market peculiarities or competitive ferocity. It is also independent of personality, being a method based on enduring principles rather than men. Once adopted, it therefore tends to be self-perpetuating as well as self-auditing. In these twin facts lie its greatest strength.

Monopologs: Management Decision Making Game Applied to Tool Room Management

Forrest M. Campbell and E. Robert Ashworth

For several years the Logistic department of the RAND corporation has been concerned with the various supply problems of the Air Force. Mathematical models have been used to present various parts of the supply system. H. W. Karr developed a model for part of the supply system of the Air Force.[2] He focused his attention on the operation of the base-depot phase of the system. He was concerned with the present policies and their improvement. W. Hamburger concentrated his attention on a less elaborate model of the base-depot part of the system.[1] His goal was to become better acquainted with the interworkings of the system rather than the finding of new policies. Monopologs is a compound name composed of "Monopoly" and "Logistics." It is an informative game that attempts to re-

At the time this article was published, FORREST M. CAMPBELL and E. ROBERT ASHWORTH were at the School of Industrial Engineering and Management, Oklahoma State University.

Reprinted, with permission, from *The Journal of Industrial Engineering*, September-October 1960.

late the gross factors with which a management would be concerned in the analysis of the high value of spare parts. The game includes the procurement, repair and shipment of spare parts to five bases in a hypothetical supply system. J. Rehkop describes some of the experiences of playing this type of game.[3]

A Pedagogical Application of Monopologs

One of the pedagogic problems which confront all who teach is the task of motivating the student. This basic problem is encountered whether the setting is academic or industrial. From the many different business games now in existence, one of the significant factors as a result of playing the game is the tremendous motivation which the game imparts to its players. The purposed tool room game will motivate the student to ask why he makes the decisions he does, what the effect of certain policies will be, and how well they meet the given situation.

The students are given a complete write-up of the tool room game to review and study before the next class period. The student's questions are answered if there are any over the previous written material which covers the sample game.

The students are asked to formulate a set of policies for themselves and to apply them to the game to be played in the classroom. At the end of play, the student will be asked to discuss how his policy was applied, and the cost of this policy for this game will be determined. The objective is to achieve the "best" results (any number of criteria might be used) with a minimum of cost or a maximum of profit. Generally, the individual with the lowest cost will be considered to be the best manager.

General Setting

The setting for this game of Monopologs is shown graphically by Figure 1. (The player should become thoroughly familiar with Figure 1.) The players assume the role of the tool room manager whose responsibility it is to see that the four production departments within a factory are adequately supplied with a particular type of die. (The specific type is not important.) The objective of the game is to supply these production departments with a sufficient number of dies so that they can maintain their production

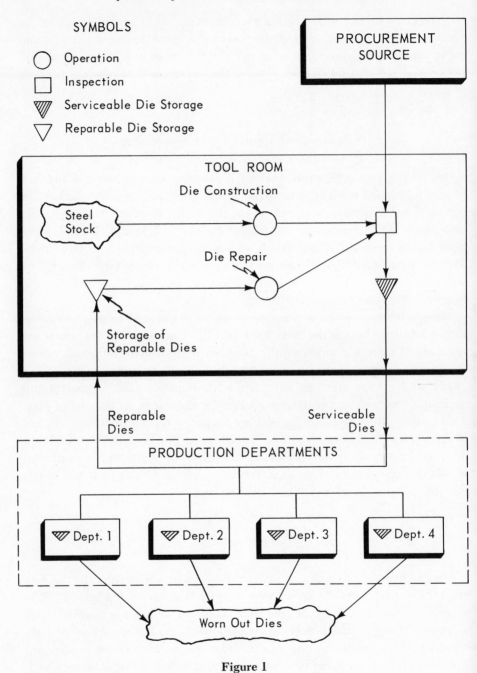

Figure 1

Flow Diagram for Dies

schedules and at the same time you, as tool room manager, can keep die storage, transportation and manufacturing costs at a minimum. Each department generates two kinds of demands for the spare dies: wearouts and

Die Construction Lead Time	5 Weeks
Die Procurement Lead Time	9 Weeks
Expedited Die Procurement Lead Time	3 Weeks
Die Repair Lead Time	3 Weeks
Expedited Die Repair Lead Time	1 Week

Table 1

Lead Times

reparables. To meet this demand, new dies may be procured from a manufacturer, new dies may be constructed in the tool room, or reparable dies may be repaired in the tool room. It is up to the tool room manager to determine which method will be used to meet the various demands which arise due to random causes during a 30 week period.

Procurement Costs and Lead Times

The cost of procuring a new die from a manufacturer is $50.00 per die. For every order (regardless of size) there is a setup cost of $50.00 per order. If the procurement is routine, it takes nine weeks for the die to reach the tool room storage from the initiation of the order. It is possible to expedite procurement at an additional cost of $100.00 per order and the lead time is reduced to three weeks. It is possible to expedite an order at the time it is placed, or at any time before the shipment arrives at the tool room. In all cases the expedited items will arrive at the tool room three weeks after the order to expedite is given.

Example: Routine procurement of 4 dies: Cost = 50 + 4(50) = $250 (9 weeks).

Example: Expedited procurement of 4 dies: Cost = 50 + 100 + 4(50) = $350 (3 weeks).

Note: In order to receive maximum benefit from the game and keep the game interesting, any procurement of new dies is not to exceed 10 per week. A further restriction on procurement is that after the initial procurement is made (during the first week), no further procurements are allowed until the eleventh week.

Construction Costs and Lead Times

The cost of constructing a new die in your own tool room is $40.00 per die. For every order (regardless of size) there is a tool room set-up cost of $115.00 per order. It is assumed that this tool room has many other tools and fixtures going through it simultaneously. For this reason a limitation has been placed on the number of dies that can be constructed simultaneously. The maximum number of dies that can be constructed in the tool room is four. Five weeks elapse from the time the order is placed until it reaches the tool room storage. There is no way to expedite construction orders going through the tool room.

Example: Construct four dies in the tool room (maximum number). Cost = $115 + 4(40) = 275 (5 weeks).

Repair Costs and Lead Times

The cost of repairing a reparable die is $20.00 per die. For every order (regardless of size) there is a set-up cost of $20.00 per order. If the repair is routine, it takes three weeks from the time the order is placed until it arrives at the tool room storage as a serviceable die. It is possible to expedite repair for an additional cost of $40.00 per order. There is no limit to the number of reparable dies passing through the shop for repair. An order may be expedited at the time it is placed or at any time thereafter, with delivery to the tool room storage one week after it is expedited.

Example: Routine repair of 4 dies: Cost = $20 + 4(20) = 100 (3 weeks).

Example: Expedite repair of 4 dies: Cost = $20 + 40 + 4(20) = 140 (1 week).

Other Costs and Lead Times

TRANSPORTATION

Serviceable dies can be shipped from the tool room storage to department or from department to department. There is no charge for transportation from the tool room storage to department. (This cost is included in procurement, construction, or repair costs.) However, there is a charge of $5.00 per shipment for transportation from department to department. In both cases the transportation time is one week.

Depletion Penalty

This cost ($200/Die/Week) is charged if a spare die is not on hand in a department at the time a demand is generated there. Of course, this is charged each week there is a shortage.

Storage

There is a storage cost of $1.50 per die per week for reparable dies on hand. There is also a storage cost of $2.50 per die per week for each service-able die in the tool room storage and for all spare dies in the four depart-

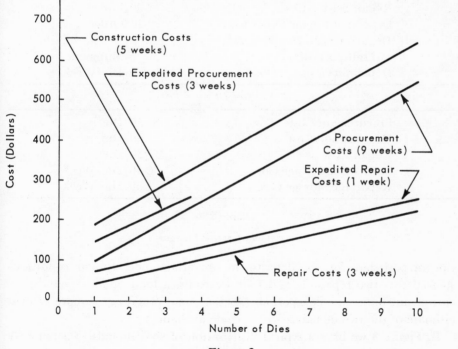

Figure 2

Comparison of Costs

ments. Figure 2 illustrates a comparison of the costs of the different activities with respect to the number of dies.

Demand Generation

Dies have to be replaced within the production departments for two reasons—some of them wear out and are discarded; others become reparable.

A reparable or wearout demand is equally likely to occur in any department in any week. The demand is erratic due to the fact that these demands arise due to random causes.

The rate at which the demands occur is not known. However, examina-

Special Charges	
Procurement Set-Up Cost	$ 50/Order
Expedited Procurement Order Cost	100/Order
Construction Set-Up Cost	115/Order
Repair Set-Up Cost	20/Order
Expedited Repair Order Cost	40/Order
Department to Department Transportation Cost	5/Shipment
Depletion Costs	200/Die/Week
Routine Charges	
Procurement Cost	$ 50/Die
Construction Cost	40/Die
Repair Cost	20/Die
Serviceable Storage Cost	2.50/Die/Week
Reparable Storage Cost	1.50/Die/Week

Table 2

Special and Routine Charges

tion of past data for one department operating under similar conditions showed that two reparable and four wearouts, a total of six demands, occurred during a ten-week period. (As the game progresses a more refined estimate of the two demands will become available.)

In Figure 3 we have a typical distribution of six demands in a ten-week period. If we tabulate our past data from the shop we might have a distribution of events as shown in the top distribution. From this Poisson distribu-

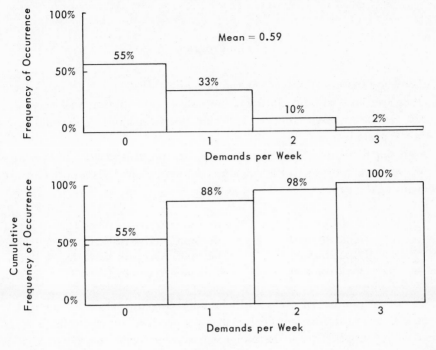

Figure 3

tion with a mean of 0.59 or 0.6 we can then determine the cumulative frequency of occurrence of our demands. Assigning a series of two digit random numbers to the cumulative distribution, we have a distribution of numbers which is unbiased and not affected by our tendencies toward favorite numbers.

To generate a series of events we can glance at the second hand on a watch and if the number of seconds is more than 50, we wait a bit and select a second number. If we have 50 or less seconds, we double the number. If our original number were odd, we would subtract from the total. Two digit random numbers can be determined without a table of numbers.

In another method, called the mid-square method, we select a four-digit number, then square the number and use only the middle four digits. This number is the next random number. The process is repeated until all numbers have been determined.

One also might write the digit 0 on 55 chips, 1 on 33 chips, 2 on 10 chips, and 3 on 2 chips. Mix the chips in a bowl and select the chips one at a time. After reading the number from the chip, replace it in the bowl, stir well and repeat the process.

The Program

The time span is 30 weeks. At the end of 30 weeks the dies will have no further use and will be considered obsolete. The player will receive no credit for either serviceable or reparable units on hand at the end of the 30 week period.

Four departments will be using the dies during this period. They will become active according to the schedule below and will remain active until the end of the game.

Department 1	Becomes Active in Week 11
Department 2	Becomes Active in Week 15
Department 3	Becomes Active in Week 18
Department 4	Becomes Active in Week 24

The same number of presses will be operating in each department. Each press has been initially supplied with a proper die, therefore, these do *not* need to be supplied from the tool room storage when the department becomes active.

From a table of random numbers we might write down the following numbers: 28, 52, 76, 48, 71, 99 . . . Interpreting these reparable and wearout demands we would have these results:

Reparables	*Wearouts*
0	0
1	0
1	3
.	.
.	.

Description of the Playing Field (See Figure 4)

PROGRAM (COLUMNS 1, 2, 3)

This information is known to the player at the start of the game. These columns are self explanatory—column 1 is the week number, column 2 shows when each department becomes active and column 3 is the total number of department weeks.

Tool Room Storage Summary

Column 4: This indicates the number of serviceable dies on hand in the tool room at the beginning of the week. This is the same as the number of dies on hand at the end of the previous week which is found in column 7.

Column 5: In this column is recorded:

1. Procurement orders—example $p4$.
2. Procurement expedite orders—example $pe4$.
3. Construction orders—$c4$.
4. Arrival of serviceable dies from the procurement source, tool room construction, or tool room repair—example 4.

Column 6: Denotes that a delivery will be made from tool room storage to one of the departments—example 4 to D_1 (4 serviceable dies will be delivered to Department 1).

Column 7: In this column is found the serviceable dies on hand in the tool room storage at the end of the week. This number is equal to B (column 4) $+ A$ (column 5) $- D$ (column 6) $= \triangledown$ (column 7).

Tool Room Activities

Column 8: This column indicates the number of dies that are being repaired during the week. Example: The player decides to repair 4 dies in a certain week. He records the number 4 in column 8 for the following 3 weeks.

Column 9: As reparable dies accumulate they are recorded in this column. When the player wishes to repair them he records R or Re beside the number of reparable dies.

Column 10: This column indicates the number of dies that are being constructed in the tool room during a particular month. The largest number of dies that can be constructed at one time is 4.

DEMAND SUMMARY

Column 11: Denotes the total number of demands, both reparables and wearouts, that have occurred to date. It is the sum of columns 12 and 13 for the particular week.

Column 12: Information for this column comes from the demand for reparables as they occur in columns 14-17. These data are kept in the form of a summation of all the reparables that have occurred to date.

Column 13: Same as column 12 except these data concern wearouts only.

DEPARTMENTS

Columns 14-17: The demands shown in columns 14-17 are covered at the beginning of the game so this information is unknown to the player. The demands are uncovered week by week as the play progresses.

DIES SERVICEABLE

Column 18: This column shows the total number of serviceable dies in the system at the end of the week. This total is equal to B (column 4) $+ A$ (column 5) $+$ (the number of serviceable dies on hand at the end of the week in each department) (columns 14-17) $= S$.

Procedure of the Game

Play progresses in the following general manner:

1. *Events* are generated by uncovering the demand data in columns 14-17. (See Figure 4.) After uncovering these data, record any deliveries to departments that were sent from the tool room or from other departments the previous week. Then, for each department, considering its inventory, demands for the week, and newly arrived items, determine and record the inventory of serviceable dies.

PROGRAM			TOOL ROOM STORAGE SUMMARY				TOOL ROOM ACTIVITIES			DEMAND SUMMARY			Dept. 1	Dept. 2	Dept. 3	Dept. 4	Dies Serviceable
Week No.	Active Depts.	Total Dept. Wks.	Dies on Hand First of Week	Orders and Arrivals	Deliveries to Depts.	Dies on Hand at End of Week	In Repair	To Be Repaired	In Construction 4 max.	Total Demand	Reparable	Wearouts	(14)	(15)	(16)	(17)	(18)
(1) T	(2) N	(3) ΣN	(4) B +	(5) A −	(6) D =	(7) ∇	(8) R	(9) ∇	(10) C	(11) Σd	(12) Σr	(13) Σw	r | w | del. | ∇	r | w | del. | ∇	r | w | del. | ∇	r | w | del. | ∇	$
1																	
2																	
9																	
10																	
11	1	1											0 | 1				
12		2											0 | 0				
13		3											1 | 1				
14		4											0 | 0				
15	2	6											0 | 0	2 | 0			
16		8											1 | 0	0 | 0			
17		10											0 | 0	0 | 1			
18		12											0 | 1	1 | 1			
19		14											1 | 0	0 | 0			
Program Known to Player													◄─── These Columns Covered ───►				

Figure 4

Example Game—Playing Field Before Game Begins

2. Bring demand summary up to date (columns 11-13). Also record the number of dies reparable (column 9).

3. *Take inventory.* This covers the dies on hand at the beginning of the week (column 4) plus the arrivals (column 5) plus the inventory in each department (columns 14-17).

4. *Make decisions* and record them. Decisions will be recorded in columns 5, 6, 8, 10, 14-17.

5. With all the information properly tabulated on the playing field for that week, then uncover the demand data for the next week and repeat the procedure.

Scoring the Game (See Table 3.)

The score of the game is not counted until the game has been completed. Below is the procedure for scoring the game.

Score Sheet	*Number*	*Cost*
1. Procurement Set-Up (50/Order)		
2. Procurement Expedite Order (100/Order)		
3. Procurement Each Item (50/Item)		
4. Construction Set-Up (115/Order)		
5. Construction Each Item (40/Item)		
6. Repair Set-Up (20/Order)		
7. Repair Expedite Order (40/Order)		
8. Repair Each Item (20/Item)		
9. Department to Department Shipments (5/Shipment)		
10. Depletion (200/Item/Week)		
11. Reparable Storage (1.50/Item/Week)		
12. Serviceable Storage (2.50/Item/Week)		
Total Cost		

Table 3

1. *Procurement set-up*—Count all the letters p which appear in column 5. Multiply this number by $50.00.
2. *Procurement expedite order*—Count all of the e's which appear beside p's in column 5. Mutiply this sum by $100.00.
3. *Procurement each item*—Find the sum of all the dies obtained by procurement (column 5) and mutiply this sum by $50.00.
4. *Construction set-up*—Count up all the letters c which appear in column 5 and multiply this sum by $115.00.
5. *Construction each item*—Find the total number of dies constructed in the tool room (column 5) and multiply this number by $40.00.
6. *Repair set-up*—Count the number of R's which appear in column 9 and multiply by $20.00.
7. *Repair expedite order*—Count the number of e's which appear beside R's (column 9) and multiply this number by $40.00.
8. *Repair each item*—Find the sum of all the dies repaired (from column 9) and multiply by $20.00.
9. *Department to department shipments*—Check columns 14-17 to see how many department to department shipments occurred during the game. Multiply the number of shipments by $5.00.
10. Check columns 14-17 to see if any minus numbers appear in the

inventory columns for the departments. Add these depletions and multiply by $200.00.

11. *Reparable storage*—Find the sum of all the numbers in column 9 and multiply by $1.50.

12. *Serviceable storage*—Find the sum of all the numbers in column 7 plus the sum of the positive numbers appearing on the inventory side of columns 14-17. Multiply this total by $2.50.

Example Game (See Figures 5 and 6.)

MONTH BY MONTH SUMMARY OF EVENTS AND DECISIONS

The following game illustrates all possible decisions that can be made and the resulting costs that arise. This game should be studied merely as a

PROGRAM			TOOL ROOM STORAGE SUMMARY				TOOL ROOM ACTIVITIES			DEMAND SUMMARY			Dept. 1		Dept. 2		Dept. 3		Dept. 4		Dies Serv-ice-able
Week No.	Active Depts.	Total Dept. Wks.	Dies on Hand First of Week	Orders and Arri-vals	De-liver-ies to Depts.	Dies on Hand at End of Wk.	In Re-pair	To Be Re-paired	In Con-struc-tion 4 max.	Total De-mand	Re-par-able	Wear-outs	(14)		(15)		(16)		(17)		able
(1)	(2)	(3)	(4)	(5)	(6)	(7)	(8)	(9)	(10)	(11)	(12)	(13)									(18)
T	N	ΣN	B	A	D	▽▽	R	▽	C	Σd	Σr	Σw	r/del.	w ▽▽	r/del.	w ▽▽	r/del.	w ▽▽	r/del.	w ▽▽	$
1	0	0	0	p4	0	0	0	0	0	0	0	0									
2																					
9																					
10				4 c4	2 to D₁	2															4
11	1	1	2		2 to D₁	0	0	0	4	1	0	1	0|1 / 2	1							3
12		2	0			0	0	0	4	1	0	1	0|0 / 2	3							3
13		3	0			0	0	1Re	4	3	1	2	1|1 / 1	1							1
14		4	0	1	1 to D₂	0	1	0	4	3	1	2	0|0 /	1							2
15	2	6	0	4 pe4	2 to D₁ 2 to D₂	0	0	2R	4	5	3	2	0|0 /	1	2|0 / 1	−1					5
16		8	0			0	2	1	0	6	4	2	1|0 / 2	2	0|0 / 2	1					3
17		10	0			0	2	1	0	7	4	3	0|0 /	1 to D₂ 1	0|1 /	0					2
18		12	0	2 4	2 to D₁ 2 to D₂	2	2	2	0	10	5	5	0|1 /	0	1|1 / 1	−1					6
19		14	2			2	0	3	0	11	6	5	1|0 / 2	1	0|0 / 2	1					4

Figure 5

Example Game—Playing Field After Game Completed

guide to properly tabulate information. *This example game should not be used as a decision making guide!*

Start of Play: This corresponds to week 1 and is the time when initial procurement order of dies is placed.

Decision: Make a routine procurement of 4 dies. Record $p4$ in column 5 for week 1 (order). Record 4 in column 5 for week 10 (arrival).

10th Week:

Events: None.

Inventory: 4 Serviceable dies. (column 5)

Decision: Construct 4 dies in our tool room. Record $c4$ in column 5. Record 4's in column 10 for 11-15th week. Record 4 in column 5 for 15th week. Send 2 dies to Department 1. Record (2 to D_1) in column 6.

11th Week:

Events: D_1 becomes active. 1 wearout in D_1. 2 dies delivered to D_1 from tool room.

Inventory: 2 (column 4) + 1 (column 14) = 3 serviceable dies.

Decision: Deliver 2 dies to D_1. Record in column 6.

12th Week:

Events: 2 deliveries to D_1 from tool room.

Inventory: 3 (column 14) = 3 serviceable dies.

Decision: None.

13th Week:

Events: 1 reparable and 1 wearout at D_1.

Inventory: 1 serviceable die (column 14).

Decision: Place repair order expedited on the one reparable die. Record Re in column 9. Record 1 in column 5 for week 14. Record 1 in column 8 for week 14.

14th Week:

Events: None.

Inventory: 1 (column 5) + 1 (column 14) = 2 serviceable dies.

Decision: Deliver 1 die to D_2.

15th Week:

Events: 2 reparables generated at D_2. 1 delivery to D_2 from tool room.

Inventory: 4 (column 5) $+$ 1 (column 14) $=$ 5 serviceable dies.

Decision: Deliver 2 dies to D_1. Deliver 2 dies to D_2. Expedited procurement of 4 dies. Record *pe*4 in column 5 for week 15. Record 4 in column 5 for week 18. Repair the two dies reparable. Place R by the 2 in column 9 for week 15. Record 2 in column 5 for week 18. Record 2 in column 8 for weeks 16-18.

Score Sheet	*Number*	*Cost*
1. Procurement Set-Up (50/Order)	2 Orders	$ 100.00
2. Procurement Expedite Order (100/Order)	1 Exp.	100.00
3. Procurement Each Item (50/Item)	8 Items	400.00
4. Construction Set-Up (115/Order)	1 Order	115.00
5. Construction Each Item (40/Item)	4 Items	160.00
6. Repair Set-Up (20/Order)	2 Orders	40.00
7. Repair Expedite Order (40/Order)	1 Exp.	40.00
8. Repair Each Item (20/Item)	3 Items	60.00
9. Department to Department Shipments (5/Shipment)	1 Shipment	5.00
10. Depletion (200/Item/Week)	2 Dep.	400.00
11. Reparable Storage (1.50/Item/Week)	10	15.00
12. Serviceable Storage (2.50/Item/Week)	19	47.50
Total Cost		$1482.50

Figure 6

Example Game—Tabulation of Score

16th Week:

Events: 1 reparable die generated at D_1. 2 dies delivered to D_1 from tool room.

Inventory: 2 (column 14) $+$ 1 (column 15) $=$ 3 serviceable dies.

Decision: None.

17th Week

Events: 1 wearout generated at D_2.

Inventory: 2 (column 14) $=$ 2 serviceable dies.

Decision: Deliver one of the serviceable dies at D_1 to D_2. Record delivery in column 14.

18th Week:

Events: 1 wearout generated at D_1. 1 reparable and 1 wearout generated at D_2. Delivery of one die to D_2 from D_1.
Inventory: 6 (column 5) $=$ 6 serviceable dies.
Decision: Deliver 2 dies to D_1. Deliver 2 dies to D_2.

19th Week:

Events: 1 reparable generated at D_1. Delivery of 2 dies to D_1 from tool room. Delivery of 2 dies to D_2 from tool room.
Inventory: 2 (column 4) $+$ 1 (column 14) $+$ 1 (column 15) $=$ 4 serviceable dies.
No decision—end of game.

Summary

A small scale decision making game has been applied to the classroom without the use of an electronic computer. The game is intended to focus attention on only a very limited area of an operational situation. The umpire of the game should be aware of the players' motivation. In the discussion which follows the game he should point out the strengths and weaknesses of the policies employed. The student should be encouraged to employ a questioning attitude on his own policies. Extensions of this type of game are limited only by one's imagination and the degree of complexity one wishes to employ.

Higher level games could be composed of a series of simpler games, which are blended into one game encompassing the broader aspects of the manufacturing enterprise.

NOTES TO THE TEXT

[1] Hamburger, W., *Monopologs, The Spare Part Manager's Game*, The RAND Corporation, RM-1579, January 1957.
[2] Karr, H. W., *Base-Depot Model Studies*, The RAND Corporation, RM-1803, January 1957.
[3] Rehkop, J., *Experience with the Management-Decision Simulation Game, Monopologs*, The RAND Corporation, RM-1917, July 1957.

Part I

D

Industry Games Readings

Here's a Realistic Way to Play
Wholesaler

In the three years since the American Management Association set off the business game fad, thousands of businessmen have piloted imaginary companies through competitive battles for imaginary markets. And skeptics have gone right on asking just what you can learn about business by playing games.

Now the Amstan Supply Div. of American Radiator & Standard Sanitary Corp. has come up with a novel answer and a novel game—one that aims to teach a practical lesson. With the marketing exercise partially illustrated here, Amstan hopes to teach its sales managers how to sell plumbing and heating supplies more profitably.

Specifically, Amstan wants to show the managers of its 63 branches how to pick the best customer mix—meaning the customers they sell to and the way they divide their sales effort among them. That's the key element in the wholesaling outfit's current drive to better its profit margins.

The Amstan game is a "micro-market simulation," according to Amstan business research manager R. C. Frazee. That means it is tailored to Amstan's own markets, and particularly to Amstan's own customers. Built into the game are some 300 "typical" Amstan customers, in effect playing against the players.

The result is a game so true to Amstan's own life that Frazee is even

Reprinted, with permission, from *Business Week*, September 3, 1960.

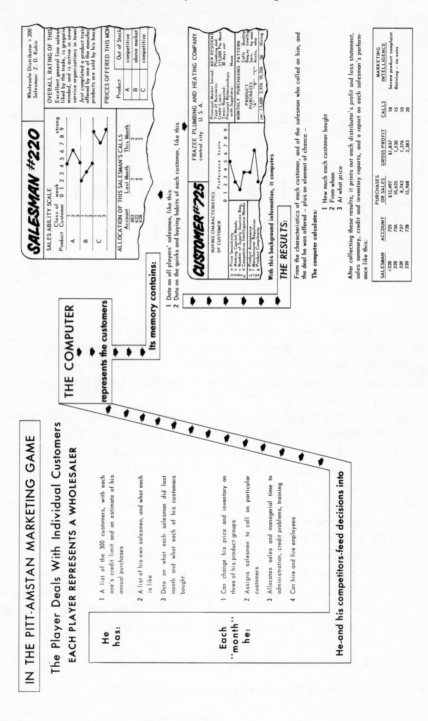

planning to use it to help solve some of the division's marketing strategy problems. That's why Amstan Pres. Robert Sells thinks the game can teach his branch managers not general business principles but exactly how to run their branches the way he wants them run.

Broad picture. Most business games have much less specific goals. Typically, they round up a group of players and put them to work making pricing and investment decisions for fictitious "companies" competing for sales in the same or overlapping markets. An electronic computer or other umpire decides what total sales volume will be, divides up the market on the basis of each company's price, advertising expenditure, selling ability, and the like, then reports back on profits. From this experience, the players are supposed to get the broad picture of what business is all about.

There are, of course, a lot of variations. There are games about marketing that concentrate on allocating sales effort, such as the marketing exercises of Pillsbury Co. and Remington Rand Div. of Sperry Rand Corp., and there are games for specific industries—Kroger Co.'s supermarket game, Dayco Corp.'s tire dealer game, oil company service station games, and so on.

But all of these are what Frazee calls "macro-market" games. They deal with generalized mass markets rather than industrial customers.

Individualized. In the Amstan game, the customer is treated as an individual. Each one has his own buying patterns and his own supplier preferences; there's even a customer who buys only from his brother-in-law. These customer profiles, based on an analysis of some 1,200 actual and potential Amstan customers, are programed into the computer. For each customer the computer runs through a separate calculation to decide how much he will buy and from whom.

That makes a lot of work for both player and computer. The player also has a list of all the customers and all his own salesmen, with quite a bit of data about them (though not so much as the computer has). He has to make separate decisions about salesmen's time and other aspects of sales effort for each customer. In game sessions so far, the players have taken about five hours to make their initial decisions.

An IBM 650 computer needs about an hour and a half to reproduce the 300 customers' decision-making processes and figure out how much they will buy and from whom; once that is done, profit-and-loss statements for the players, and reports on salesmen's efficiency, can be calculated in a few minutes. In the ordinary management game, a computer of the same size can do the whole scorekeeping job in a matter of minutes.

Amstan and the University of Pittsburgh are now busy reprograming the game for an IBM 7070 that the university will be getting in the fall. The giant computer will do all the calculations in about 10 minutes, and it will also take over a lot of the players' routine work.

Double problem. Even so, many management development specialists think Amstan's game is too complicated and cumbersome for a training program. Amstan's executives don't agree. Amstan's game took the form it has because the division was facing two closely related problems at the same time—one of marketing profitably, and one of management development.

Since World War II, as Amstan's vice-president of field operations, C. Gilmore Ruston, points out, growing competition, and the collapse of prices in economic slumps, have combined to pinch profit margins in the heating and plumbing supply business.

And Amstan has no competitive advantage on product line. Though it's the wholesale supply division of American-Standard, its franchise is not exclusive for its parent's plumbing and heating supply equipment. In Pittsburgh, Amstan's headquarters city, American-Standard has four other wholesale outlets; in Chicago it has 20 others.

Besides, two-thirds of Amstan's sales are of related "roughing-in" items (such as steel pipe, soil pipe, fittings) the parent company doesn't make.

In this situation, Vice-Pres. Ruston thinks, the only way Amstan can increase its profitability is to improve its customer mix.

Finding the customers. After a careful look at its profit margins, Amstan has decided the branches are "either doing business with too few people or not calling on the right type of accounts." So, says Ruston, the division got to work "to get the customer brought to light—who he is, where he is, and why we weren't selling him." Then each branch manager could figure out "how to rearrange his sales efforts to get the best mix to assure profitability."

That is the goal of Amstan's current "account census" program—a market research and analysis project aimed at pinpointing the customers who will produce the most profitable business. The branch managers will have to do the final job, and the game is supposed to show them how.

Market studies. Three members of Amstan's headquarters research staff did a pilot market study for one branch in 1958. They dug up present and potential accounts (contractors and factories). They interviewed customers and branch employees.

Then they made out a sales card for each account—its market (residential, commercial, industrial), buying potential, credit rating, five-year buying history with the branch (if any), and the branch's past efforts to sell it. They also recorded a lot of information on each customer's buying attitudes—whether he bought on price alone, how much he was influenced by salesmanship, special services, and the like.

Later, other branches did their own account censuses, though most gathered only basic quantitative data.

Using the data. With the market research done, "We really knew for the first time," says Vice-Pres. Ruston, "who our customers were, the type of business, and what their potential was so we could make decisions on how best to get the business." The next step was, of course, to get the right people to make the right use of it. That's where the game came in.

Business research manager Frazee originally was attracted to games for management training when he read about the American Management Assn.'s top management decision simulation (BW—Jul.25'59,p56). Amstan had been concerned about a lack of depth in management and Pres. Sells had launched an effort to develop new talent and beef up the old.

But there's a lot to teach a wholesale manager. "There are so many little details about running our business," says Sells. "They get a new manager confused."

Starting a game. Frazee thought a game might provide synthetic experience. Sells recounts that Frazee said one day, "I don't suppose you'd like to play this game they have at Pitt." This was a highly abstract general management game. "It was fun," Sells admits, "but I wanted a game that specialized in our business."

So Frazee and Dr. William Kehl, director of the University of Pittsburgh's computation and data processing center, worked out the Pitt-Amstan Market Simulator.

Except for the customer decision-making process (based on the Amstan account census), it's much like any other marketing game. Six competing distributors are selling three product lines to 300 potential customers. Each distributor has six salesmen of varying abilities (which can be improved by training) and other workers. He can hire and fire. He sets prices and terms of sale; spends money on salaries and inventory; allocates time.

Each distributor has basic financial information about customers and descriptive reports of his salesmen's talents; after each round of play he gets financial statements from the computer. From time to time he gets other facts. The Builders Exchange Newsletter (signed by Ima Builder) tells him what contractors are bidding on which jobs. Occasionally the computer provides such tips as "Customer 801 normally employed two office girls, just released one."

Without the profile of Amstan's own market, Frazee thinks, this game could apply to any marketing organization. In fact, an auto manufacturer is thinking of adapting it for dealers.

Controversial. The Amstan market model is the game's unique—and controversial—feature. Some game designers think it's much too detailed.

Frazee disagrees. Most training games, he says, teach by analogy; the player gets a general idea that he is supposed to apply to his own similar problems. But Amstan's branch managers are supposed to be able to make a literal transfer from game to job.

Applying the lesson. Right now, what they are supposed to have learned (at meetings last winter) is how to balance the cost of serving a customer against revenue he can bring in.

Branches began applying the lesson in April, and some managers are already reshuffling their salesmen. It's too early to see any concrete payoff. But branch managers were enthusiastic, and Executive Vice-Pres. Joseph Salamone is sure they'll come up with a better customer mix eventually.

More to come. There's more to customer mix, of course, than just sales cost vs. revenue. Amstan wants its branch managers to learn how to balance their accounts geographically, by size, and among industries. It wants them to give a lot of attention to customers' credit standing ("The worst thing in our business," according to Sells).

That will come up early next year, and the branch managers will learn their lesson by playing the game again.

Other uses. Meanwhile, Amstan is finding other uses for the game. It has been trying out candidates for branch managerships by letting them play, through the mail. Some are now on the waiting list for such jobs; others are getting additional training.

Amstan's executives, while not calling the game a selection device, admit it influences them, giving "an insight into a man's thinking abilities."

Amstan has also been using the game to give divisional staff personnel and executives of other American Standard divisions a better idea of branch managers' problems.

The most ambitious application is scheduled this fall. In one of its big markets, Amstan has a price-cutting problem. Frazee wants to test alternate pricing strategies, using actual rather than typical customers. Amstan executives well acquainted with competitors will play their roles.

The way it is. Amstan's advisers at Pitt regard the game as a "major breakthrough in being able automatically to generate computer simulations of micro-models of large business systems."

But is the game actually realistic enough to be a basis for decision-making? Frazee is convinced it is, though the only proof so far is the reaction of the 100 or so Amstan people who have played it. All of them, he says, have echoed Pres. Sells' remark: "This is just the way our business is."

Your Wits vs. the Computer's

BANKERS, we understand, have a new, informal game that's as up to date as the Automation Age. Played with a computer, it's called variously "Bank Management Simulation," "Bank Simulation," "Men and Machines," or maybe just "The Game."

The players are teams of bankers, sometimes called "banks," which pit their management decisions against a national economy situation that has been built into the machine. Thus the game, which is just beginning to evolve, is a gimmick for exposing management people to banking problems and solutions, a training device for sharpening judgment and developing potential.

The idea was developed by McKinsey & Company, Inc., a New York management consultant firm, and a group of West Coast banks, with an important assist from International Business Machines Corporation. It has been tested, we're told, by groups of bank officers, and several banks around the country are now experimenting with the novel training technique.

How to Play

McKinsey explains it this way:

"The game is played by one or a number of teams, four to six members to a team, each representing a bank of $50,000,000 in assets. The teams do

Reprinted, with permission, from *Banking*, August 1960.

not compete directly; one team's decisions do not affect another's. Instead, each bank plays against a fluctuating national economy. However, at the end of play some teams in some respects—assets buildup, net profits, usage of funds—will naturally do better than others.

"Each bank begins with equal statements of condition showing commercial accounts broken down into three types, a real estate portfolio of 5-year real estate loans, consumer loans of five quarters' duration, and certain holdings in 90-day Treasury bills and 2-year U.S. Government bonds.

"At the beginning of each quarter the banks are given the gross national product, manufacturers' trade inventory, and consumer price index figures for the previous quarter, plus the average going interest rates of various types for that quarter. Each bank then makes its own decisions on commercial accounts (including officer additions, removals, and assignments to various accounts), real estate loans, consumer loans and investments, and advertising and promotion expenditures. These interacting factors are checked against shifts in the economy by the computer which returns to the banks a new quarterly statement, new economic and new average rate data.

"Over a series of 20-minute quarters the separate teams take their banks through four or more years of asset management decisions."

ONE BANK'S EXPERIENCE

Mellon National Bank and Trust Company of Pittsburgh, where the game has been played, reports on the experience.

Three "banks" or teams of three bank officers each started operations with equal assets, capital, and deposits, competing against the economy built into the computer. As they made their decisions affecting commercial loans, demand deposits, increasing and decreasing the number of officers, assignments of officers, loan rates, service charges, real estate loans, consumer credit, advertising expenditures, and investments, the information was punched on cards and fed into the IBM 650 computer. The report continues:

THE PROGRAM

"The computer was programed to calculate the effects of the decisions, apply results to the previous condition of the bank, and compute current quarterly income. A simple but realistic model of the economy was built into the simulation and, as it progressed, various economic factors fluctuated, as did required bank reserves and the Federal Reserve rediscount rate. The teams had no advance knowledge of the ups and downs of economic activity, but had to recognize various indicators encountered during the course of the action.

"A critique conference, where officers of each team or 'bank' explain their management philosophy and how they arrived at their decisions, closed the session. Progress charts were discussed, compared, and strategies evaluated. Each 'bank' had taken a different approach to the problem, and all participants were enthusiastic about the possibilities the experiment promised."

Commenting on the game, Mellon's president, John A. Mayer, said:

"It broadens the scope of management decisions beyond those many officers face in their daily work and gives them a greater appreciation of the myriad and interrelated problems of bank management."

FROM MILITARY TO BUSINESS

The bank recalled that simulation as a means of providing experience stemmed from the military, which for years has played war games to help in the training of officers. "However," adds Mellon, "the harnessing of a computer makes it possible to simulate several years of actual operating conditions in a single day of real decision-making based on real problems. Now simulation is applied to business situations, too."

HOW IT STARTED

The McKinsey consultants in November 1958 had evolved a "general management game" that operated manually. Then the firm's San Francisco office joined with Crocker-Anglo National Bank, Bank of America, Bank of California, and First Western Bank & Trust Company in doing the research on a banking game. IBM was called in to program the game for a computer.

The firm's W. H. Dennick, one of the game's originators, says: "It's a lot of fun. Especially for banks, it is an important training device, but it's really exciting in that it points to predictive simulation for actual banks."

Computer Simulates
Executives' Problems

Russell Hawkes

Use of computer simulation to train business executives and develop management techniques in a compressed time scale and without attendant losses due to learning errors has been developed and is being used by Lockheed Missiles & Space Co. in Sunnyvale, California.

Aerospace business environment simulator (ABES) has been developed during the past two years by the LMSC information processing staff headed by Roger K. Summit to subject competing teams of managers to many of the same factors which real aerospace firms encountered in doing business with the government.

Four Lockheed competitors, Philco Corp., Aerojet-General Corp., Boeing Co., and Douglas Aircraft Co., have taken part in ABES exercises by mail and all have expressed interest in using the simulator under license in their own organizations. Douglas used ABES to give the people in its new top management structure experience in working together as a decision team. Boeing used its ABES exercise to test operations research techniques the

Reprinted, with permission, from *Aviation Week & Space Technology*, June 18, 1962.

IBM Computer

ABES is a mathematical and logical model programed for the IBM 7090 computer which was developed in a program during the past two years to apply quantitative techniques and electronic data processing to management problems.

To conduct an exercise, separate teams of managers are assembled to represent aerospace companies in competition with each other for business. The computer reacts to decisions by printing out the results that presumably would occur in the real world. Teams compare the results of each round of decision-making to the objectives of their simulated companies and adjust their decisions during the next round to get improved results. The game lasts about two weeks, though the length is arbitrary. This period of time represents a number of years.

The teams begin with identical companies and the decisions each makes affect its standing in the simulated industry. Decisions involve procurement of resources, including labor, operations and contract bidding. Results are in the form of financial and operating reports, contract awards and new proposals to be bid. Research and development contracts are funded on a cost-plus-fixed-fee basis and production is done on a fixed price. Space systems and missile systems are treated as separate product lines.

During a game team members have the opportunity to evaluate the factors and the sometimes contradictory inter-relationships that must be manipulated to produce success. For example, improved facilities, internal research, and employee training tend to improve productivity of the company but can be obtained only at a certain increase in the cost of operation. As team members learn how contract awards are influenced by other factors such as bid price, past performance, etc., they can decide whether to accept the increased cost of additional productivity or save the money so as to make a correspondingly lower bid.

Some Factors Revised

The inventors of ABES in the LMSC information processing staff have revised some factors in the simulator model on the basis of participant reaction. Among the revisions were reductions of the weighting assigned to availability of resources and the inclusion of company financial condition as factors in determining contract awards.

Past games show that experienced teams make individual decisions within a framework of basic policies that express the degree of risk the team is willing to assume and the alternatives of short-range payout versus long-range payout.

Typical risk considerations are the amount of backlog to be maintained and the degree of diversification to be sought. High backlog is security against running out of work but requires that the company bid more daringly because it is government policy to maintain some sort of balance in the award of contracts to keep competitors in the field.

The game divides operations on a functional basis between R&D work which is funded by cost-plus-fixed-fee contracts and production which is funded by fixed-price contracts. Operations are also divided along product lines into missile systems and space systems. If a company specializes in one function or product area, it can become more efficient in that area but runs the risk that a contract in the area might not be available when the company needs business. Each team must also weigh the desirability of high current profits against the gain in efficiency and competitive position during future rounds that can be obtained by investing a large part of profits to improve or expand capabilities.

Results of ABES games often fail to produce clear-cut winners and losers. In an exercise involving five teams and covering a simulated span of three years, one team was the apparent winner by the criterion of total equity at the end of the period. However, it achieved this at least partially by sacrificing some efficiency in research and development which might have caused later procurement difficulties had game been continued indefinitely as in real life. The apparent winner also had bid on only a few contracts which kept indirect administrative costs low but allowed backlog to approach zero frequently which could have necessitated a major lay-off.

Lockheed has had more than 200 of its executives run ABES exercises to acquire experience in top-level decision-making. Company officials say it is analogous to aircraft and spacecraft simulators used to enable pilots to make their learning errors without disastrous results or excessive costs. Specific benefits of the simulation listed by participants are that it:

- *Enables team members* to work in unfamiliar decision roles.
- *Gives participants* an understanding of broad company objectives that is often lacking in their real life jobs.

- *Gives competing executives* an awareness of the interacting forces in the aerospace business.
- *Teaches the advantages* of long-range planning compared with brush fire planning.
- *Teaches techniques* of analyzing numerical business information.
- *Makes team members aware* of the distinctions between relevant and irrelevant information.
- *Illustrates the difference* between cost-plus-fixed-fee and fixed-price contracting and emphasizes the importance of cost control in the latter.

Part II

Selected Business Games

The game abstracts in this section have been classified into three divisions: general purpose games, special purpose and functional games, and industry games. Each abstract covers the following information:

    I. Game description
   II. Training purpose
  III. Decisions made by the participants and the game administrator
  IV. Method of administration—manual or computer
   V. Source of information
  VI. Reference code

The latter provides a ready reference to determine if the game is manually or computer scored; the numbers refer to articles listed in the bibliography which discuss the particular game. For example, the AMA General Management Business Simulation game is referenced (C, 12, 22, 87, 152, 162, 165, 209, 214, 215, 216, 219, 239, 247, 281). This indicates the game is computer scored and articles numbered 12, 22, 87, 152, 162, 165, 209, 214, 215, 216, 219, 239, 247, and 281 in the bibliography include some additional information concerning the game.

General Purpose Games

GENERAL PURPOSE games are especially useful in broadening the decision-making experiences of the participants. These games require the participants to make top-management decisions related to the overall operation of their company. The games stress strategy formulation and long-range planning within a competitive environment. General purpose games are integrative—they demonstrate the interrelationships of the functional areas of marketing, finance, and production. Such games are designed to force the participants to deal with the factors of risk and uncertainty. The influence of the economic climate on the level of business activity is clearly illustrated. General purpose games require heuristic problem solving by the players because of the multiplicity of variables, components, and parameters of the game model.

The "A" Game

1. DESCRIPTION

This is a total enterprise game that is flexible and can be tailored to emphasize any particular discipline by variation of approximately 100 parameters. Decisions are usually made in two phases—a planning phase and an operational phase. The planning phase has to be done under conditions of uncertainty with respect to future operations such as production, research and development, actual price, and sales performance.

Teams may sell a single product in four regions, each of which includes six districts. The actual number of units sold depends on market potential and competitive action. Sales are made through company salesmen who have different levels of abilities. Salesmen are assigned to particular districts each period. Sustained and adequate research and development can result in product improvements. Participants decide how much to spend on advertising and in which regions they will advertise. Plant capacity decisions are incorporated in the model by accentuating declining plant efficiency and depreciation. Computer output includes income and balance sheets along with other information necessary for operating a business.

II. Training Purpose

Since the game is flexible and can be tailored to particular needs, the general training purpose is to provide a decision-making model which demonstrates the interrelationships of the key variables in a business system. Emphasis can be shifted by changing the parameters.

III. Decisions Made by Participants

Phase I

1. Hire sales trainees
2. Hire and terminate qualified salesmen
3. New plants to build
4. Plants to scrap
5. Information purchases
6. Accounts receivable factored
7. Long-term loans

Phase II

1. Units of production
2. Research and development
3. Price by region
4. Units advertising by region
5. Salary and location of salesmen

1. Economic index
2. Game parameters

IV. Administration

This is a computer game programmed in FORTRAN for both the IBM 7094 and CDC 6400.

V. Source

Hector R. Anton, *General Information and Rules of Play Manual,* School of Business Administration, University of California, Berkeley, California.

(*C*)

The A.B.C. Management Exercise Game

I. Description

This is a noncomputerized, integrated management game in which teams composed of six members attempt to maximize the value of stockholders' equity.

The game begins with each team having quantitative information on costs, price demand, and a ten-year market survey. The teams produce three perishable products which are not stocked. Teams make such major decisions as pricing, production quantity, and purchase quantity at the beginning of each quarter. At the end of the fourth quarter each team is given a report summarizing operating information.

The maximum time allowance between decisions is one hour and real time is one day.

No face-to-face interaction among team members is allowed during the experiment—communications are written.

II. Training Purpose

The training purpose is to allow the participant to apply such techniques as cost analysis, EOQ formulae, funds flow, and price demand analysis in a laboratory situation calling for applications in the areas of planning, communication, and decision making. The game also tests the participant's willingness to innovate.

III. DECISIONS MADE BY PARTICIPANTS

1. The product unit price
2. The units of product to be produced
3. The number of orders for raw materials
4. Quantity of raw materials to be purchased per order
5. The amount of desired borrowing

IV. ADMINISTRATION

Administrators score work sheets and quarterly report blanks. They are furnished with the price demand schedule, the solution letter, the critical values in the exercise by the game source, and necessary forms.

V. SOURCE

A. A. Robichek, *Imede,* Management Development Institute, P.O. Box 1059, 1001 Lausanne, Lausanne, Switzerland.

(*M*)

AMA General Management Business Simulation

I. DESCRIPTION

Any number of company teams may be formed to manage a typical American corporation, the Mose Company. The number of members per company team may range from five to eighteen. The Mose Company is an industrial firm with two manufacturing plants and a choice of one, two, or three products. The firm may serve both the industrial and/or the consumer market.

Raw material procurement is handled through a central warehouse serving both manufacturing plants, with production output of the two manufacturing plants shipped to each of two, four, or six possible sales-product regions in the East and in the West.

At the beginning of the simulation exercise the Mose Company management is faced with a situation of low profit performance expressed in terms of return on invested capital, poor utilization of capacity, and an overcapitalization in relation to the size of the volume transacted. Each team is required to make decisions in the areas of marketing, production, research and development, corporate financing, and survey information on competitive actions regarding price, advertising, and share of the market. Planning, organizing, and controlling are very important, with particular emphasis on financial management including investment, borrowing, cash-flow in profit planning, and accountability. Performance is evaluated on the basis of quarterly statements and analyses.

II. TRAINING PURPOSE

This game is designed to provide participants with realistic experience in managing a (simulated) company through identifying and utilizing optimal tactical tools and information for strategic decision making.

III. DECISIONS MADE BY PARTICIPANTS

1. Raw material purchases
2. Raw material conversion and inventorying
3. Plant equipment and depreciation
4. Labor force, wages
5. Production level
6. Warehousing and shipping
7. Marketing research
8. Advertising
9. Pricing
10. Sales: bookings, back orders, deliveries, lost orders
11. Sales force: level, remuneration
12. Administrative expenses: production, sales, research and development, corporate

13. Borrowing, emergency loans
14. Loan repayments, dividends

DECISIONS MADE BY ADMINISTRATOR

1. Price and availability of raw material
2. Number of competitors
3. Wage competition
4. Time scheduling

IV. ADMINISTRATION

The game was designed for the IBM 650 and was later programmed for the IBM 1410. It is currently programmed for the Honeywell 1200 (via Data-Phone link) using Honeywell Assembly Language.

V. SOURCE

The game is the proprietary property of the American Management Association and is reserved for use in its executive development programs. An appraisal of the similar predecessor-game can be gained from AMA's publication *Top Management Decision Simulation: The AMA Approach,* Elizabeth Marting, Editor—now out of print, but obtainable in photocopy from University Microfilms, Ann Arbor, Michigan.

(*C,* 12, 22, 87, 152, 162, 165, 209, 214, 215, 216, 219, 239, 247, 281)

The Arizona Business Game

I. DESCRIPTION

In this game a domestic based capital goods manufacturing concern is involved with the functions of engineering, manufacturing, marketing, and financing one product in a competitive environment. The product is quite technical and requires one-half year to manufacture. It is sold in a market characterized by product differentiation and mutual interdependence of sellers.

A minimum of two and a maximum of four teams, each ideally composed of four men, may play the game. However, it is possible to play with only one man per team. Each team is an entity and represents one company.

The first game period, six months of game time, is utilized in organizing the company. The second six months of game time are utilized for operation of the firm. Each company begins with $800,000.

Sufficient marketing information is given to allow each team to prepare forecasts.

II. Training Purpose

The game is designed to help participants develop the ability to do business planning with emphasis on formulation, parameters, and revision and to become cognizant of the necessity to develop information about market conditions, advertising, research and development, and manufacturing costs.

III. Decisions Made by Participants

1. Construction and size of plant
2. Securing and resolving bank loans
3. Product research and cost reduction
4. Determining size of sales force and hiring and firing
5. Product promotion and selling price
6. Administrative expenses
7. Number of shifts per day the plant will operate

Decisions Made by Administrator

1. The trend of the market at the beginning of the game
2. The trend of the market at the beginning of each subsequent quarter of play

IV. Administration

This game, designed for an IBM 1401 computer, includes detailed discussion for each officer and necessary equations and exhibits in the game manual. A policy book and decision sheet are also part of the manual.

V. Source

Department of Management, College of Business and Public Administration, The University of Arizona, Tucson, Arizona.

(*C*)

Boston College Decision-Making Exercise

I. Description

This is a total enterprise game in which three firms compete for sales of a single consumer durable product in four market areas. Different competitive situations exist in each area. Firms may develop improved versions of their product through research and development; such improvements usually improve sales. Management also controls salesmen's salaries and advertising to optimize sales and profit margin. Careful consideration must be given to production scheduling of the numerous plants each firm may have. Since the economy is assumed to be growing in the long run, capital improvements and acquisitions become necessary; firms may finance such projects through borrowing long-term funds, issuing stock, or with working capital. The computer output includes the profit and loss statement, funds statement, position statement, stock price, and industry report.

II. Training Purpose

The game is designed for use in teaching participants to appreciate the interrelationships of marketing, finance, and production in short-run decisions and long-range planning.

III. Decisions Made by Participants

1. Price for each area
2. Advertising for each area
3. Number of active salesmen

4. Training and relocating salesmen for each area
5. Research and development—product and process
6. Production scheduling
   A. Plants producing
   B. Number of shifts
   C. Number of lines
   D. Weeks of production
   E. Hours per week
7. Sales salary and commission
8. Executive compensation
9. Change in stock shares
10. New issue price
11. New plants
12. Additional lines
13. Deactivation and reactivation of lines
14. Other expenses
15. Bank loans
16. Bonds issued or redeemed
17. Dividends

DECISIONS MADE BY ADMINISTRATOR

1. Economic factors—trends, seasonal and cyclical
2. Price for additional information and "other expenses"
3. Starting position of firms
4. Demand elasticity

IV. ADMINISTRATION

The game is programmed for the IBM 1620 computer in machine language.

V. SOURCE

John Van Tassel and Vincent Wright, 1620 General Program Library (10.2.005), *Boston College Decision-Making Exercise,* 1962. Requests for manual and computer documentations should be directed to Program Information Department, Program Distribution Center, International Business Machines Corp., 40 Saw Mill Road, Hawthorne, New York.

(C)

Burroughs Economic Simulator

I. DESCRIPTION

This game is a total enterprise game that demonstrates the interrelationships and interaction of the marketing, finance, and production areas. The structure of the game is based on the UCLA Executive Games, Models 1, 2, and 3.

This simulation is a single industry, single product one with firms competing against each other. Each management team is told that its company has suffered from poor communication channels between executives and has had difficulty in providing executives with current information about operations. The teams are charged with establishing corporate policy, including devising an effective internal organization and allocating cash assets. Each quarter six decisions regarding the allocation of funds may be made. Before each decision period, each team is provided with a report showing its profit or loss, receipts and disbursements, assets, and owners' equity for the previous period. Every four quarters an annual report is also provided showing the net cash assets, inventory value, net book value of the plant, and owners' equity of each competing firm. The success of each team depends upon the effectiveness of its decisions made in view of economic and competitive patterns.

II. TRAINING PURPOSE

This game shows the importance of team effort and good communications, the value of long-range planning, and the complexity and interrelationship of many factors confronting managers in making decisions.

III. DECISIONS MADE BY PARTICIPANTS

1. Organizational structure
2. Pricing

3. Capital investments
4. Production
5. Research and development—product
6. Dividends
7. Advertising

DECISION MADE BY ADMINISTRATOR

1. Economic index

IV. ADMINISTRATION

The game is programmed for Burroughs B200, B300 data processing systems and the B5500 information system.

V. SOURCE

Player's Manual, *Burroughs Economic Simulator,* Equipment and Systems Marketing Division, Burroughs Corporation, Detroit, Michigan.

(*C*, 196)

Business Game III, Executive Decision Making

I. DESCRIPTION

This is a competitive game simulating multiproduct firms serving two available markets in the same industry. Participants are divided into three to five groups of four to six participants each. These groups become managers of competing firms. The game itself may be played from ten to twenty meetings with each meeting representing a business quarter.

The members of each firm meet privately at the end of each business quarter to make decisions for the future quarters. All business is obtained through competitive bidding on various types of contracts involving manufacture of products for the two available markets—aircraft components and components for missiles and space vehicles. A firm may serve both markets or choose to specialize and serve one market. A firm specializing has a slight bidding advantage in its single market.

Managers are required to state their firm's long-run objectives, organize their firm, prepare a yearly letter to stockholders, and prepare information on new contracts received to be published in *The Eagle*.

Each quarter managers are given financial statements, company position information (current backlog, current inventory, number of employees, etc.), a trade publication, *The Eagle,* and requests for bids.

II. TRAINING PURPOSE

This game is designed to provide participants with simulated competitive-bidding and decision-making experience gained under the pressure of time and changing circumstances.

III. DECISIONS MADE BY PARTICIPANTS

1. Bid or no bid
2. Amount of bid
3. Personnel hiring, termination, and transferring
4. Overtime work
5. Sell, buy, or maintain plant and equipment
6. Research and development
7. Dividend
8. Inventory of raw materials

DECISIONS MADE BY ADMINISTRATOR

1. Requests for bids (number and type)
2. Industry index
3. Economic index
4. Material prices, labor rates, interest rates, and other items of interest (published in *The Eagle*)

IV. ADMINISTRATION

This is a manual game. Decision sheets, proposal sheets, and record-keeping sheets are provided. Four to twelve hours should be provided for a critique session following completion of the game.

V. Source

Instruction Manual, *Rohr Management Development, Business Game III, Executive Decision Making,* Rohr Aircraft Corporation, Chula Vista, California.

(*M*)

Business Management Game

I. Description

The game simulates the operation of a one-product capital goods company. Two or three teams (three to four members per team) compete in the same market. A playing board is employed which is divided into a market section and an operations section. The market section of the board is further divided into 24 squares in a combination of four geographical areas and rural and urban markets. Each square represents a potential customer. Each team makes decisions on dispersement of its sales force in contacting these customers, hiring new salesmen, enlarging plant capacity, advertising, and spending for market information and research and development. The operations section of the board is similarly divided into squares which allow time lags for training of new salesmen, production lead time, enlarging plant capacity, and collection of receivables. A random number table is used to determine the success of sales contacts, the effect of research and development, and the loss of salesmen. Emphasis is not placed on winning the game, but an evaluation session to discuss the results of the game is recommended at the conclusion of play.

II. Training Purpose

Participants learn to organize and plan the operation of a simulated capital goods company. In two hours they can observe and evaluate the effect that their decisions would have in a two-year period, and they can develop insight into the consequences of their decisions.

III. DECISIONS MADE BY PARTICIPANTS

    1. Dispersement of salesmen
    2. Hiring of salesmen
    3. Research and development
    4. Advertising
    5. Marketing research
    6. Plant capacity
    7. Factoring accounts receivable

DECISION MADE BY ADMINISTRATOR

    1. Trend of market

IV. ADMINISTRATION

Decisions and results are recorded on a decision form. Scoring is manual and takes from five to seven minutes. Fifteen to twenty minutes are allowed for participants to make decisions. Ten runs may be completed in about two and one-half hours.

V. SOURCE

The game is described in detail in G. R. Andlinger, "Business Games—Play One!" *Harvard Business Review*, Vol. XXXVI, No. 2 (March-April 1958), pp. 115-125.

Reprints of the game and copies of the game board are available from A-1 Readers Service Department, *Harvard Business Review*, Boston, Massachusetts.

(M, 10)

The Business Management Laboratory

I. DESCRIPTION

The Business Management Laboratory allows three to eight teams, each having four to six members, to compete for sales of two products in a domestic economy. Each product has its own marketing characteristics. The simulation assumes a period of three months for each decision set. The firms must consider the stated general economic conditions in planning their decisions. There are two marketing areas, with each team permitted to locate sales activity and/or production facilities in either area or both areas. Transfer of goods, capital, and salesmen between areas is permitted. Marketing research is permitted. Production is a two-stage process with many variations of scheduling and materials usage possible. Several options are available for financing the operations of the firms. Emphasis is placed on planning ahead for two or more periods in several areas of the decision-making process. An auxiliary program allows the administrator to obtain a fairly extensive evaluation of each firm at the end of any given period.

II. Training Purpose

The Business Management Laboratory gives the participants experience in coordinating many facets of a complex business enterprise. Emphasis is on the need to balance management activity without slighting important areas. A less obvious but equally important emphasis is on the need to consider management decisions as they are interpreted by concerned persons outside of the firm. Many decisions will require both short- and long-range planning.

III. Decisions Made by Participants

1. Prices
2. Advertising and promotion
3. Marketing research
4. Assignment of salesmen
5. Sales training
6. Sales compensation
7. Choice of markets
8. Transfer of goods
9. Raw materials management
10. Selecting an inventory accounting system
11. Research and development
12. Production levels
13. Shift and overtime operations
14. Production load balancing

15. Plant capacity
16. New plant construction
17. Factoring accounts receivable
18. Borrowing: loans and bonds
19. Common stock sales
20. Dividends
21. Executive compensation

DECISIONS MADE BY ADMINISTRATOR

1. Determining costs and charges
2. Establishing the economic cyclical pattern
3. (Optional) Approving loans, stock sales, etc.
4. (Optional) Rating quality of promotional activity
5. (Optional) Supervising intercompany transactions such as sale of surplus inventory or equipment

IV. ADMINISTRATION

The scoring is handled by a computer. Almost any system capable of using FORTRAN II or FORTRAN IV may be used. The administrator is given considerable control over the complexity of the simulation, and auxiliary programs reduce administrative intervention to a minimum, if desired.

V. SOURCE

Ronald L. Jensen, Graduate School of Business Administration, Emory University, Atlanta, Georgia.

(C)

Business Simulation Game

I. DESCRIPTION

The game is a simulation of general management decision making, illustrating the problems of management policy formulation and how to coordinate decision making of the major functional departments of the company. Three to five teams may be formed of eight to twelve members. Participation of all members of the team increases if membership is kept to the minimum.

The objective of the game is to teach general management policy, the elements of policy, and their interrelationships. The industry represented in the simulation is nationally oriented and the firms are few and compete under conditions of oligopoly. The participants are taught the techniques of policy formulation by top management in large companies in a complex industry, operating in an uncertain world. Students learn the importance of teamwork in policy formulation and how management tries to assess the future and the possible reactions of competitors to decisions. Having products when needed and scheduling output to satisfy sales demand while maintaining adequate inventories are key decisions each operating period.

Allocation of sufficient funds to research and development in order to develop new products, new production equipment, and production processes is a basic decision to keep costs in line and retain market share and, hopefully, to gain market expansion at the expense of competitors. A quarterly evaluation of the results from decisions is shown in computer output of a consolidated operating statement; for the noncomputer model, the statement may be prepared in a referee center.

II. Training Purpose

This game provides participants with experience in preparing and coordinating top management decisions in key areas and management of large companies in an industry that serves the domestic market exclusively.

III. Decisions Made by Participants

1. Volume of output
2. Advertising
3. Selling outlays
4. Price
5. Research and development
6. Investment in capacity
7. Short-term cash borrowed

DECISIONS MADE BY ADMINISTRATOR

1. Selection of historical series for economic index of U.S. economy
2. Liaison with computer center
3. If noncomputer game, operation of referee center

IV. ADMINISTRATION

The scoring is done by the computer, Burroughs 220, or by the referee center.

V. SOURCE

John L. Fulmer, *Business Simulation Games*, Monograph C-12, South-Western Publishing Company, Cincinnati, Ohio.

(*M, C,* 97)

Compuman

I. DESCRIPTION

In this total enterprise game up to nine teams (three to five or more per team) manage a firm within a competitive industry. Each firm manufactures and sells up to three products (different qualities of the same basic product). Each team makes decisions regarding plant expansion, manufacturing quantity and quality for each product, prices of each product for sale in market, marketing allocation, design and styling, and research and development budget. Additional decisions are made by each team as to handling of financial matters such as investments and plant expansions. Loans and loan restraints are voluntary and have involuntary emergency loan possibilities built in.

Decisions cover one quarter of the year. A seasonal index and an estimated economic index are given for forecasting purposes. Printout consisting of profit and loss, balance sheet, cash flow, and operational statements is furnished each team after every decision for total firm operation along with operational information for each product. Industry information is furnished on all firms with built-in random error for all items except price.

II. TRAINING PURPOSE

Compuman gives training in bringing together the use of functional disciplines learned in a student's four years of work in a school of business.

III. DECISIONS MADE BY PARTICIPANTS

1. Purchase of plant and equipment
2. Purchase (or sale) of long-term securities
3. Purchase (or sale) of short-term loan
4. Application for (or repayment of) long-term loan
5. Application for (or repayment of) short-term loan
6. Amount of research and development
7. Price for product (for each of three products)
8. Marketing budget (for each of three products)
9. Design and styling budget (for each of three products)
10. Production volume (for each of three products)
11. Production budget (cost per unit) (for each of three products)

DECISIONS MADE BY ADMINISTRATOR

1. Purchasing cards (if students are not taught how)
2. Limits of change per periods of variables for price, marketing, design and styling, and cost per unit

IV. ADMINISTRATION

Scoring and printout are done by computer; the game is programmed in FORTRAN IV.

V. Source

Paul **D**. Miller or Jay A. Craven, School of Business, University of Miami, Coral Gables, Florida.

(*C*)

The Conopoly Industry

I. Description

In this total enterprise game the participant or team selects decision rules or strategies at the beginning of the game; from that point on the computer uses programmed subroutines for the selected strategies to calculate output for each period without intervention. As an example, price may be set by strategy rules such as the following: Teams may set a constant price, set their price as a multiple of the last period industry average with specified upper or lower limits, or set their price as a multiple of their own last period price with specified limits. Once the team determines its decision strategies for price, marketing production, capital investment, and loan payments, the computer carries the strategies out for the entire game.

The participants represent teams in *The Conopoly Industry,* which has a competitive market for the one product produced by the companies. The total market is affected by the normal factors—marketing expenditures, economy changes, and price—while each company's market share is determined by its marketing expenditures and price in relation to those of its competitors. Balance sheets, profit and loss statements, and statements of cash flows are provided to the participants to allow them to evaluate their performance.

II. Training Purpose

As a change from most business games, this game forces the participant to concentrate on long-range plans rather than period-by-period decisions. It also emphasizes the importance of long-range planning in a general management context.

III. Decisions Made by Participants

1. Price per unit strategy
2. Marketing expenditures strategy
3. Production rate strategy
4. Plant and equipment purchases strategy
5. Loan repayments

IV. Administration

This is a computer-programmed game in which the computer plays all the periods of the game during one run.

V. Source

Robert C. Meier, *The Conopoly Industry* (Mimeograph), University of Washington, Seattle, Washington, 1966.

Robert C. Meier, "Decision-Making Versus Strategy Determination: A Gaming and Heuristic Approach," *University of Washington Business Review,* Vol. XXV, No. 4, April-June 1966, pp. 34-41.

(C, 186)

Decision Making

I. Description

Teams of four to five players are formed. Competition is between teams and between members within each team. Each team represents managers in a manufacturing company employing 150 to 200 people. All managers are competing to be selected for the presidency of the company in six years, when the current president expects to retire. Questions for decisions are referred to the participants one at a time. The decisions are high level and reflect long-range planning. Once made, the decisions must be implemented by management. Managers are asked to recognize opportunities in potential new products, acquisitions, and various management programs.

Both personal and team decisions are called for. The team decision is evaluated against those of other teams. The game provides instant feedback informing participants which of their decisions were unsound and why. Additional feedback is provided through the technique of "peer rating," whereby discussion leads to interchange of ideas and judgments of performance of team members.

II. TRAINING PURPOSE

This game is intended to provide middle managers with some practice in higher level decision making. They are asked to recognize risk and opportunities in potential new products, acquisitions, and in various management programs. The game places emphasis on personal development as a means for achievement and superior performance.

III. DECISIONS MADE BY PARTICIPANTS

1. Training assistants
2. Risk evaluation
3. Personal development
4. Acquisitions
5. Communication consultants
6. Management by objectives
7. Human relations in management (leadership style)

IV. ADMINISTRATION

This game is manually scored by participants. A guide booklet is provided for administering the game. The administrator leads pregame and postgame discussions. The game requires one and one-half to two hours of playing time.

V. SOURCE

Erwin Rausch. Direct inquiries to Science Research Associates, Inc., 259 East Erie Street, Chicago, Illinois.

(*M*)

Decision Simulation of a Manufacturing Firm

I. DESCRIPTION

Three to ten companies are required for the simulation, with four or five members recommended for each team. Each company manages a small domestic manufacturing company engaged in the production and sale of two standard items made from metal castings.

The members of each team make decisions regarding production, including days of operation and number of employees; marketing, including prices, salesmen's compensation, expenses, advertising, and commission on sales; licensing; storing; financing; inventory control; contract bids; wage negotiations; and raw materials and equipment purchases. Two products are manufactured and the companies operate in two distinct sales areas. Introduction of an improved product and entry into the second area are controlled by the simulation administrator.

Decisions are made in a dynamic business environment, which may vary according to a quarterly index of seasonal business activity. Marketing research information may be purchased from the administrator.

Companies are required to submit bids on contract awards which are released at the discretion of the administrator. The bids are a separate part of the market structure.

Timing and scheduling are important considerations in the simulation. The variables are completely interacting, and decisions made by each of the teams affect the decisions of the other teams. Performance is evaluated quarterly through the use of income statements and financial reports. A yearly statement comparing all companies is also furnished.

The construction of the game produces the type of problems most frequently encountered in the real world by small firms and places the burden of developing the entire company strategy upon the participants.

II. TRAINING PURPOSE

The decision simulation provides the participants with experience in making top management decisions as required in the operation of a small manufacturing firm in a typical environment.

III. DECISIONS MADE BY PARTICIPANTS

1. Production
2. Plant capacity
3. Product mix
4. Borrowing
5. Advertising
6. Markets
7. Market research
8. Pricing
9. Equipment replacement
10. Maintenance
11. Sales-force composition
12. Salesmen's compensation
13. Administrative detail
14. Raw-material purchase plan
15. Factory expansion
16. Training program for salesmen
17. Contract bid-prices

DECISIONS MADE BY ADMINISTRATOR

1. Determining costs, changes, and time lags
2. Opening second sales area for company use
3. Releasing product "B" for production and sale
4. Releasing contracts for bid
5. Input variables for marketing, production, and finance which determine the economic and competitive environment

IV. ADMINISTRATION

Scoring is by computer; the program is written in FORTRAN IV.

V. SOURCE

The simulation procedures are contained in two volumes. The administrator's manual and the student's manual are both entitled *Decision Simula-*

tion of a Manufacturing Firm. The simulation is administered by the Graduate School of Business, College of Business Administration, The University of Texas at Austin.

B. H. Sord, The College of Business Administration, The University of Texas at Austin, Austin, Texas.

(C)

Duquesne University Management Game

I. DESCRIPTION

The game is designed as a basic part of a two-semester course intended to provide skill in business decision making under relatively complex conditions. Forty-two decisions, covering a span of four years, are made (the first two decisions are for months seven and eight of the first year).

The firm operates in an economy such as that of the United States, in four marketing areas, with competition from two other American firms and one foreign importer; it manufactures and distributes carbon and alloy steel from three plants and four warehouses (one in each marketing area).

Decisions are made monthly. The corporate management sets broad company policies with regard to prices, capital expenditures, research and development, and so on. The plant managers make decisions about such things as operating levels and plant maintenance. Control of decisions of plant managers must be attained through advance planning of the corporate management. The corporate managers meet three hours each week to make their "monthly" decisions. Prior to these meetings they prepare any policy directives which are necessary for the guidance of the plant managers, who are meeting at the same time to make their decisions.

The game is programmed for a computer which handles that part of the real world background which can be described by mathematical equations, but assumes human administrators who are the banker brokers, labor unions, etc., with whom all financial and labor matters are negotiated. The board of directors reviews the performance of the student managers and executives. They may require any reports which are necessary to evaluate the management.

II. Training Purpose

The game attempts to provide experience in handling a multitude of business experiences within the broadest possible framework. Specifically, the game and the course of which it is a part are designed to give experience in group leadership; strengthen competency in procedural areas; develop an awareness of the complexity and interrelationships in business management; help develop ability to seek out, evaluate, and use data; and provide an opportunity to work effectively in a group and to participate effectively in group discussions of policy and procedures.

III. Decisions Made by Participants

1. Allocation of funds within the firm
2. Modernization programs and maintenance expenditures
3. Production and quality control
4. Research and development
5. Labor force and overtime
6. New production facilities (if desired)
7. Marketing expenditures
8. Price of product line
9. Other information required (if desired)
10. Financial needs (securities, short-term loans, and investment policies)
11. Buying schedules for raw materials and inventory balances
12. Company organization and objectives
13. Performance ratings of managers

Decisions Made by Administrators

1. Evaluate performance
2. Set market price of stock
3. Set terms of loans
4. Set bond issue details
5. Handle labor contract negotiations

6. Answer any questions regarding appropriateness of specific actions of the participants

IV. ADMINISTRATION

The game is programmed for a modern computer. A manual is provided which gives the students participating the necessary information with regard to raw materials, labor costs, market conditions, etc., and the reports and decisions required of them. Forms are available for decisions.

V. SOURCE

Student's Manual, J. J. Miller and B. Meyer, *Duquesne University Management Game,* Duquesne University, Pittsburgh, Pennsylvania.

(C)

Dynamic Executive Simulation

I. DESCRIPTION

This is an interactive game containing probabilistic and deterministic elements. It employs the concepts of both decreasing returns and marginal utility.

The game may be scored either manually or by computer. If computer scored, ten teams may participate.

In the game each team manages a manufacturing plant which makes small, multipurpose electric motors. They make decisions in the functional areas of finance, production, and marketing, and through these decisions attempt to enlarge their share of the market.

II. TRAINING PURPOSE

The purpose is to give the participants experience in making and analyzing decisions, both their own and the actions of competitors. Through study of this feedback from previous decisions, the participants are expected to make better decisions.

III. Decisions Made by Participants

1. Price
2. Level of production
3. Plant capacity
4. Research and development expenditures
5. Allocation of salesmen

Decisions Made by Administrator

1. Determine game parameter
2. Substitute or alter suggested procedures

IV. Administration

This game may be hand calculated or IBM 1620 computer scored. The computerized version will take up to ten teams, prints out complete financial records, and keeps records of each team's quarterly and accumulative operating results. The player's and umpire's manuals and computer program are available from game source.

V. Source

Department of Industrial and Personnel Management, The University of Tennessee, Knoxville, Tennessee.

(M, C)

Executive Decision-Making Through Simulation

I. Description

This game is a case-simulation exercise. Through the study of cases, the participants become familiar with the external environment with which rubber companies cope. In the simulation phase the participant is presented with the problems of the interrelationships of the marshaling and allocation of the internal resources of the firm. The firm's position must be changed through strategies developed to handle shifts in the environment.

This competitive situation game is played with a minimum of three and a maximum of eight teams comprising four or five members. Game time is three years; real time is eight to ten hours in meetings and nine to fourteen hours outside meetings.

The teams make plans, forecasts, and decisions in overall performance, finance, assets, personnel and labor problems, sales and costs, and production.

II. Training Purpose

The game is designed to teach the participants the interrelationships of functional fields and the effect of the external environment on the strategies of the firm. Also, emphasis is placed on the concepts of cash budgeting and planning.

III. Decisions Made by Participants

1. Forecast sales in units and dollars
2. Selling price per unit
3. Number of sales personnel to hire and fire
4. National and local advertising budgets
5. Research and development cost
6. Number of units to produce and cost per unit
7. Production capacity and percent of capacity to use
8. Expansion of facilities and automation
9. Increase or reduce dividends
10. Increase or reduce long-term debt

Decisions Made by Administrator

1. Loan rate
2. Labor costs
3. Doubtful account losses
4. Units on private brand contract
5. Economic lever

    6. Effectiveness of advertising and salesmen
    7. Price elasticity
    8. Research and development effect
    9. Automation effect

IV. ADMINISTRATION

This game may be either computer or hand scored. The computer version is programmed in FORTRAN II.

V. SOURCE

Instructor's Manual, Douglas C. Basil, Paul R. Cone, and John A. Fleming, *Executive Decision-Making Through Simulation,* Charles E. Merril, Inc., Columbus, Ohio, 1965.

(*M,C*)

Executive Simulation Game

I. DESCRIPTION

The participants in this game represent the management of a manufacturer of transistorized production equipment competing in a multifirm market. The product sells for $40,000 and is sold on the basis of error free, quality production rather than cost savings.

The game is played by opposing teams competing for the limited sales potential in 48 market areas. Each team is organized by its members; however, a chief executive and directors of sales and marketing, finance and accounting, personnel, and production are suggested.

Mathematical probabilities affect the flow of the game to a large extent. Wise expenditures for research and development, advertising, sales training, and bonuses improve the firm's probabilities but do not guarantee results. Umpires decide, on the basis of amounts spent for training, bonuses, research, advertising and probability, the outcome of a firm's decisions. Data are provided regarding training costs, advertising costs, and the current and residual values of these expenditures. The umpire evaluates sales activity and informs each company of its results. Success or failure of the company depends on the probability of sales being made under competitive interaction of the several companies.

A number of forms are provided to keep a record of advertising expenditures, salesmen used and calls made, units sold, and revenue for each sales area. Additional forms keep track of the "game flow" by quarters, the financial condition, sales and inventories, expenses, and cash flow and other financial data. Decisions are normally made in 20 minutes, with some variation specified by the umpire depending upon the skill of the players. The game may be played over any number of years.

II. Training Purpose

This game assumes that by "doing" an individual increases his knowledge and his ability to perform in a business environment. The author has attempted to demonstrate the necessity for the integration of the essential elements of business organization and the principles of management.

III. Decisions Made by Participants

1. Market information to be purchased
2. Advertising expenditures
3. Salesmen used in each area and calls made
4. Sales training programs and bonus plans
5. Production schedules and levels
6. New production facilities
7. Product research expenditures and information needed
8. Amounts spent for cost data

IV. Administration

The game may be scored manually or through the use of a computer. The game umpire provides information (for specified fees) regarding total sales dollars available in all areas, in specific market quadrants, and in each state. He also evaluates sales calls and reports on their success, notifies companies when salesmen resign, and advises each company of the results of its research. He may audit a firm's books and assess audit fees if the records are incorrect.

V. Source

Participant's Manual, W. D. Heier, *Executive Simulation Game,* College of Business Administration, Arizona State University, Tempe, Arizona.

(*M*,*C*)

The Firm

I. Description

In this manually scored game, five or six participants compose a team which operates a store. The relationship among revenue, cost, and profits is highlighted; diminishing returns, alternative costs, balance sheets, and earnings (profit and loss) statements are covered.

Merchandise price decisions trigger auxiliary decisions on quantity of merchandise to buy, number of salesmen to employ, and sales money to borrow (or repay).

Success is measured by profit; the best group is the one operating the most profitable store.

II. Training Purpose

The training purpose generally is to acquaint the participants with the language of business and some of the attendant problems, and specifically to give the participants experience in deciding the prices at which to offer their merchandise when business conditions change.

III. Decisions Made by Participants

1. Selling price of merchandise
2. Amount of money to borrow

1. Business conditions (slow, moderate, busy)
2. Interest rate

IV. Administration

Instructions for the game's administration are provided. Worksheets to record decisions and their computed results are included. Fact sheets giving details pertaining to the game are provided.

V. Source

Direct inquiries to Science Research Associates, Inc., 259 East Erie Street, Chicago, Illinois.

(*M*)

General Business Management Simulation (Computer)

I. Description

This dynamic, interacting, total business game is played by eight or more teams, each composed of from four to seven players. Each of these teams represents the management of an existing company which manufactures a new consumer expendable product. All firms start with the same economic position—cash, assets, inventories, plant capacity—and compete in the same market.

The teams are furnished the decision form for the last period and then make interdependent decisions on a quarterly basis for a simulated four- to five-year period. While there is no absolute goal which determines the winner, measures of relative success are share of market, total sales, total assets, return on sales and investment, and dividends paid.

II. Training Purpose

The training purpose is to give participants the opportunity to analyze the variables comprising a business situation and then to experiment with different allocations of available resources and to provide an understanding of the interacting processes involved in these decisions.

III. Decisions Made by Participants

1. Price
2. Quantity of product to be manufactured at normal operations during the period
3. Quantity of product to be manufactured at overtime operations during the period
4. Advertising and selling expenditures
5. Methods engineering expenditures
6. Research and development expenditures
7. Market research information expenditures
8. Plant expansion
9. Liquidation of excess plant capacity
10. Short-term investment of surplus funds
11. Bank loans
12. Dividend payments
13. Long-term debt loans
14. Common stock issue
15. Labor agreement

IV. Administration

The game is computer scored. All necessary forms and administrative instructions are available from the game source.

V. Source

Participant's Manual, E. T. Hellebrandt and John E. Stinson, *General Business Management Simulation,* Department of Management, Ohio University, Athens, Ohio, 1965. Direct inquiries to E. T. Hellebrandt, Management Research Associates, P.O. Box 747, Athens, Ohio.

(C, 124, 125)

General Business Management Simulation (Manual)

I. DESCRIPTION

In this competitive total enterprise game the teams operate a company producing one consumer expendable product. The participants may organize their team in any way they see fit and can set their own goals. Although the market shows a long-run growth trend, seasonal variations do affect decisions. Sales are determined by such things as the number of innovations produced by research and development, price, and advertising. The teams may borrow short-term funds or invest excess funds on a short-term basis. Although some information is available as to competitors' actions and the future trends, the companies may wish to purchase additional information. Rather specific information is provided to the players as to the effects of price and advertising, as well as the variable costs associated with each production level.

One somewhat original feature of this game allows the teams to take part in union bargaining. At the beginning of Period 2 management makes a final counter offer to the union local. If the union rejects this offer, it will call a strike and the umpire will mediate the dispute. The differences between the offers will determine to a large extent the length of the strike and the final settlement.

II. TRAINING PURPOSE

This game allows decision making in a competitive environment. It teaches the players the importance of making sound and coordinated decisions.

III. DECISIONS MADE BY PARTICIPANTS

1. Price
2. Quantity produced

3. Marketing
4. Research and development
5. Marketing research
6. Plant size
7. Investment of excess funds
8. Short-term borrowing
9. Labor contract negotiation

IV. Administration

In this hand-scored game the umpire provides the decision form with information about fixed and variable costs, inventory levels, and plant capacity, as well as each company's price and number of innovations. The supplementary information form gives the marketing research information purchased. The statement of assets shows the company's present position.

V. Source

Edwin T. Hellebrandt, *General Business Management Simulation* (5th ed.), College of Business Administration, Ohio University, Athens, Ohio, 1962.

(M, 124, 125)

General Electric Management Game (III)

I. Description

This is a competitive-interactive game which essentially consists of allocating scarce resources under conditions of uncertainty in a competitive context. Both bad judgment and good strategy by competition can end in bankruptcy and loss of the game. The game is so designed that it is difficult for a firm to recover once it is far behind; it is easy for it to go bankrupt; and those firms which plan poorly or do not respond quickly to competitive action are penalized.

Ten to twenty simulated periods can be played in an hour or two; the game may thus be used in short sessions.

There must be two competing teams and each team should have six members. These include general, marketing, engineering, manufacturing, and financial managers and a treasurer.

II. TRAINING PURPOSE

The training purpose is to develop the capability of making better plans, especially profit planning. The team which plans better usually gets into a dominant position very quickly and is hard to overtake.

III. DECISIONS MADE BY PARTICIPANTS

1. Set advertising and marketing dollars
2. Forecast sales, competitive strategy, variable costs, and profits under different competitive situations, and cash requirements
3. Set design dollars, construction budget, price policy, and dividend policy
4. Set production schedule

IV. ADMINISTRATION

The model is designed for the GE-265 Time Sharing System and is programmed in ALGOL. Tape is available from Information Systems Service. Printouts of a typical play are appended as is a marked-up copy of the program listing.

V. SOURCE

R. W. Newman, Consultant—Economic Division Models, Information Systems Service, General Electric Company, 570 Lexington Avenue, New York.

(*C*, 152)

Harvard Business School Management Simulation

I. DESCRIPTION

This general business game allows teams of four or five men to compete in a consumer goods market against zero up to four other firms. Decisions are made in all the functional areas of business. In the area of manufacturing teams must purchase and warehouse raw materials, schedule production, and determine labor utilization. Marketing decisions are made concerning number of products, prices, quality, advertising, and market research. Both short- and long-term loans are available. Companies can issue common stock, buy securities, and pay dividends.

This game is designed to reward consistent decision making. Those teams which develop and follow through on coordinated strategies usually achieve adequate profits. They must utilize the past information about their firm, other firms, and the industry trends.

II. TRAINING PURPOSE

This game was created to allow the players to coordinate their knowledge of the functional areas of business in a complex situation. It also allows the use of analytic decision-making techniques. Finally, the "team" nature of the game develops skills of communication and cooperation among the players.

III. DECISIONS MADE BY PARTICIPANTS

1. Number of products
2. Price
3. Quality
4. Plant size
5. Labor utilization
6. Production scheduling
7. Financing

IV. Administration

This simulation was designed to allow the administrator to use the model without any programming knowledge. It is programmed in FORTRAN II or IV for an IBM 7094 computer. The computer prints out income statements, balance sheets, product statements, and industry information.

V. Source

James L. McKenney, *Simulation Gaming for Management Development,* Division of Research, Harvard Business School, Boston, Massachusetts, 1967. Inquiries should be directed to F. W. McFarlan, Harvard Business School, Soldiers Field, Boston, Massachusetts.

(C, 140, 171, 172, 174, 258)

The Imaginit Management Game

I. Description

Any manufacturing industry may be simulated in either man-computer or all-computer runs with this game vehicle. All parameters for products, firms, elasticities, and industry configurations are under control of the game administrator. Industries that have been successfully simulated in man-computer management game runs include typewriter, tire, automobile, dentifrice, hairdressing, home heating and air conditioning, appliance, and detergent.

Each firm starts with one or more products in one or more markets and may end the game with up to three products in a total of two markets. From two to five firms (of any number of players) make up an industry. Simulated decision periods may be years, quarters, or months, or any combination of these with changes in period size permitted during a run.

Teams may write reports for the policy areas of marketing, production, finance, administration, and labor relations. Numerical grades, called qualitative indexes, given to teams on these reports may be input for the computer run where the grades affect the consequences of decisions.

Data tape options permit simulation of an entire past live run in a single computer pass.

II. Training Purpose

The Imaginit Management Game is intended to serve the integrating or "capstone" function in business curricula, or as a stimulus device early in a curriculum, or in management development programs. The complexity of the game and the kind of industry are adjustable to fit given players.

III. Decisions Made by Participants

A. For each of up to three products:
1. Price
2. Materials input per unit
3. Salesmen
4. Advertising
5. Product research and development
6. Materials to be ordered
7. Units to be produced

B. For the firm as a whole:
1. Employee fringe benefits per hour
2. Dividends per share to be paid
3. Operations research
4. Short-term loans
5. Bonds
6. Shares of stock to be sold
7. Factory capacity

Decisions Made by Administrator

1. Initial histories and starting values
2. Control of 102 game parameters
3. Evaluation of performance

IV. Administration

The game is operating on an IBM 7040 (16K) and on a GE 625. It is written in FORTRAN IV, and operable versions are filed at the computing centers of the Universities of Nebraska and of Kansas and at Texas Technological College.

V. Source

Richard F. Barton, Department of Management, Texas Technological College, Lubbock, Texas.

(C)

Integrated Simulation

I. Description

Two to twenty teams are formed (four to eight members per team). Each team manages a corporation which may have sales in the home country (domestic market) and in foreign countries (foreign market). Each team makes decisions regarding production, price, plant expansion, research and development, and the purchase or sale of stock. Only one product is produced and sold, but the quality of the product can be changed from one quarter to the next. Decisions are made with regard to business and economic conditions in the market. Performance is evaluated on the basis of quarterly income statements and balance sheets. In the final analysis, the company with the highest value for the variable rate will be the most efficient and prosperous company.

II. Training Purpose

The game gives participants experience in top management decision making. All areas of business management, from human relations to economics, are involved in the decisions.

III. Decisions Made by Participants

1. Production level
2. Product quality level
3. Price
4. Units offered for foreign sale
5. Stock issues
6. Bonds
7. Dividends
8. Credit (borrowing)
9. Plant capacity
10. Plant capacity in two quarters
11. Research and development
12. Raw material purchase

Decision Made by Administrator

1. Forecast of domestic sales

IV. Administration

Scoring is by computer, either IBM 1620, IBM 1401, IBM 360 Model 30, or higher 360 models.

V. Source

W. N. Smith, E. E. Estey, E. F. Vines, *Integrated Simulation,* South-Western Publishing Company, Cincinnati, Ohio, 1968.

(C)

A Management Decision Game

I. DESCRIPTION

In this production and marketing game, four teams of from three to six members compete for three products in a common market. All teams begin with identical financial and operating structures. They make decisions in advertising, price change, and research and development. The results of these decisions affect their sales and market share.

Four quarters of game time are equal to approximately two hours and fifteen minutes of real time. The results of each quarter are returned to the teams within ten minutes of their submission. The teams then make the current quarter decisions based on these results.

II. TRAINING PURPOSE

The purpose is to give the participants experience in decision making in the functional areas of production and marketing as well as in coping with chance circumstances that can affect company operations.

III. DECISIONS MADE BY PARTICIPANTS

1. Place salesmen
2. Advertising expenditures
3. Price changes
4. Research and development expenditures
5. Number of units of each product to be produced each quarter
6. Services to be purchased

IV. ADMINISTRATION

In this manually scored game each team must be furnished a referee who will answer questions on game rules and collect and deliver decision sheets.

A chief referee is also necessary. He will compile results for each quarter on decision sheets and return them to teams. Manuals for the players and referees are available from the game source.

V. SOURCE

J. W. Gavett, Department of Industrial Engineering, Cornell University, Ithaca, New York.

(M)

Management Decision-Making Laboratory

I. DESCRIPTION

Three teams of four to six participants are formed, each to act in competition, manufacturing and marketing a single product. Each team has a home marketing area but is free to compete in a competitor's home area and in a fourth area which has no similar business. Each team sets price, production level, plant capacity, transportation, and expenditures for marketing and research and development. Twenty minutes are allowed for decision making, after which a quarterly summary report is distributed showing a new balance sheet and income statement, area market information, area sales analysis, and production. The cycle may be repeated every half hour.

II. TRAINING PURPOSE

This game is designed to provide experience in making decisions concerned with adjusting production and marketing variables to meet competition.

III. DECISIONS MADE BY PARTICIPANTS

1. Price
2. Markets

3. Production
4. Transportation
5. Marketing expenditure
6. Research and development
7. Plant investment

DECISIONS MADE BY ADMINISTRATOR

1. Economic conditions
2. Production costs
3. Transportation costs
4. Effect of research and development
5. Price and marketing sensitivities
6. Objectives

IV. ADMINISTRATION

The game is programmed for several IBM computers.

V. SOURCE

Participant's and Administrator's Manual, *Management Decision-Making Laboratory,* International Business Machines Corporation, Technical Publications Department, 112 East Post Road, White Plains, New York.

(*C,* 20, 52, 130, 137, 139, 174, 203, 239)

Management Decision Simulation

I. DESCRIPTION

This game was developed for use in an introductory course in business administration in conjunction with *Introduction to Business: A Management Approach,* by Arthur M. Weimer.

The participants are divided into teams, each to represent the top management of manufacturing companies, all in competition with the same product in the same market. The teams are asked first to establish company objectives and to assign organization responsibilities to their members. Five decisions are made each game quarter. The success of a team will depend upon its effectiveness in decision making in relation to the decisions made by the other teams.

Decisions are recorded on forms and returned to the referee. He then returns to the teams their quarterly sales figure, from which they compute an income statement, a statement of cash flow, and a balance sheet. The referee also provides a quarterly statistical report showing the industry sales potential, the economic forecast, and the prices, sales, and marketing effectiveness of each team. Every four quarters he provides a report showing the assets of each team. From these reports, the teams are able to make subsequent decisions.

II. TRAINING PURPOSE

The game shows how production, marketing, finance, and accounting are related and must be integrated for effective decision making in a competitive situation.

III. DECISIONS MADE BY PARTICIPANTS

1. Objectives of company
2. Organization of team
3. Production level
4. Plant capacity
5. Dividends
6. Price
7. Marketing expenditures

DECISION MADE BY ADMINISTRATOR

1. Economic index

IV. Administration

The game is manually scored, and 20 minutes are allowed for each team to compute reports and make new decisions for each quarter. An evaluation session normally follows the play, during which each team analyzes its objectives and performance.

V. Source

E. W. Martin, Jr., *Management Decision Simulation*, Richard D. Irwin, Inc., Homewood, Illinois, 1960.

(*M*, 181)

Management Decision Simulation

I. Description

When first published in 1960, this game was designed for hand scoring. Later it was adapted to the computer, at which time several new modifications were introduced. In both versions three teams with five to eight members per team are organized, each to market a common product in the same area. The teams are asked to make quarterly decisions regarding the production, financial, and marketing operations of their companies. Their success depends upon their ability to analyze and predict the consequences of these decisions and to react to the decisions made by competitors. The game is repeated once a week for eight weeks, simulating two years' results.

The computerized version of the game offers the possibility of several changes. A business index, which requires that the participants plan ahead and adjust their decisions to meet cyclical variations in the economy, may be used. A strike threat simulation is available, which requires teams to alter decisions in the face of a possible strike when the labor contract expires. The administrator may make the demand more sensitive to price changes. Individuals may be allowed to run a company, rather than be part of a team.

In the manual-scoring version, each team computes a new share of the market, a new balance sheet, and new stock quotations after each run. The computerized version provides for the determination of a "total game performance" or "learning curve," which is based on the success of each team in meeting the following company objectives: share of market, profit, cash account, inventory level, net worth, and dividend payment.

II. TRAINING PURPOSE

This game provides participants with experience in making top-level management decisions for a company in a competitive environment. Each participant can see the effect his decisions would have on the company over a period of two years and can gain insight into the problems of planning production and finances.

III. DECISIONS MADE BY PARTICIPANTS

1. Price
2. Production level
3. Plant capacity
4. Product quality
5. Borrowing
6. Dividends
7. Effectiveness of distribution
8. Liquidation of inventory

DECISIONS MADE BY ADMINISTRATOR

1. Elasticity of demand
2. Business index

IV. ADMINISTRATION

Hand scoring requires about thirty minutes. The program is written in FORTRAN II.

V. Source

Student Manual, Stanley C. Vance, *Management Decision Simulation,* McGraw-Hill Book Company, New York, New York, 1960.

Stanley C. Vance and Clifford F. Gray, *Management Decision Simulation: A Computer Manual,* School of Business, University of Oregon, Eugene, Oregon, 1965.

(M, C, 104, 277, 278, 279, 280)

Management Game

I. Description

Two to four players run a corporation geared to market mass-consumer merchandise. Each player, acting as corporation president, must decide on capital expansion and the extent of inventory carryover in relation to drain on gross income. Gross income is determined by the selling price which each corporation president sets for his finished inventory in competition with opponents. In addition, competitive bidding for raw materials determines the market price for these materials, with the optimum situation derived from "buying low and selling high." Each player's current operating condition is reflected on a running record pad which must be completed after each turn (equal to one month in time). How much a player is willing to pay for raw material and how low he is willing to sell finished inventory determine, in general, the profit or loss and ultimately his ability to run a corporation on a profitable basis.

II. Training Purpose

The purpose is to teach the proper relationship between gross and net income in regard to fixed expenses and current operating costs which vary according to the fluctuations in the economy and with variations in degree of competition.

III. Decisions Made by Participants

1. Production capacity
2. Plant expansion
3. Financing
4. Warehousing costs
5. Stock issuance
6. Pricing of finished inventory
7. Purchasing of raw materials
8. Quality of competition

IV. Administration

The scoring is done by the participants, and performance is measured by the largest contribution to "surplus" derived when players complete profit and loss statements and year-end balance sheets.

V. Source

Avalon Hill Company, 4517 Harford Road, Baltimore, Maryland.

(M, 105)

Mansym

I. Description

In the game there are one to five competing firms in an industry producing and marketing basically the same products. Each team acts as top-level management. Firms start with equal profits and market share. Firms may produce and sell from one to six products described as durable consumer goods. (The hand-scored version uses only one product and is played by one to three teams.) These product lines are somewhat similar to minor electric household appliances, but are not substitutes.

Eighteen factors determine total demand. Some of these include product differential through physical changes, general economic environment, prices, promotional expenditures, secular trend, seasonal factors, etc. The game evaluates performance in the areas of profitability, marketing effectiveness, production planning, financial planning, and position for continued play; the composite game score may be used for evaluating performance and may be returned to the team as additional feedback for improving performance.

II. Training Purpose

The training purpose is to give the participant practice in analyzing and considering variables and arriving at decisions in the functional areas of business; additionally it is designed to allow the participants to become familiar with and prepare sales and raw material forecasts, cash budgets, pro forma income statements, and pro forma balance sheets.

III. Decisions Made by Participants

1. Pricing
2. Promotion expenditure
3. Raw materials ordered
4. Production first month of period
5. Production second month of period
6. Capacity additions
7. Changes in loans
8. Change in quality level

Decisions Made by Administrator

1. Economic index
2. Many parameters

IV. Administration

The game may be scored manually or electronically on any 40K IBM computer. Decision sheets, referee information for both manual and electronic versions, inventory forms, and other necessary forms are included in the participant's manual. An instructor's manual and computer programs are also available. A discussion of parameter values which the administrator may vary is included in the instructor's manual.

V. Source

Participant's Manual, Robert E. Schellenberger, *Mansym,* School of Business Administration, University of Maryland, College Park, Maryland. Published by Wm. C. Brown Book Co., 135 S. Locust Street, Dubuque, Iowa, 1965.

(M, C, 207)

Mark XIV Executive Decision Simulation

I. Description

This total enterprise game simulates competitive industry with four firms, each developing, producing, and selling a single scientific product. At the outset, each team must decide upon its organizational structure and its own goals. The simplified model used in this game allows the teams to formulate long-range plans in their attempts to achieve their goals. Each team is given a form showing the effects of its decisions. For example, an increase in research and development expenditures increases the industry's market slightly, increases the firm's share of the market quite slowly, reduces its fixed and variable costs per unit quite slowly, and increases total expense. The impact of this decision covers a seven-quarter period and is maximized in the third and fourth quarters.

The *Mark XIV* game is designed so that 16-20 quarterly decisions can be made in a single day. Hopefully the players will devise a long-range strategy and adjust their plans as they discover the effects of their decisions. After the game is completed, the participants discuss their plans and the effects of their decisions.

II. Training Purpose

This game demonstrates the complex interaction of the many factors which must be considered to achieve management goals. Emphasis is placed on long-run goals and strategy formulation.

III. Decisions Made by Participants

1. Price per unit
2. Production volume
3. Marketing and sales promotion
4. Research and development
5. Plant investment
6. Dividends

IV. Administration

This game is computer processed.

V. Source

Manual, Rodney Luther, *Mark XIV Program Management Workshop,* Lockheed California Company. Direct inquiries to Management Personnel Department, Lockheed California Company, Burbank, California.

(C)

The Marman Management Game

I. Description

Four to fifteen teams are formed. Each team manages a manufacturing company which produces four products, utilizing three types of component parts which are purchased from vendors. Various decisions are required which affect plant productivity. Three of the four products are distributed through regional warehouses. For these three products sales are influenced by the various marketing decisions taken by the companies. A market-clearing mechanism is built into the game which insures that a company's sales are affected by the competitive actions of other companies (other teams playing the simulation).

The simulation stresses the training of the players in planning and making operating decisions under certainty and uncertainty in the following areas: advertising and sales promotion, production control, plant and sales personnel management, distribution of finished goods, raw material purchasing, inventory control, plant productivity, cost and financial accounting. Performance is evaluated on the basis of income statements and balance sheets.

II. TRAINING PURPOSE

This game gives participants experience in facing complex business decision problems in a simulated business atmosphere. In particular, it serves to emphasize the interrelated nature of complex business operations. It also stresses necessity for adequate planning to deal with the repercussions throughout a firm's operations of a change in one particular area of its operations.

III. DECISIONS MADE BY PARTICIPANTS

There are 48 decisions made by participants in the following areas:
1. Advertising
2. Prices
3. Sales personnel
4. Credit policy
5. Borrowing
6. Securities transactions
7. Production scheduling
8. Production levels
9. Raw materials purchases
10. Plant productivity
11. Wages

12. Workforce
13. Finished goods shipments to regional warehouses

DECISION MADE BY ADMINISTRATOR

1. General level of economic activity

IV. ADMINISTRATION

The model is programmed in FORTRAN for the IBM 7040, 360 model 40, and 360 model 65.

V. SOURCE

Jerome J. Day, Jr., Department of Statistics and Operations Research, Wharton School of Finance and Commerce, University of Pennsylvania, Philadelphia, Pennsylvania.

(C)

MSU Management Game

I. DESCRIPTION

The *MSU Management Game* is a total enterprise game patterned after the UCLA Executive Decision Game No. 2. This game adds maintenance problems, production control, and a more elaborate market.

The teams in this game make eight quarterly decisions for their company, which produces one product in a highly competitive industry. A company's sales are determined by its price, marketing, and product quality; the latter is determined by its research and development expenditure. Per-unit costs are dependent upon such things as maintenance, raw materials purchases, overhead, carrying costs, plant size, and financing. Although no specific measurements of performance are prescribed, profits and market share are among the usual measures employed for evaluation.

II. Training Purpose

This general management game is designed to emphasize top-level planning and policy formulation. It also requires that the participants adjust to a changing environment and their competitors' actions.

III. Decisions Made by Participants

1. Price
2. Marketing
3. Research and development
4. Maintenance
5. Production
6. Plant size
7. Raw materials purchase
8. Dividends

Decisions Made by Administrator

1. Economic index
2. Game parameters

IV. Administration

This game is scored by the MISTIC electronic computer, which simulates the quarter's operations. It produces a tape and card deck from which the IBM 407 prepares balance sheets, income statements, cash flow statements, and other information concerning each firm's market share, production, and inventory.

V. Source

James R. Jackson and Richard C. Henshaw, Jr., *MSU Management Game: Instructions for Players,* Michigan State University, East Lansing, Michigan, 1961.

(C)

Oklahoma Business Management Game

I. DESCRIPTION

In this total enterprise game, ten teams of three to seven players compete against each other, first in the acquisition of one raw product (A) and then in the sale of two processed products (B and C). Before play begins each team sets up a statement of objectives such as maximizing net worth, profit, or share of market. When the game is over the teams are evaluated on the basis of accomplishing their objective.

Each team completes a decision sheet for each one-year time period. They are given past performance, balance sheet, and income statement for the previous time period. After each play, each team prepares a complete balance sheet and income statement.

The firms may expand by borrowing from the bank (if their loan request is approved). They must present appropriate financial statements and projections with the loan request.

II. TRAINING PURPOSE

The training purpose is to give the participants experience in top management decision making in both the functional and general management areas.

III. DECISIONS MADE BY PARTICIPANTS

1. Quantity of raw product to be purchased
2. Price paid for raw product
3. Product mix
4. Advertising expenditures per product
5. Storage facilities to be purchased
6. Short-term note payments
7. Dividends to be paid

IV. ADMINISTRATION

This is a noncomputerized game. At the end of each time period the administrator gives the teams additional information so that they may prepare a new balance sheet and income statement to be used the following period. He also acts as the banker and approves or rejects loans for expansion of firms. At the termination of play the administrator leads the evaluation process and critique.

V. Source

R. W. Schermerhorn, Cooperative Extension Service, Division of Agriculture, Oklahoma State University, Stillwater, Oklahoma.

(M)

The O.U. Executive Management Game

I. Description

In this total enterprise game each team operates a multifirm, one-product industry. Management must make plans in the early stages of the game since stable policies are more effective than fluctuating ones. The members of the team acting as the firm's top management set their own goals. Game managers influence their share of the market by price adjustment, design, and advertising expenditures.

Plant and equipment decrease in efficiency at 10 percent per year; thus reinvestment in capital equipment must be included in long-range plans. Matching units of production to uncertain demand is the key to minimizing operating costs.

Decisions are made on a quarterly basis. After decisions have been turned in, each firm announces its current price and dividend.

II. Training Purpose

The training purpose is to help managers and students of management learn more about the work of top-level planning and policy formulation in business.

III. Decisions Made by Participants

1. Price of product
2. Production volume
3. Advertising budget
4. Research and development budget
5. Investment in plant and equipment
6. Dividend

IV. Administration

This game is run on a Control Data G-15. After receiving quarterly decisions, the computer prepares reports for each firm which indicate sales volume, percent of industry sales, inventory, the next quarter's production capacity, profit and loss statement, receipts and disbursements statement, dividends, and financial condition. Decision forms are supplied with the game.

V. Source

L. Doyle Bishop, Department of Management, Oklahoma University, Norman, Oklahoma.

(C)

The Pillsbury Company Management Game

I. Description

In this interactive, competitive game five teams of three persons each operate firms making similar products. The managements choose output levels, price, and advertising expenditures and develop long-range plans.

Each team starts with identical data and decision-making alternatives and has control over seven decision variables. The value of other variables is determined by the model. The teams are given statements after each quarter and an annual statement after four quarters. Decision alternatives change from quarter to quarter as a result of past decisions. The game usually runs for 20 to 40 decision-making periods.

II. TRAINING PURPOSE

The training purpose is to give the participants experience in choosing objectives, developing strategies to obtain these objectives, making long-range plans, and deciding courses of action with only a vague knowledge of the outcomes of such actions. Additionally, the participant must remain flexible enough to reverse plans if a change seems indicated.

III. DECISIONS MADE BY PARTICIPANTS

1. Price
2. Marketing expenditures
3. Research and development expenditures
4. Investment in additional plant and equipment
5. Discard of plant
6. Expenditures on market research
7. Output
8. Dividends

IV. ADMINISTRATION

The program for this computer-scored game is run on an IBM 650. The statements with necessary additions for printing should be applicable to FORTRANSIT II and III and FORTRAN. The game includes a player's manual, forms, description of the model, and operating procedures.

V. SOURCE

The Pillsbury Company (File No. 0650-01-04), Minneapolis, Minnesota.

(*C*, 203, 209, 239, 292, 293)

Scarcity and Allocation

I. DESCRIPTION

The participants, in groups of five or six, are to assume that they are the only survivors of a shipwreck and have been fortunate enough to land on a small island, rich in vegetation and wildlife. They are to consider themselves reasonable people who try to make their own lives as comfortable as possible without taking advantage of others. All are assumed to be equally efficient in all tasks, from food gathering to shelter and tool building. Without tools most of the day is needed for the search of food; however, as the little "free" time available is used to build these tools, more discretionary time is developed.

Success is measured by a combination of the amount of food stored for emergencies and the productive capital accumulated. Both the best group and the most resourceful individual are given recognition.

II. TRAINING PURPOSE

The training purpose is to highlight scarcity as a fundamental fact of economic life and to show that productive processes are subject to both social and natural restrictions, while allocation is entirely up to society. The game is also designed to emphasize the greater productivity of the division of labor, the usefulness of capital equipment, the role of savings in capital formation, and the meaning of value.

III. DECISIONS MADE BY PARTICIPANTS

    1. Time each participant spends on each occupation
    2. Quantity and type of tools to build

DECISIONS MADE BY ADMINISTRATOR

    1. Type of disturbing disasters such as drought or flood
    2. Distribution system—market or command

IV. Administration

Administrative instructions for this manual game are given in a teacher's manual; fact sheets and worksheets are included. The fact sheets include the time needed to provide a daily food requirement for one person by various means with various tools; the time required to build these tools, singly and in two's and three's; and the time required to tailor clothing and to build shelter.

V. Source

Erwin Rausch. Direct inquiries to Science Research Associates, Inc., 259 East Erie Street, Chicago, Illinois.

(M)

Simulett

I. Description

Three to 25 teams may be formed, preferably with four to six members per team; each team manages a company producing and marketing a product in three areas. Quarterly decisions are generally made for two or more years. Potential sales for each company, by area, are based upon a predetermined program adjusted by the *Business Week Index* and sales promotion, sales effort, and prices of the company.

The teams start with a production plant in one area and must decide when and where to add additional capacity. Decisions must be made as to purchasing of raw materials, hiring of employees—production and sales, buying pages of local and national advertising, and warehousing the finished goods. Union negotiations may be introduced, generally in the latter quarters of the game. Market information is available; the costs vary according to the type of information purchased. Short-term and long-term borrowing are available with the interest rate on the latter being determined by the administrator. Performance is judged mainly upon stock market prices; dividends to stockholders; retained earnings; and the administrator's rating of the rationale of the team's decisions, participation of each team member, and the final reports of each team.

II. TRAINING PURPOSE

Simulett helps the participants to use the material presented in various courses and particularly to integrate economics, accounting, finance, marketing, organization, and industrial management.

III. DECISIONS MADE BY PARTICIPANTS

1. Production capacity
2. Number of workers
3. Inventory
4. Plant location
5. Sales promotion
    a. Salesmen (number)
    b. Amount of local advertising
    c. Amount of national advertising
6. Sources of financing
    a. Stock issuance
    b. Long-term bonds
    c. Short-term loans
7. Product pricing
8. Purchasing
9. Purchase of market information
10. Dividend policy
11. Pay of workers

DECISIONS MADE BY ADMINISTRATOR

1. Preliminary plan for market potential
2. Union negotiations
3. Number and type of reports

IV. Administration

The game can be processed manually or processed by computer. The program is written in FORTRAN IV and has been used on the UNIVAC 1107 and IBM 1101 and 1620 computers.

V. Source

Robert L. Trewatha. See Hargrove, Harrison, and Swearengen, *Business Policy Cases,* Richard D. Irwin, Inc., Homewood, Illinois, 1966.

(*M, C*)

Small Business Executive Decision Simulation

I. Description

This is a total enterprise game designed to portray a small business. All of the strategies available are not initially made obvious to the participants. For example, during the early quarters of play the company sells "Product A" in the "local region." By purchasing information the team can learn of a new product and a new region in which it can market. The products are sold to contractors through salesmen. Competitive pressure is maintained by large national firms that sell slightly below the average market price; this price is controlled by the administrator. Demand is seasonal. On occasion a large development firm will invite bids for a special number of units of the product; the contract is usually awarded to the lowest bidder. Raw materials may be purchased on long-term or short-term contracts. Quarterly information concerning market conditions is provided each team. The computer provides the traditional balance sheet, the income statements, and the status report.

II. Training Purpose

This model is developed to emphasize the interrelationships among functional specialties (marketing, finance, and production) in the decision-making process.

III. Decisions Made by Participants

1. Product price
2. Output
3. Product mix
4. Purchase quantity of raw materials
5. Number of shifts
6. Capacity utilization
7. Sales quota
8. Sales commission rate
9. Salaries of salesmen
10. Hiring and termination of salesmen, foremen, clerical workers
11. Contract quantity and price
12. Machine purchase or renovation
13. Machines sold
14. Borrowing
15. Information purchases

Decisions Made by Administrator

1. Economic index
2. Price elasticity
3. Effectiveness of salesmen
4. Penalty costs
5. Contract units requested
6. Information purchases available

IV. Administration

The model is programmed in FORTRAN II. Forms are provided for the participant and administrator.

V. Source

Administrator's Manual, John R. Stockton, Alfred G. Dale, Francis B. May, Charles T. Clark, and P. John Lymberopoulos, *The Small Business Executive Decision Simulation: Administrator's Manual.* Copies available through Small Business Administration, Washington, D.C., or Bureau of Business Research, The University of Texas, Austin, Texas.

(*C*, 65, 66, 243)

Top Brass

I. DESCRIPTION

Top Brass is based on the "Business Management Game" by G. R. Andlinger described in the July 1958 issue of the *Harvard Business Review*. This is a total enterprise game, played between teams of four players. Each team is charged with making manufacturing and merchandising decisions for a multiproduct firm in competition with firms of similar structure. The four players on each team take the roles of president, treasurer, controller, and general manager. The president is charged with keeping activities moving in the right direction. The treasurer keeps a record of cash flow and changes in assets. The controller prepares a profit and loss statement. The general manager keeps a record of sales, inventory, and production costs.

The market consists of six customers in each of four cities. Each team attempts to deploy its sales force in the manner which will produce the greatest volume of sales. Sales occur on a random basis, but the chance for success increases with repeated customer contact, advertising, investment in research and development, and the lowering of prices. Results from investment in R&D are also a random process, but the probability of an improved product increases with the amount of expenditure.

II. TRAINING PURPOSE

Top Brass provides training in top-level decision making for a total enterprise business; increases knowledge of the marketing, production, engineering, and accounting aspects of a business; and provides insight into the importance of planning and the effects of competition.

III. DECISIONS MADE BY PARTICIPANTS

    1. Price
    2. Plant capacity

3. Research and development—product
4. Hiring and firing
5. Advertising
6. Marketing research
7. Placement of salesmen
8. Buying of inventory
9. Factoring receivables

DECISIONS MADE BY ADMINISTRATOR

1. Trend of market
2. Resignation of salesmen
3. Consultant services

IV. ADMINISTRATION

The game is manually scored. Players record decisions on the special report forms for the treasurer, comptroller, and general manager. The game is played for ten quarters. Thirty minutes are allowed for the first quarter's decisions, and 15 minutes are allowed for each quarter thereafter.

V. SOURCE

Participant's Manual, *Top Brass*, Honeywell, Inc., 2701 Fourth Avenue South, Minneapolis, Minnesota.

(M)

Top Management Decision-Making Simulation
(Wayne State University)

I. DESCRIPTION

This is a total enterprise, competitive, manually scored game played with five teams. Each team takes over as management of a newly acquired manufacturing plant. Each team operates a plant which is the same size as the other four and produces a similar product—an original equipment part for automobiles. All teams will begin with the same capital and operational structure and will compete in the same markets.

Decision periods are in terms of a quarter year. After decisions are made during this period, they are compared and evaluated against those of the four competitors. Results are then fed back to the team.

Each team may purchase market research information and is also supplied with competitors' balance sheets at the end of each year.

II. TRAINING PURPOSE

The training purpose is to provide participants with an experience involving the application of management and business principles such as planning, organizing, and making decisions in the areas of marketing, manufacturing, and research and development.

III. DECISIONS MADE BY PARTICIPANTS

1. Pricing product
2. Expenditure for advertising
3. Sales promotions
4. Size of field sales force
5. Quantity and cost of product to be produced
6. Inventory level
7. Expenditure for research and development

DECISIONS MADE BY ADMINISTRATOR

1. Manipulation of economic environment variables
2. Labor relations
3. Cost of capital

IV. ADMINISTRATION

The simulation is hand scored against a mathematical model developed from operating results of companies in the automobile parts manufacturing industry. All necessary materials are available from game source.

V. Source

Participant's Manual, Bruce E. DeSpelder and John J. Rath, *Top Management Decision-Making Simulation,* School of Business Administration, Wayne State University, Detroit, Michigan, 1962.

(*M,* 174, 209)

Top Management Decision Simulation
(The Top Man Game)

I. Description

The game places the participants in the role of top management of a business firm. The size of the competing firms can be varied from small operations to very large ones. The unique feature of this game is its division into "phases" which are sequentially introduced to the participants and which progressively increase the complications they must face. The computer simulation is structured for three to six teams, each consisting of up to six participants.

The instructor is easily able to change parameters of the game equations as part of the input data and to use actual economic data from any selected period, which are automatically camouflaged by the computer program. At the start of the game, the participants receive a three-year history of their company. They then proceed to make key decisions that cover a three-month period. These decisions result in typical financial statements prepared by the computer program and then form the basis for the next set of decisions.

Each company is permitted to obtain funds from a number of sources: accounts receivable, borrowing from several sources, sale of common stock and treasury stock, etc. There is a single product and a single market, each of which can be identified at the instructor's option, or left unnamed. The game includes a simulated stock market phase, in which the game and action in the real market are interactive.

Federal income taxes are based on U.S. tax laws, including special provisions for the normal taxes and the surtax. Monte Carlo techniques are used to establish distribution patterns for the quality of marketing expenditure and research and development expenditures.

At the end of each simulated year of play, the computer program provides a special statistical summary for the participants, and at the end of the game, a complete summary of the game is provided. The output data from the regular plays of the program provide input data, which can be used at the end of the game to prepare large charts of the variables on standard computer output paper that can be mounted for display purposes.

II. Training Purpose

The Top Man Game is designed to help participants integrate the various functional areas of business in an industrial setting where they must deal with factors of certainty, risk, and uncertainty. The game is also designed to provide important experience in group dynamics so that each participant can evaluate his role involving leadership and followership.

III. Decisions Made by Participants

Phase A:
1. Prices
2. Marketing expenditures
3. R&D expenditures
4. Market research information expenditures
5. Plant expansion
6. Plant contraction
7. Production operating level
8. Purchasing quantities

Phase B:
1. Notes payable
2. Long-term debt
3. Investment in treasury bills
4. Investment in certificates of deposit
5. Random number determination for quality of market
6. Random number determination for R&D expenditures

Phase C:
1. New stock to be issued
2. Treasury stock to be bought or sold
3. Sale of company facilities to other participating companies
4. Sale of raw or finished inventory to other companies

5. Mergers and consolidations
6. Change in character of company from manufacturing to a marketing organization or an investment organization

Phase D:
1. Response to plant catastrophe by scrapping or reconditioning part of facilities

IV. ADMINISTRATION

The scoring is done by computer, and the program is written in FORTRAN IV language which can be used on any computer able to handle this language with a memory capacity of 16K in the core. Decisions by each team can be submitted on punched cards; this minimizes the work of the instructor. Copies of the output can be prepared to provide each participant with a complete set of records. Further development is under way to print the output reports in any language using the environmental setting and currency of any country.

V. SOURCE

Professor Albert N. Schrieber, School of Business Administration, University of Washington, Seattle, Washington.

(C, 52, 80, 229, 239)

Top Management Game

I. DESCRIPTION

Four teams are formed, with four to seven members each. Each team manages a company operating in five sales territories, with each team at home in a separate territory and the fifth territory a common territory. They are American domestic corporations.

Each team makes decisions quarterly concerning production, prices (by territories), marketing, research and innovation, dividends, and the sale or repurchase of common stock or company bonds. Each team also may negotiate a bank loan for the given quarter (repayable the first day of the following quarter). One product is manufactured and marketed throughout the five areas. Team decisions are made in the light of economic conditions currently prevailing. Timing and scheduling are of great importance. Construction of and adherence to a company strategy are essential (although modifications should be made in the light of operating results). Performance is evaluated on the basis of quarterly statements: income statement, analysis of cash flow, and balance sheet. Copies of these for the given team are supplied to that team and to the administrator; there is a separate six-page administrator's summary which shows the operating results and the currently applicable parameters, scaling factors, sensitivity factors, and so on.

II. Training Purpose

This game challenges the participants to make top-level decisions under conditions of competition and subject to cyclical fluctuations. By thus affording practice in decision making, with regular evaluation of outcomes, it tends to improve materially the decision-making skills of the participants.

III. Decisions Made by Participants

1. Bank loan
2. Bond sales
3. Stock sales
4. Production spending
5. Research and development spending
6. Marketing spending (areas and total)
7. New plant spending
8. Repurchases of bonds outstanding
9. Repurchases of treasury stock
10. Dividends
11. Prices (by areas)

Decisions Made by Administrator

1. Value of business cycle index, quarter by quarter
2. Operation of control game

IV. Administration

Processing is by IBM 1620 computer, FORTRAN programmed. Evaluation (or grading) is done by the administrator at the termination of the game (comparing actual team results with control game—or standard—results).

V. Source

H. N. Broom, Baylor University, Waco, Texas.

Players' instructions and general data on gaming will appear in *Business Policy and Strategic Action* (tentative title) to be published by Prentice-Hall, Inc., in 1969.

(C)

Top Management Simulation
(TMS)

I. Description

Four to ten teams are formed (four to seven members per team), with each managing a manufacturing firm producing heavy equipment and selling it in 36 different regions within the United States. Each team makes decisions regarding objectives, price, scheduling of production, research and development, plant capacity, advertising, hiring salesmen, placing salesmen in the regions, and buying market information. The total market potential changes from quarter to quarter and decisions are made in light of how these changing conditions affect the marketing potential of each of the 36 regions. Taxes, factoring, and penalties for both excess inventory and lack of inventory are also employed in the game. Performance is evaluated on the basis of quarterly income statements and balance sheets, how realistic the team's objectives are, how well the team accomplishes its predetermined objectives, and how each team member is rated by the rest of the team.

II. Training Purpose

The game provides the participants with experience in making top management decisions while operating a manufacturing organization, setting objectives, assuming functional roles, and competing within a common environment against other teams.

III. Decisions Made by Participants

1. Objectives
2. Price
3. Production scheduling
4. Research and development
5. Advertising
6. Hiring salesmen
7. Placing salesmen in regions
8. Purchasing market information
9. Factoring receivables
10. Ordering increased plant capacity
11. Paying back outstanding loans

Decisions Made by Administrator

1. Choosing assistant game umpires
2. Setting guidelines for
   a. attaining sales product improvements
   b. losing salesmen
   c. effect of advertising and research and development on sales
   d. trend of economic cycle

IV. Administration

Scoring is computed by hand, with the assistant game umpires gathering the decisions from the teams and determining which salesmen have made sales. The chief umpire determines how many units each salesman has sold.

V. SOURCE

Richard M. Hodgetts, College of Business, Management Department, University of Nebraska, Lincoln, Nebraska.

(*M*)

Top Operating Management Game

I. DESCRIPTION

In this total enterprise game companies compete for industrial business. All companies offer a similar product. The sales volume is determined largely by the price and promotional effort. Participants gain experience in forecasting, balancing inventory levels and production, adapting to competition, and predicting the price elasticity of demand. Teams plan plant capacities and calculate the manufacturing costs at each level of planned capacity. Company profits are also affected by the point of trade-off between high inventory carrying charges and large income losses due to inventory shortages and lost sales.

II. TRAINING PURPOSE

The game provides experience in top management decision making. The game demonstrates the need to evaluate the company's manufacturing and inventory problems with respect to market conditions.

III. DECISIONS MADE BY PARTICIPANTS

1. Product price
2. Promotion expenditure
3. Amount of plant expansion
4. Volume of raw material to put into production

Decision Made by Administrator

1. Economic trends

IV. Administration

The game is manually scored. The administrator prepares income and cash available statements and provides market information. First period decisions require about 50 minutes. Later rounds require less time.

V. Source

Jay R. Greene and Roger L. Sisson, *Dynamic Management Decision Games,* John Wiley & Sons, Inc., New York, 1959, pp. 58-69.

(*M*, 109, 174, 286)

The UCLA Executive Decision Game

I. Description

This game is set up to simulate a manufacturing industry. Teams act as top management of several competing firms. Team organization is left up to the members of the individual teams. The game entails decisions pertaining to most aspects of business, and the resulting information is quickly fed back so the participants can evaluate their own performance and use it as a guide for future decisions. The simulated time period is a quarter year, during which time each team makes decisions pertaining to the firm as a whole and to each individual product. Each firm may manufacture up to three products which must belong to the same product family. More specifically, the decisions made may be classified in the following categories: marketing, production, plant and equipment, and finance. After each quarter the teams receive reports which include data covering the industry as a whole, their respective firms, and each of their products. From this information the teams make decisions for the next quarter. The environment in which these firms operate is quite real, including economic fluctuations and seasonal cycles in the demand for their products.

II. TRAINING PURPOSE

The purpose of this game is to give participants practice and experience in making decisions as top management. The game emphasizes the analysis of complex problems using mathematical techniques.

III. DECISIONS MADE BY PARTICIPANTS

Firm as a whole
1. Purchase of plant and equipment
2. Purchase (or sale) of securities

For each product
1. Price of product
2. Marketing budget
3. Design and styling budget
4. Production volume
5. Production budget

DECISIONS MADE BY ADMINISTRATOR

1. Market fluctuations
2. Limitations in budgets
3. Evaluation of changes in the decisions
4. Limitations in production

IV. ADMINISTRATION

The game is computer scored and has been programmed for several modern computers.

V. Source

Participant's Information Manual, James R. Jackson, *UCLA Executive Decision Game No. 2*, Graduate School of Business, University of California at Los Angeles, Los Angeles, California.

(*C*, 52, 137, 142, 144, 165, 170, 172, 202, 203, 209, 239, 252, 259)

University of Nevada Management Game

I. Description

This total enterprise competitive model simulates the durable goods industry. Each of the three to six firms in the industry sells one product, which is differentiated from the competitors' products, in a home area and in three other areas adjacent to the home area. The participant is exposed to several of the problem areas in which top management must make decisions and formulate policy such as economic and sales forecasting, cash flow, plant expansion, production planning and scheduling, research and development, dividends, marketing programs, and many others. In this simulation exercise the credit rating of a firm influences the cost of obtaining cash from external sources. For example, a poor credit rating for the firm increases the interest rate for bank loans or bond issues; or if management wishes to issue stock, the issue price of the stock would be lower for a firm with a low credit rating.

Production planning and scheduling are important because of the storage charges on all items in inventory. Several plant expansion alternatives are available to the management team. The computer output provides standard balance sheets, profit and loss statements, and other information, including a summary of competitors' positions. Twenty quarterly decisions permit simulated operations for a period up to five years.

II. Training Purpose

This model is designed to demonstrate the interrelationships between the various functional departments of a business firm and between the firm and the competitive economic environment in which it exists. The simulation exercise allows the participants to apply principles of management decision making and policy formulation.

III. Decisions Made by Participants

1. Price for the product in each area
2. Advertising in each area
3. Hiring and termination of salesmen
4. Research and development
5. New model production
6. Production units
7. Overtime
8. Activation or deactivation of second shift
9. New plant or plant expansion
10. Activation or deactivation of production lines
11. Bank loans
12. Sale of bonds
13. Sale of new stock
14. Dividends
15. Salesmen's salaries and commissions
16. Executive compensation

Decisions Made by Administrator

1. Economic indices
2. Price elasticity
3. Interest rates
4. Production costs
5. Credit ratings
6. Starting position may be adjusted by changing historical "decisions" and regenerating two years of historical data. Initial values of many variables may be adjusted before regeneration if desired.

IV. Administration

The simulation is computer scored. The program is written in FORTRAN II for IBM 1620 with 60K core storage and FORTRAN IV for SDS Sigma 7.

V. Source

Participant's Manual, *University of Nevada Business Game*. For information contact Richard V. Cotter, College of Business Administration, University of Nevada, Reno, Nevada.

(C)

Venture

I. Description

Three to five teams are formed (three to five members per team), each to manage a U.S. consumer products company. Each company makes and markets a single consumer product (such as synthetic detergent or cake mix); together, they make up the leading national competitors in their product field.

Each company operates for three years in half-year periods; it decides how much to produce, sets prices, and allocates operating funds to marketing, research and development, market research, and depreciation costs. Following each period, companies receive sales results, calculate profits, and allocate profits to taxes, dividends, and "plowback" alternatives for new or improved facilities and equipment. The game requires four hours to run.

II. Training Purpose

Venture provides practical experience in making the operating decisions of a firm and its profit allocations. It was designed for, and has been used with, Procter & Gamble production employees.

III. Decisions Made by Participants

1. Production level
2. Marketing

3. Research and development
4. Depreciation costs
5. Market research information
6. Prices
7. Dividends
8. "Plowback" into
   a. cost saving equipment
   b. capacity expansion
   c. R&D facility expansion
   d. working capital

DECISIONS MADE BY ADMINISTRATOR

1. Changes in total market potential
2. Changes in production cost (due to external factors: raw material prices, etc.)

IV. ADMINISTRATION

Venture is manually operated using scoring tables and an "economy wheel." A scorer is required in addition to the game administrator.

V. SOURCE

Student Manual. Note: *Venture* is available on a limited basis to schools only. Economics educators may direct requests to Director of Educational Services, Procter & Gamble Company, P. O. Box 599, Cincinnati, Ohio.

(*M*, 80, 137)

Washington University Management Game

I. DESCRIPTION

This is a competitive total enterprise game in which the teams of six to eight members produce and market a specialized product for various industrial plants in the Midwest. The market, composed of thirty customers, is growing slightly, but not consistently. These thirty customers are located in five geographical regions, two urban and three rural.

As the game begins, the teams find themselves operating companies which have shown only mediocre performance over the past three years. Each team must begin play by building a plant which takes nine months to complete and has a capacity of five units per quarter. Additional units may be produced in plant additions which take nine months to build. Financial problems of the companies are increased because it takes six months to manufacture units and an additional year to collect accounts receivable. Each company's sales are determined by its allocation of salesmen, advertising, quality of product, and price. Two market indicators are provided to assist the teams in forecasting total market performance. The playing period usually covers between ten and sixteen quarters.

II. Training Purpose

The game stresses the functions and interrelationships of the management process. It demonstrates principles and problems top managers must face.

III. Decisions Made by Participants

1. Allocation of salesmen
2. Hiring and terminating of salesmen
3. Price
4. Advertising
5. Inventory levels
6. Plant expansion
7. Borrowing or factoring
8. Research and development

Decision Made by Administrator

1. Number of periods to play

IV. ADMINISTRATION

This game requires an experienced chief umpire for coordination of all the activities of the game and an additional team umpire for each competing team. The ten to sixteen quarters of play can be carried out in one day.

V. SOURCE

Powell Niland, Player's Manual, *Washington University Management Game,* Graduate School of Business, Washington University, St. Louis, Missouri.

(M)

Special Purpose and
Functional Games

Contrary to general purpose games, these games are restricted to problems narrow in scope. These games are usually designed to teach specific skills in particular management areas: accounting, inventory control, transfer taxes, marketing, maintenance, and so forth. Although such games are more limited in scope than general purpose games, they allow for more in-depth examination of specific problem areas. Special purpose and functional games often stress techniques and have optimum solutions.

The games in this division range from those that are very specialized—such as the *Production* and *Capertsim* games—to those that are general purpose with special emphasis in a functional area such as marketing—as the *Carnegie Tech* and *INTOP* games. (The distinction between the latter type of game and general purpose games is a fine line; there may be some disagreement with this classification.)

ABKEM Game

I. DESCRIPTION

This noninteractive finance game was designed to be used as a research tool to test hypotheses concerning the use of financial data by people who seek different objectives. Half of the players seek to maximize funds while the others concentrate on maximization of earnings as shown by net profits after taxes. During the four quarters of play, each individual player manages his own wholesale firm, making decisions as to methods of depreciation and inventory, investments, dividend policy, means of company expansion, and performance measurement. For each of the decisions the players tell how they reached their decision, what statements were most useful, and what their decision was. Forms for preparing statements are provided, but the players are not forced to use them. Generally the funds statement was most frequently used by both groups.

II. TRAINING PURPOSE

Although this game was designed as a research device, it can easily be used to provide practical experience in preparing and using financial statements and making financial decisions.

III. DECISIONS MADE BY PARTICIPANTS

1. Inventory and depreciation methods
2. Investments
3. Dividend policy
4. Capital budgeting
5. Performance measurements

IV. ADMINISTRATION

In this manually scored game the players begin the play with financial information about the ABKEM Company, an instruction sheet, a financial position statement, an earnings statement, and a funds statement.

V. SOURCE

Abdellatif Khemakhem, "A Simulation of Management-Decision Behavior: Funds and Income," *The Accounting Review*, Vol. XLIII, No. 3, July 1968, pp. 522-534.

(*M*, 151)

Accounting in Action: A Simulation

I. DESCRIPTION

This accounting simulation introduces the participant to the accounting process. The simulated company acts as a wholesaler of a single product. Participants balance supply of purchased goods with demand of final consumers; however, the primary task of the participant centers in the preparation of journal entries, cash flow, cost of goods sold, income statements, and balance sheets. The simulation stresses the relationship between transactions and financial statements for several decision periods.

II. TRAINING PURPOSE

This simulation is designed to provide the participant with experience in preparing accounting reports and to stress the relationship between transaction and financial statements.

III. DECISIONS MADE BY PARTICIPANTS

1. Units and price of purchased goods
2. Selling price and units offered for sale
3. Loans

IV. ADMINISTRATION

The administrator monitors the prepared journal entries and financial statements from output provided by the computer. (In some cases the computer output is given to the participants.) Forms are provided for the participant requirements. The simulation is programmed in FORTRAN.

V. SOURCE

Participant's Manual, John J. Willingham and Robert E. Malcom, *Accounting in Action: A Simulation*, McGraw-Hill Book Company, New York, 1965.

(*C*)

Accounting for Decisions: A Business Game

I. Description

This is a manual accounting game that provides the participant with experience in making top management decisions concerning the operations of a business and experience in preparing budgets and financial statements for an on-going business. The hypothetical business sells portable power tools to contractors and homeowners. Model A is sold to contractors through salesmen, and Model B is sold to hardwares through wholesalers. The game is not interactive among the teams.

The primary task of the participant is the preparation of the budgets and the financial statements which are monitored by the game administrator. Various accounting methods are available to the participant—for example, LIFO or FIFO method, depreciation methods, and others.

II. Training Purpose

The purpose of this accounting game is to provide an on-going problem that requires the game participant to make operating decisions for key areas of the business and to prepare traditional accounting reports.

III. Decisions Made by Participants

1. Prices
2. Advertising expenditures
3. Production units
4. Direct labor hours
5. Parts purchased

Decision Made by Administrator

1. Economic index

IV. ADMINISTRATION

The game is manual. Forms are provided for the participants to prepare their accounting reports. The game administrator determines sales and checks and evaluates the accounting reports turned in by participants.

V. SOURCE

Participant's Manual, William J. Bruns, Jr., *Accounting for Decisions, A Business Game,* The Macmillan Company, New York, 1966.

(*M*)

Accounting Information and Business Decisions

I. DESCRIPTION

This simulation can be run with as few as four teams and as many as fifty. Each team consists of four to seven people who compete within industries (maximum of six teams per industry) in the purchase of raw materials and the production and sale of finished goods.

The companies compete in the market for purchases of raw materials which are available in limited quantities. After a production decision has been made, each company competes to sell its manufactured goods. All companies start with the same financial position, and all have the opportunity to borrow funds from the bank at any time.

At the beginning of each period, each company prepares a cash budget. At the end of each quarter each company prepares a balance sheet and income statement. At the beginning of the game, teams can choose their organization structure and decide whether they wish to use accelerated or straight line depreciation, FIFO, LIFO, or average costs for inventory, and direct or absorption costing for inventory accounting purposes. Each industry can choose its own criteria for success. Capital budgeting options may be introduced, such as the purchase of equipment, the entry into a foreign market, and so on.

II. Training Purpose

The purpose of this game is to give participants experience in using accounting information in decision making and to illustrate the effect of management decisions on accounting statements.

III. Decisions Made by Participants

1. Organization structure
2. Accounting policies
3. Borrowing
4. Raw materials to purchase
5. Price paid for raw materials
6. Production level
7. Finished goods to sell
8. Timing of repayment of debt
9. Capital budgeting options

Decisions Made by Administrator

1. Length of game
2. Economic cycle
3. Options to introduce

IV. Administration

This is a noncomputer game and is scored by the administrator on the blackboard or on prepared scoring sheets which can be posted.

V. Source

Jack Gray, Kenneth Johnston, John Willingham, R. Gene Brown, *Accounting Information and Business Decisions,* McGraw-Hill Book Company, New York, 1964. Direct inquiries to R. Gene Brown.

(M)

The Action Corporation

I. DESCRIPTION

Any number of teams, each of one to four members, are formed. The teams manage a corporation manufacturing two products in a relatively simple environment. The game is manually operated, though reference is made to a set of computer-generated, demand-supply function tables. The primary audience for the game will be students and others to whom business administration is a relatively new field. Performance of the teams is evaluated on the basis of income statements and balance sheets which the teams prepare annually after each four quarters of results.

II. TRAINING PURPOSE

The game is intended for use as part of an introductory accounting course and is of assistance in improving the students' understanding of business.

III. DECISIONS MADE BY PARTICIPANTS

1. Production level
2. Advertising
3. Selling price
4. Prices bid for subassembly

Each decision made for both products.

DECISIONS MADE BY ADMINISTRATOR

1. Introduction of special events into the game and selection of economic climate
2. Selection of demand function of each product
3. Selection of supply function of each product

IV. ADMINISTRATION

The game is completely manually operated. (Complete generated demand function tables are available which may be employed by organizations having no computer handy. A game administrator wishing to adjust demand functions would need a copy of the program which is presently listed in FORTRAN IV.)

V. SOURCE

Andrew M. McCosh, Graduate School of Business, University of Michigan, Ann Arbor, Michigan. The game by W. G. Kell and A. M. McCosh will be published by Ronald Press.

(M)

BIG
(Business Investment Game)

I. DESCRIPTION

This is a production investment game in which teams attempt to maximize profits while competing with other teams. Each team begins with $4 million which it uses to purchase factories and raw materials and for production. There are four products each team may produce. Each product has a storage cost and depreciation factor. The raw material units for these products involve purchase cost, storage cost, and deterioration costs.

Each team is divided into two sections. While one section is participating in management decision making, the other team observes.

II. TRAINING PURPOSE

The game is designed to give participants experience in making production and investment decisions in order to maximize profits in a competitive environment.

III. Decisions Made by Participants

    1. Amount to bid on contracts
    2. Amount of production to schedule
    3. Amount of production units to store
    4. Amount of raw material to purchase
    5. Number of factories to purchase
    6. Number of fixed fee contracts to purchase
    7. Set schedules for factories

IV. Administration

In this manually scored game, each two hours of real time is equal to one year in game time. Contracts are issued quarterly in the game. All necessary forms and contracts are included in the player's manual.

V. Source

John L. Kennedy, Department of Psychology, Princeton University, Princeton, New Jersey. Direct inquiries to Robert Graham, School of Business and Technology, Oregon State University, Corvallis, Oregon.

(*M*)

Business Game for Using Accounting Information

I. Description

This game introduces the participant to the accounting process by requiring him to make operating decisions, to prepare accounting reports, and to use these reports for decisions in future periods. The simulated company is a single product firm operating in a competitive environment; firms compete for both raw materials and sales of final product.

II. TRAINING PURPOSE

This game is designed to introduce the participant to accounting methods used in preparing financial statements and to stress the importance of financial statements in the managerial decision-making process.

III. DECISIONS MADE BY PARTICIPANTS

1. Purchase of raw material—units and price
2. Units of production
3. Price and units offered for sale

DECISIONS MADE BY ADMINISTRATOR

1. Units of direct material available for sale
2. Total market demand

IV. ADMINISTRATION

The game is administered manually. The administrator monitors the financial statements prepared by the participant—cost of goods sold, cash flow, earnings, and balance sheet. Forms are provided for preparing these financial statements.

V. SOURCE

Participant's Manual, Paul E. Fertig, Donald F. Istvan, and Homer J. Mottice, *Business Game for Using Accounting Information: An Introduction,* Harcourt, Brace & World, Inc., New York, 1965.

(*M*)

Business Logistics Decision Simulation
(BULOGA)

I. DESCRIPTION

This competitive business logistics game involves four companies which make gamets, a consumer durable product, for sale in five market areas. Each team has a manufacturing plant in one of the four regions which are equidistant from the larger central region. Each also owns a warehouse in each of the five regions.

A gamet is manufactured from three raw materials in fixed proportions, each with differing costs, transportation charges, and lead times. Weekly decisions must be made regarding such things as raw material purchases, warehousing capacity for both raw materials and finished goods, shipments to each of the warehouses, and production. Production costs are essentially uniform, except in the case of underutilization, rush orders, or excessive production.

Performance is measured by two indices: (1) average per unit gross profit on delivered gamets and (2) total gross profits. The administrator can discount a firm's performance if it has "end-played" the game; that is, if it has placed itself in a precarious future position for the sake of current profits.

II. TRAINING PURPOSE

This game was designed to emphasize problems encountered in business logistics. Players must concentrate on solving supply scheduling, production, and distribution problems.

III. DECISIONS MADE BY PARTICIPANTS

1. Raw material purchases
2. Raw material warehouse capacity
3. Production
4. Finished goods warehouse capacity
5. Finished goods warehouse shipments

IV. ADMINISTRATION

This computer game has been programmed in FORTRAN. Participants are provided with logistics operating statements and logistics operations planning reports.

V. SOURCE

Business Logistics Simulation Participant Information, Graduate School of Business Administration, University of Minnesota, Minneapolis, Minnesota.

(C)

Business Logistics
Facility Location Simulation

I. DESCRIPTION

This game simulates the manufacturing, marketing, and distribution of a consumer product in the 38 major markets in the United States. Participants, each of whom is given a fixed amount of capital to invest, compete singly or in teams with an objective of maximizing individual return on investment over a series of plays of the game. Each company makes decisions regarding major facility locations, including the number, size, and location of plants and warehouses, as well as decisions regarding those markets in which the company will compete. As logistics managers, participants are called upon to specify sources of raw materials, methods of transportation, size and location of inventories, and frequency of customer service. Consumer demand is basically a function of population, with the capability provided for simulating growth rates for markets individually or with a national average. Shares of markets are determined competitively in each market, the major influences being price, promotion, and customer service.

II. Training Purpose

This simulation is designed to describe the competitive environment and conflicting economic factors within which a firm's major resource allocation and facility location decisions are made. The role of logistics and facility location decisions is identified with special attention given to the trade-offs between marketing needs for readily available goods and production and distribution needs for cost minimization. Strategic factors involving timing, market entry, and competitive investment strategies are represented as being as important as technical questions.

III. Decisions Made by Participants

1. Plants:
   a. Number
   b. Location
   c. Capacity
2. Warehouses:
   a. Number
   b. Location
3. Raw materials, two types:
   a. Sources for each plant
   b. Alternative sources, if desired
4. Markets in which to compete
5. For each market:
   a. Price
   b. Promotion
   c. Mode of transportation and frequency of shipment
6. Market research (e.g., Neilsen reports)
7. Timing of investments

Decisions Made by Administrator

1. Sensitivity factors, especially regarding competitive influences of price, promotion, and service

2. Number of three-month periods over which the game is to be played
3. Total investment capital to be made available to participants
4. Setting of prices for the purchase of market research information
5. Demand growth rates of individual markets

IV. ADMINISTRATION

The simulation is currently designed to be run on the Call-A-Computer Time-Sharing service. The computer programs are written in GE Time-Sharing FORTRAN and may be modified if desired to FORTRAN II or FORTRAN IV for the IBM 7094. Input by game participants is made directly to the computer via teletype installations at any time up to a deadline set for each play of the game. Actual running of one period of the game involves the successive execution of a series of programs which will operate on the input files already created on the time-sharing system.

V. SOURCE

Direct inquiries to J. L. Heskett, Logistic Systems, Inc., 10 Arrow Street, Cambridge, Massachusetts; or Stephen Cotler, Computer Associates, 380 Putnam Avenue, Cambridge, Massachusetts.

(C)

Business Management Simulation

I. DESCRIPTION

Each of the five team members in this total enterprise game serves his company by assuming specific roles; that is, as president or as vice president of finance, marketing, production, or research and development. These players also make up the board of directors for a new company which hopes to produce a new desk computer for sale in a very competitive market.

Information is presented to each of the vice presidents concerning the department under his direction. All decisions are made in quarterly meetings by the board of directors. This simulation allows only oral communication between the members and thus brings up problems of organization and communications. The teams may also purchase information from the game administrator. Decisions to be made concern initial plant construction, plant additions, production, allocation of salesmen, and advertising. The quarterly decisions are usually made for from four to ten years.

II. TRAINING PURPOSE

This simulation is designed to point out communication and organizational problems to the players. It also allows the players to sharpen their communication skills in an interactive environment. It also allows them to set expectations and to see how well these are achieved.

III. DECISIONS MADE BY PARTICIPANTS

1. Plant size
2. Scheduling
3. Production
4. Allocation of salesmen
5. Advertising
6. Research and development
7. Financing

IV. ADMINISTRATION

This is a manually scored game in which the game administrator presents quarterly reports of a company's past performance. A game board is also provided to allow the teams to evaluate their operations.

V. SOURCE

Players' Manual, *Business Management Simulation,* Douglas Corporation, Missile and Space Division, Space Systems Center, 5301 Balusa Avenue, Huntington, California.

(*M*)

Buying Game

I. Description

Any number of players may participate. They act individually as buyers in a paint department and use whatever methods they like for making decisions. Their goal is to maximize long-term profits without neglecting customer service. They buy eight items from two manufacturers, a restriction being that all orders must be in multiples of 100 since both manufacturers pack their items 100 to a case.

At the start of the game each player is given the total dollar sales for the department for each of the preceding three years, the total dollar sales for each month of the preceding year, and the cost, selling price, and description of each item.

More detailed information is available, but at a cost to the player since the information would have to be compiled and analyzed by the player or by someone else. The additional information includes last year's total dollar and unit sales of each item, the number of units of each item sold each month, and detailed information on lead times.

The game is played over 24 two-week periods. It emphasizes forecasting sales rates and lead times, setting safety stocks, determining order quantities, dealing with seasonal factors in sales rates, deciding on the type of unit control data which should be generated and analyzed, and making decisions under pressure.

II. Training Purpose

The game was designed originally to train buyers in the purchase of products to be retailed. It gives participants experience in forecasting, setting safety stocks, determining what information they require, and making decisions under pressure. It also highlights the importance of good buying strategies.

III. Decisions Made by Participants

1. Additional information purchase
2. Quantity to order

IV. Administration

At the end of each period, the administrator provides data on receipts and demands for the period and ranks each player by means of a simple manual-scoring procedure.

V. Source

J. G. F. Wollaston, Greatermans Stores Limited, P. O. Box 5460, Johannesburg, South Africa.

(*M*, 288)

CADISIM
(Computer Assisted Disposal Simulation)

I. Description

The participants represent the program section of the offices of the property disposal officer of a large aeronautical material depot. The depot is involved in the disposal, through donation, scrap, sale, or transfer, of excess materials. The National Inventory Control Point generates, by stock number and quality, forecasts of excesses. The participants make two major decisions each month: (1) the number of items to process and (2) the size of the labor force. These decisions are based on the forecasts of excesses given on the overall effect of regular labor costs, overtime costs, hiring and layoff costs, and inventory carrying costs on the cost per item processed by the activity.

The simulation covers a 12-month period, with decisions required monthly. Each group is given from ten to fifteen minutes to make its decisions for the coming month. Data on the effect of the production rate per month and size of the labor force on overtime costs, hiring and layoff costs, and inventory costs are provided, along with forecasts of excesses. Monthly reports are generated showing the excesses forecast and actually received, the number of items processed, and the inventory, the size of the labor force, and the resulting payroll, hiring (and layoff), overtime, and inventory carrying costs. Cumulative costs-to-date are given. Competing groups are judged on their ability to minimize cost per unit processed.

II. TRAINING PURPOSE

The game is designed to illustrate the problems involved in managing a large property disposal activity, such as those which dispose of excess aeronautical or military material through donation, scrap, sale, or transfer. The objective is to minimize the cost per item to dispose of the materials through the control of labor force, overtime work, and level of work in process.

III. DECISIONS MADE BY PARTICIPANTS

1. Number of items to be processed (donated, sold, scrapped, or transferred)
2. Number of employees in labor force
   The amount of overtime work and the level of work in process are determined by Decisions 1 and 2 and by the data given.

DECISIONS MADE BY ADMINISTRATOR (DATA GIVEN)

1. Regular and overtime payroll costs
2. Hiring and layoff costs
3. Inventory handling costs
4. Items to be generated (forecast and actual)

IV. ADMINISTRATION

The simulation exercise is programmed in FORTRAN. Reports on costs and items processed are produced "monthly" for one year.

V. SOURCE

CADISIM (Computer Assisted Disposal Simulation ALM-2017-Sim). Request for copies should be directed to Commandant, U.S. Army Logistics Management Center, Fort Lee, Virginia.

(*C*)

A Computer-Oriented Game Simulating the Combined Production
Scheduling—Inventory Control Activity

I. DESCRIPTION

This production game can be played by individuals or teams. The players must purchase raw materials and schedule production for a small job shop operation and subcontract a limited number of jobs. This is a noninteractive game in which the various individuals or teams face similar period demands. Decisions are made every two weeks concerning such things as scheduling of departments, priorities, and authorization of overtime. Each team tries to minimize its costs by choosing consistent policies.

II. TRAINING PURPOSE

This game is designed to give the participants experience in running a job shop operation. Emphasis is placed on the costs involved with various policies.

III. DECISIONS MADE BY PARTICIPANTS

1. Purchases of raw materials
2. Scheduling and priorities
3. Subcontracting
4. Overtime authorization

IV. ADMINISTRATION

This computer-scored game is programmed on an IBM 1410, 60K digital computer. Daily printouts cover job movements, jobs completed, orders received, and changes in finished products inventory. More detailed reports are prepared biweekly concerning such things as total sales, raw materials inventory, down time analysis, and cost analysis for the period.

V. SOURCE

"A Computer-Oriented Game Simulating the Combined Production Scheduling—Inventory Control Activity" (a thesis), John V. Sodem, North Carolina State University, Raleigh, North Carolina.

(*C*)

CAISIM
(Computer Assisted Industrial Simulation)

I. DESCRIPTION

This is a production management game in which participants attempt to minimize total production costs by selecting the optimum monthly production schedule. The major costs considered are regular payroll, overtime, hiring and layoff, and inventory costs. Participants select the units to produce and the size of the workforce that best meets a somewhat variable demand and minimizes costs.

II. TRAINING PURPOSE

The computer-assisted simulation model is designed to demonstrate typical problems in managing an industrial production system.

III. DECISIONS MADE BY PARTICIPANTS

1. Number of units to produce
2. The size of the labor force

IV. ADMINISTRATION

The computer game is programmed for the RCA 501 computer and in FORTRAN IV.

V. Source

Participant's Manual. *CAISIM: Computer Assisted Industrial Simulation (ALM*-1248-*SIM [A]).* Request for copies of the manual should be directed to Commandant, United States Logistics Management Center, Fort Lee, Virginia.

(C)

CALOGSIM
A Computer Assisted Logistics Simulation

I. Description

This logistics simulation game is used to train military and civilian personnel of the Defense Department. The setting and decisions are similar to those found in any wholesale supply system. The game presents the total system approach by integrating all of the functional areas into the wholesale supply system. Each management team of six to ten participants is responsible for supplying eight depots located in the United States. Inventory is divided into three major classes—major items, secondary items, and repair parts. Teams have complete control over the major aspects of the supply systems; they control the forecasting model, review model, and ordering model—the basic elements of any inventory system. There are charges for changes made in the system and paperwork. The computer provides monthly reports on the complete status of the system and costs. The game is usually played for 48 time periods.

II. Training Purpose

The model is designed to illustrate and provide experience in making decisions in a wholesale supply system.

III. Decisions Made by Participants

    1. Purchase—normal, emergency, and cancel
    2. Repair—normal, emergency, and cancel

3. Reports requests
4. Surplus disposal
5. Inventory policies—system or depot
    a. Service level
    b. Something constant (alpha)
    c. Trend adjustment
    d. Reorder cycle
    e. Safety stock level
    f. Estimated quarterly demand
6. Transfers—normal, expedited

IV. ADMINISTRATION

The game is computer scored and programmed for the RCA 501 computer. The model is to be programmed in FORTRAN IV in the near future.

V. SOURCE

Student Manual, *CALOGSIM* (A Computer Assisted Logistics Simulation) (ALM-1348-H-C).
CALOGSIM—How to Read and Use Background Data Sheets (ALM-2285-PI).
CALOGSIM—How to Prepare Computer Decision Cards (ALM-2286-PI).
Requests for this material should be addressed to Commandant, United States Army Logistics Management Center, Fort Lee, Virginia.

(C)

CAMSIM
(Computer Assisted Maintenance Simulation)

I. DESCRIPTION

The participants represent the production control division of the directorate for maintenance of a U.S. Army depot which provides depot maintenance and supply support for the Army installations in its area. Forecasts of requirements for the overhaul of unserviceable equipment are received monthly, but actual requirements may vary by up to 15 percent of the forecast. The goal of the management team is to meet the demands placed on the depot by the depot maintenance control center at the minimum cost.

Decisions of the group are based on the forecasts of overhaul requirements and on the overall effect of the size of the labor force and the number of overhauls completed on the payroll and inventory carrying costs. Data are provided on regular labor costs, the overtime resulting from various combinations of labor force size and overhauls made, hiring and layoff costs, and inventory carrying costs.

Each team receives a monthly report showing the overhauls forecast and the number actually required, the number of units repaired and the inventory of unfinished jobs, the size of the labor force, regular payroll costs, and total costs incurred. Cumulative year-to-date costs are also given. These costs result from the group's decisions regarding size of labor force and units to be repaired, and the actual work load required by the DMCC.

Participants are allowed from ten to twenty minutes to consider the forecast, the costs involved, and the processing time data given, and make their monthly decisions regarding the labor force to be used and the number of jobs to be completed. The decisions are then given to the computer for the computation of the monthly report. Success is measured by the total cost of meeting the demands placed on the depot by the DMCC.

II. Training Purpose

The purpose of this exercise is to give the participant experience in handling typical problems involved in managing a maintenance activity, such as an army depot which provides maintenance and supply for the installations in its area.

III. Decisions Made by Participants

1. Number of employees
2. Number of overhauls to be completed
   These decisions control labor and overtime costs, hiring and layoff costs, and costs of holding an inventory of unfinished jobs.

DECISIONS MADE BY ADMINISTRATOR

1. Data on costs and performance are provided
2. Forecast and actual overhaul demands are given
3. Performance of the group is judged on the basis of total cost of meeting the workload imposed

IV. ADMINISTRATION

All necessary data are provided. The computations of costs resulting from decisions of the group are made on a computer, but could easily be made manually.

V. SOURCE

CAMSIM (Computer Assisted Maintenance Simulation ALM-1246-SIM [B]). Request for copies should be directed to Commandant, U.S. Army Logistics Management Center, Fort Lee, Virginia.

(*C*)

CAPERTSIM Decision Simulation Program

I. DESCRIPTION

Several teams can participate with approximately five to eight members on a project management team. The simulation uses a project network of 43 activities. The duration time for each activity may vary within a stated restricted range—but with accompanying increases in cost for shortening the duration time. For example, in activity 26-27 the expected time may have a restricted range of 10 to 15 days for the duration time, and total costs would range from $50,000 for 10 days to $30,000 for 15 days.

The simulation presents a situation in which each project management team must shorten activity times to meet an imposed early completion date. The teams submit trial decisions to test various possible courses of action for the best time-cost relationships in meeting the early completion date. The computer calculates the results of such changes, and the team then decides if any of these changes should be incorporated into the permanent schedule. The computer also prints out the updated schedule, unforeseen occurrences, total project costs, and pertinent correspondence relative to the project.

II. Training Purpose

CAPERTSIM is designed primarily to acquaint participants with the principles and uses of PERT and to provide experience in making time-cost trade-off decisions.

III. Decision Made by Participants

    1. Duration time for each activity

IV. Administration

The programs for CAPERTSIM are available through the IBM "SHARE" and RCA "PAL" libraries.

V. Source

Student Manual, CAPERTSIM (ALM-1439-SIM-A). Requests for copies should be addressed to Commandant, U.S. Army Logistics Management Center, Fort Lee, Virginia.

(C)

Capital Budgeting Simulation

I. Description

This is a game in which two companies, a medium-sized conservative one whose position in the industry is declining and a small, expanding company whose president wants to sell out and retire, operate in the highly competitive chemical industry. Each of the two teams is composed of six players. The conservative company (A) has a new management team whose objective is to expand and diversify. One alternative for meeting this objective is to acquire the smaller company (B). In the simulation the two presidents talk about the acquisition and the vice presidents negotiate short-term budgets.

The game takes approximately four hours to play. The players should play the game twice, once as management of each company.

II. TRAINING PURPOSE

The training purpose is to give participants experience in situations which require such investment evaluation techniques as cash flow (present value), pay-back, and return on investment. They apply the investment analysis techniques while evaluating the relative desirability of various alternatives.

III. DECISIONS MADE BY PARTICIPANTS

Company A:
1. Plant expansion
2. Build new plant (or)
3. Acquire Company B
4. Divert funds from short-term projects to major investments
5. Draw down on current assets to finance short-term alternatives

Company B:
1. Make new machinery purchases
2. Hire new salesmen
3. Increase research and development budget
4. Whether or not company should be acquired by A

DECISIONS MADE BY ADMINISTRATOR

1. Acceptability of loan
2. Feasibility of players' decisions

IV. Administration

The game is manually scored and ideally would have three administrators but could be run with only one. The administrator collects, records, and evaluates decisions, then determines players with highest scores. Instructor's manual and players' materials are furnished by game source.

V. Source

Participant's Manual, *Capital Budgeting Simulation,* Abt Associates, Inc., 55 Wheeler Street, Cambridge, Massachusetts.

(M)

CARESIM
(Computer Assisted Repair Simulation)

I. Description

This management exercise considers each group as an ad hoc committee to select the parts replacement policy for each of four items of equipment to minimize the overall cost of maintenance. Four different replacement policies are considered for each of the four equipment items. When the group reaches agreement as to a tentative policy decision, they may ask for a simulation run on the computer. The effects of various policies (e.g., replace individual parts as they fail, replace all parts when one fails, etc.) are studied and a final recommendation is made for each equipment item.

Data are provided for each item showing hours tested, mean time between breakdowns, standard deviation, labor costs to replace parts, parts costs, and down-time costs. Reports generated by the simulation runs show the same data plus the net effect of following the designated policy. These results include the number of parts replaced; down time; preventive maintenance time; costs for labor, parts, and down time; and the final cost.

No time limits are specified for decisions, nor is there a stated limit on the number of simulation runs which may be asked for by the participants, but a final recommendation is required for each item before completion of the simulation.

II. TRAINING PURPOSE

The exercise uses simulation to provide an understanding of the considerations involved in selecting sound parts replacement policies to provide optimum maintenance of equipment and weapons systems. As members of an ad hoc committee, each group studies the effects of four different replacement policies on four different items of equipment and makes a recommendation for the policy which will minimize the overall cost of maintenance per period for each item.

III. DECISIONS MADE BY PARTICIPANTS

A parts replacement policy is required for each of four items of equipment. Four possible policies are considered, two of which include a variable number of hours. Final decisions may be based on the results of computer simulation of cost experience using a prescribed policy.

DECISIONS MADE BY ADMINISTRATOR

Data are provided for each item of equipment. Results are judged on the basis of total cost of maintenance per period.

IV. ADMINISTRATION

Computer scored, RCA 501 and in FORTRAN IV.

V. SOURCE

CARESIM (Computer Assisted Maintenance Simulation ALM-1246-SIM [B]). Request for copies should be directed to Commandant, U.S. Army Logistics Management Center, Fort Lee, Virginia.

(C)

CARMSIM
(Computer Assisted Reliability Maintainability Simulation)

I. DESCRIPTION

This simulation presents a cost reliability problem of determining an optimal maintenance service level. Participants are given a minimum reliability level for an item which is a component part of a larger system. By using the Monte Carlo simulated sampling technique, the participant is able to use the computer to assist him in finding the desired reliability based on the trade-off costs between reliability and maintenance. The participant may submit as many trial runs as desired.

II. TRAINING PURPOSE

This simulation provides a model by which the relationship between specified reliability and maintenance costs can be studied objectively.

III. DECISION MADE BY PARTICIPANTS

    1. Percent reliability

IV. ADMINISTRATION

The simulation is run on the computer. Participants select a card which represents their decisions and submit it to the computer which has the program on call. The simulation is presently programmed in RCA 501 machine language and FORTRAN IV.

V. SOURCE

CARMSIM Student Manual (ALM-2594-SIM). Request for copies should be addressed to Commandant, U.S. Army Logistics Management Center, Fort Lee, Virginia.

(*C*)

Carnegie Tech Management Game

I. Description

The Carnegie game is a marketing game with teams composed of up to ten members; each member assumes a specialized role in the operation of the company. There are three companies located in four geographical regions which produce up to three products in the detergent market. The game begins with each company producing one detergent from its plant which can be used to provide other given product mixes. They also have research and development facilities, raw materials and finished-goods warehouses, and regional warehouses in each of the four areas.

The different products are produced from seven basic raw materials with varying lead times and costs. The teams must schedule production and authorize overtime. Sales are made directly from the factory and from each of the regional warehouses to wholesalers and retail chains. Teams may vary price and advertising expenditures in the different regions in efforts to increase their market share. Market share may also vary according to product characteristics, promotions, and sales force allocations. New products can be developed and produced for sale after market research and laboratory tests are conducted. Several means are available for gaining both temporary and long-range funds. To assist the players in making decisions, a great deal of information is available (probably more than most players can effectively utilize). The teams must sort through this information and any other they purchase to find what is most meaningful for their decisions.

II. Training Purpose

This game is designed to allow the participants to test and develop management skills. Teams must organize activities to use available information effectively and work effectively on their company's problems. Teams also must meet the problem of proper utilization of the members' specialized skills while each member retains a general outlook.

III. Decisions Made by Participants

1. Raw materials purchases
2. Labor force size

3. Overtime authorized
4. Maintenance
5. Production level
6. Allocation of goods to warehouses
7. Price
8. Advertising expenditures
9. Promotional expenditures
10. Financing
11. Dividends
12. Market research
13. Product research and development
14. Regions to be entered
15. Product characteristics

IV. ADMINISTRATION

This computer-scored game provides a great deal of very specific information to the participants. Performance is evaluated and, to some extent, guided by the administrators. Annual reports to the stockholders are required along with a forecast of future plans.

V. SOURCE

The Carnegie Tech Management Game, K. J. Cohen, R. M. Cyert, W. R. Dill, A. A. Kuehn, M. H. Miller, T. A. Van Wormer, and P. R. Winters, Carnegie Institute of Technology, Pittsburgh, Pennsylvania, 1960.

(*C*, 37, 41, 42, 45, 46, 47, 63, 74, 77, 78, 79, 172, 174, 203, 239, 259)

City I

I. DESCRIPTION

In this game nine teams (three to five members per team) act as entrepreneurs who own economic developments in part of a partially urbanized county which is divided into four political jurisdictions. The playing board contains 625 squares (each square represents one square mile), most of which are unowned at the beginning of play. These land parcels may be purchased and developed by the teams during the course of the game. There are nine types of private land use which the teams can develop on a parcel of land: heavy industry, light industry, business goods, business services, personal goods, personal services, high-income residences, middle-income residences, and low-income residences.

Each of the nine teams is elected or appointed by elected officials to assume the duties of one of nine governmental roles: these are played simultaneously with the entrepreneurial functions common to all teams. The elected officials (the county chairman and the central city councilman) must satisfy the electorate (the other teams) in order to stay in office each round. The chairman team appoints other teams to play the roles of the school, public works and safety, highway, planning and zoning, and finance departments. The two residual teams play the mass media and citizens' organizations. The governmental departments build schools, provide utilities, build and upgrade roads and terminals, maintain roads, buy parkland, zone land, and estimate revenues.

Teams set their own objectives for both the public and private actions they undertake. Team decisions are recorded each round (approximately two hours in length) by a computer, which acts as an accountant and indicates the effects of the teams' actions on one another and on the county itself. The interaction of public and private decisions and their influence over time are illustrated by regularly provided computer printouts. Even though conflicts may develop between urban and suburban interests, among businesses, and among governmental departments, teams often find that cooperation is as important as competition in fulfilling their objectives.

II. TRAINING PURPOSE

Participants who play this game receive a comprehensive view of central city and suburban growth and development. Teams are free to try alternative solutions to problems created within the model by their own actions in previous rounds. The governmental, economic, and social systems of the model are defined broadly enough so that they may be altered by a team majority vote. Through their own actions players become aware of the interrelation of public and private decisions, the interdisciplinary scope of urban problems, and the effect over time of public and private decisions.

III. Decisions Made by Participants

1. Vote for political officers
2. Acquire land
3. Sell and trade land
4. Build nine types of private land-use developments
5. Operate businesses
6. Set prices for commercial establishments
7. Set wages for businesses
8. Operate residences
9. Maintain or demolish land uses
10. Expand density of land-use development
11. Raise local taxes from three sources
12. Use federal-state aid
13. Balance local budget
14. Request and expend funds for four departments
15. Build schools
16. Hire and assign teachers
17. Build municipal services
    (police, fire, etc.)
18. Hire and assign personnel
19. Provide utility service
20. Build, upgrade, and maintain roads
21. Relieve road congestion
22. Build and upgrade terminals
23. Change zoning
24. Appeal zoning changes
25. Purchase parkland
26. Hold referendums

IV. Administration

The game has no formal scoring system, but the teams receive computer output (from an IBM 1130 using FORTRAN IV) at the end of each round which indicates whether or not they have accomplished their own objectives.

V. Source

Peter House, Director, Urban Systems Simulations, Washington Center for Metropolitan Studies, 1717 Massachusetts Avenue, N.W., Washington, D.C.

(*C*)

Collective Bargaining

I. Description

The game requires only two or three hours playing time during which the participants have an opportunity to represent both union and management positions in a collective bargaining situation. Any number of groups of six persons can play. Each group initially acts as management personnel facing two difficult grievance problems. Subsequently, two of the groups remain management people while the remaining four take the union position. In these assumed roles the teams negotiate contract clauses and settle wages and benefits covered by the contract. The game goal is for each union or management team to negotiate a "better" contract.

While decisions are made in a conflict context, the final scoring compares only union teams against other union teams and management against other management teams. This design avoids the possible emotional spillover which might result from comparing management against union.

II. Training Purpose

The game is essentially designed to provide supervisors and managers with practice in a collective bargaining situation. Emphasis is placed on the wording of contractual clauses. Prescribed decisions very closely simulate those made in actual bargaining situations. The game play also points out the political nature of the collective bargaining process.

III. Decisions Made by Participants

1. Subcontracting grievance
2. Overtime grievance
3. Contract clauses pertaining to subcontracting and overtime
4. Wage rates
5. Fringe benefits (holidays, vacations, pensions, insurance)

IV. Administration

All necessary directions for administering the game are included in an administrator's manual. The administrator leads pregame and postgame discussions to evaluate and critique game performance. Administration does not require any mathematical computation.

V. Source

Erwin Rausch. Direct inquiries to Science Research Associates, Inc., 259 East Erie Street, Chicago, Illinois.

(M)

The Community Land Use Game

I. Description

CLUG is the urban systems game that involves three to fifteen players in a sequence of highly interdependent decisions concerning real estate development, transportation, taxes, utilities construction, and building maintenance. The player's decisions themselves result in foreseen as well as unforeseen consequences for community land use, economic base, level of employment, and financial position.

Aside from the fact that CLUG is one of the few games dealing systemically with urban factors, the game has advantages not found in many games: (1) no two plays of CLUG are the same, so it can be played repeatedly; (2) the outcome of play is determined by player decisions and is not predetermined or due simply to luck; (3) CLUG can be modified to meet a wide variety of needs; and (4) the game is designed to be played manually and does not normally require computer assistance.

II. Training Purpose

The general purpose of CLUG is to provide intense experience with the growth, development, and resulting problems of urban growth—all in a very short period of time.

CLUG is used widely by professionals, researchers, and educators in the fields of law, planning, architecture, business, public administration, political science, sociology, urban studies, economics, and engineering. Each user tends to find his own purposes and ways of using the game depending on his own substantive interest in the urban areas.

III. Decisions Made by Participants

1. Assess real property
2. Receive income
3. Pay employees
4. Pay stores and officers
5. Pay transportation
6. Pay taxes
7. Set tax rate
8. Buy and sell land
9. Provide utilities
10. Renovate buildings
11. Construct or demolish buildings
12. Designate place of employment
13. Set prices for suppliers
14. Sign trade agreements
15. Receive interest

DECISION MADE BY ADMINISTRATOR

1. Locate existing highways, shipping points, and public service supply plants at the beginning of play

IV. ADMINISTRATION

CLUG is designed to be played manually with two administrators. For
extended plays and for research a computer program in FORTRAN IV for
the IBM 1130 has been written.

The Center for Housing and Environmental Studies at Cornell University
sells the CLUG rule book. A variety of other CLUG related materials are
also available from this source. A *Community Land Use Game* kit including
all the materials needed to build a city of one-half million population is
available for $125 from Systems Gaming Associates, Apt. A-1-2, Lansing
Apartments, 20 N. Triphammer Road, Ithaca, New York.

V. SOURCE

A. G. Feldt, Department of City Planning, Cornell University, Ithaca,
New York.

(C, M)

Cornell Hotel Administration Simulation Exercise
(CHASE)

I. DESCRIPTION

This game simulates the hotel industry; participants manage a hotel in a
competitive environment. The firm competes with three other hotels for
business in four markets—commercial, tourist, group, and local. Game success depends heavily on optimizing the allocation of available funds to com-

pete with the other three firms. In the first quarter the participants must determine the depreciation method, whether to lease or self-operate the restaurant, and whether to franchise or be independent. Other quarterly decisions concern room rates, marketing expenditures, operations expenditures, and finance. The computer provides feedback in the form of profit and loss statements, balance sheets, and industry reports.

II. TRAINING PURPOSE

This game is designed to demonstrate typical problems of a hotel. It stresses long-range planning and the need for the establishment of operating goals.

III. DECISIONS MADE BY PARTICIPANTS

1. Room rates—single, double, group single, group double, and commercial single
2. Operations expenditures—housekeeping, maids, wage rate, and maintenance
3. Marketing expenditures—local, tourist, group, and commercial
4. Dividends
5. Borrowing
6. Additional rooms

IV. ADMINISTRATION

The game is computer scored and is programmed in FORTRAN IV, for an IBM 360-65 computer.

V. SOURCE

Participant's Manual, Robert M. Chase, *Cornell Hotel Administration Simulation Exercise,* School of Hotel Administration, Cornell University, Ithaca, New York, 1968.

(*C*)

An Economic Strategy Analysis Game

I. DESCRIPTION

The economic strategy analysis game is an analytical device that can assist government policymakers or students of economics in testing their respective roles in national economic affairs. As a computerized game, operating in an interactive mode, this device becomes a dynamic and adaptable model of the national economy.

The major components of the game are:

1. The Core Macroeconomic Model: The core econometric model simulates the U.S. economy. It is a basic Keynesian model with a series of defined fiscal and monetary policy instruments, some key economic indicators as its primary output, and a data bank containing current and past values of the more important economic variables.

2. A Shock Generator: Exogenous changes are introduced to the gaming environment by the referee. These changes or shocks specify the magnitude and direction of changes imposed on certain variables. Players react to changes or to anticipated changes.

3. The Rules of Play: The roles for two policy players are defined. The rules for manipulating policy instruments and the rules of communication between players are described.

4. The Rules of Operation: The rules of operating the game include descriptions of allowable model modification, information retrieval and dissemination, and the rules governing the referee. Each round of play consists of plotting strategies, testing policies by forecasting players' decisions (or moves), selected exogenous events, and the determination by the core model of the new state of the economy. The game provides the basis for analyzing strategies employed by players relative to stated objective functions or player-modified preferences. The introduction of exogenous events provides a basis for testing decision theories and allows players to test alternative strategies. The gaming-simulation also provides insight into evaluating the decision-making process by analyzing the information requests of the players. In this manner, policy-makers and econometricians are communicating with each other in a gaming environment.

II. TRAINING PURPOSE

The economic strategy analysis game is designed to be used by current and potential economic decision makers and planners who are concerned with formulating and evaluating national economic policies. The gaming simulation techniques employed can be used for educational purposes as well.

III. DECISIONS MADE BY PARTICIPANTS

    A. Fiscal Decisions
        1. Government purchases
        2. Government transfer payments
        3. Debt administration
        4. Tax rates on personal income
        5. Tax rates on business income
        6. Indirect business taxes
    B. Monetary Decisions
        1. Discount rate
        2. Bank reserve requirements
        3. Open market operations
    C. Information Requests

DECISIONS MADE BY ADMINISTRATOR

    A. Exogenous Shocks
        1. Environmental changes
        2. Information exchange
    B. Model Parameters
        1. Variable coefficients
        2. Scoring weights

IV. ADMINISTRATION

This game is computerized with the core model and data bank in storage. Players plot strategies, request information, and make decisions by typing inputs to the system. Outputs show results of decisions, period by period, and scores for objective functions. Period scores are accumulated automatically and summed with bonus scores or penalties at the end of the game.

V. Source

Game descriptions and specifications may be requested from Arnold H. Packer, Senior Analyst, or James A. Zwerneman, Senior Analyst, Operations Research and Economics Division, Research Triangle Institute, P.O. Box 12194, Research Triangle Park, North Carolina.

This work was performed under contract with the U.S. Army Corps of Engineers. Contract No. DA-18-020-ENG 3673.

(*C*)

EEDEMAS
Engineering Economies Decision-Making Simulation

I. Description

The game managers manage a moderate-size but rapidly growing conglomerate. Each team acts as a corporate staff group with responsibility to make recommendations concerning the various capital investment proposals which arise in any of the four divisions of the hypothetical firm.

The actual structure of EEDEMAS differs from the usual notion of gaming and perhaps is more closely related to the concept of the case method. The game might best be characterized as a "game-case." The game is designed for use primarily in relatively small classes so that team size and number of teams may be kept relatively small. (Teams should have no more than four members and the number of teams should be four or five, though the optimal number of teams is a function of the number of administrators.)

Each team must compose a formal report including its analysis and recommendations on each proposal presented to it. The teams receive a memorandum from the division which originated the proposal. The memorandum includes the division's action on the committee's recommendation and, on occasion, the division's request for further clarification, etc. Communication between the game administrator(s) and the players then occurs through a sequential series of proposals, reports, recommendations, and memoranda. Class sessions also include time spent in the detailed critique of a particular team's past decision. Throughout the course of the simulation each team is responsible for all of its previous recommendations.

II. TRAINING PURPOSE

The game is designed to create an experience which mirrors as closely as possible the experience of an engineer or manager who is involved with capital investment decision making.

III. DECISIONS MADE BY PARTICIPANTS

1. Reports
2. Analysis
3. Recommendations

DECISIONS MADE BY ADMINISTRATOR

The administrator is responsible for presenting decision alternatives (capital investment proposals which have arisen in one of the four divisions of the hypothetical firm) to the teams at each meeting. In addition, he prepares memoranda from each division to the teams which include a detailed analysis of each team's recommendation.

IV. ADMINISTRATION

The game is manually scored.

V. SOURCE

John J. Neuhauser, Computer Laboratory, Rensselaer Polytechnic Institute, Troy, New York.

(*M*)

FINANSIM
A Financial Management Simulation

I. DESCRIPTION

The game is a noninteractive financial management game in which the participants make decisions concerning the acquisition and use of capital in a simulated, generalized environment. The game can be played by individuals or teams. The participants in this game must make decisions concerning production scheduling and plant and machine capacity which show the interrelationship of these aspects with financial management. They can finance their company's operations by any of several means normally available to managers—for example, common stock, bank term loans, and debentures.

FINANSIM is designed to be used in conjunction with a text which discusses various aspects of financial management. This text covers the following general areas: financial objectives, financial planning, investment decision making, fund acquisition, and policies for debentures, dividends, and marketable securities.

II. TRAINING PURPOSE

This simulation, when used with the text, is designed to allow the participants to apply the general concepts of financial management.

III. DECISIONS MADE BY PARTICIPANTS

1. Production schedule
2. Marketable securities purchased and sold
3. Ten-year debentures floated and retired
4. Term loans obtained
5. Common stock issued
6. Plant capacity
7. Capital improvements
8. Dividends paid

DECISIONS MADE BY ADMINISTRATOR

1. Number of firms
2. Number of participants per firm
3. Number of periods of play
4. Changing model parameters if desired (e.g., economic index)

IV. ADMINISTRATION

This computerized game can be run on any of four IBM computer systems: 1620, 700/7000, 360, or 1130. Upon adoption, the Publishing Department of the International Textbook Company will provide programmed computer decks free of charge. The computer prints out income statements, position statements, and supplemental information with data about such items as a firm's past performance, its current operations, and forecasts about the future state of the industry. The basic program language is FORTRAN.

V. SOURCE

Paul S. Greenlaw and M. William Frey, *FINANSIM: A Financial Management Simulation,* International Textbook Company, Scranton, Pennsylvania, 1967.

(*C*)

The Gaming Company

I. DESCRIPTION

Individual participants play in identical companies and situations and seek to outperform each other. The company manufactures games (like Parker Brothers) and each player takes the position of final goods warehouse manager. In order to illustrate the concepts of inventory management the player is concerned about the ordering and storage of one of the company's representative games, "The Big Game." The objective of the game is to minimize total costs of inventory storage, ordering, and stockouts over the period of play.

II. TRAINING PURPOSE

This game is used as an introduction to inventory control to illustrate the nature of the costs involved and the utility of developing inventory control decision rules.

III. DECISIONS MADE BY PARTICIPANTS

1. Quantity to order
2. Timing of orders

DECISIONS MADE BY ADMINISTRATOR

1. Sequence of actual sales
2. Length of play

IV. ADMINISTRATION

This is a hand simulation game and has been run in class with the students doing their own scoring on a standard scoring sheet. It is possible to simulate 40 to 50 weeks of company operation in a single class period.

V. SOURCE

D. Clay Whybark, Krannert School, Purdue University, Lafayette, Indiana.

(*M*)

General Electric Management Game (I)

I. Description

This is a manufacturing production scheduling game which can be played with up to ten teams with three to six persons on a team. Game managers attempt to optimize total variable costs associated with inventory holding costs and changes in the size of the workforce by proper selection of quantity to produce.

To start the game, a team will type "RUN" at the remote terminal and specify the number of sets of instructions required, the length of time to be played, and the number of competing firms. In the competition each team answers a series of questions and decides to accept or reject several options. The game objective is to minimize four costs—payroll, hiring and terminations, overtime, and inventory—in an environment where increasing sales are forecast and where there are high penalties for stockouts.

II. Training Purpose

The simulation attempts to give the participant an appreciation of the problems management faces in scheduling and an awareness of the major costs that need to be minimized.

III. Decisions Made by Participants

1. Quantity to be produced
2. Number of employees
3. Purchase of new sales forecasts
4. Purchase of estimates of competitors' results

Decision Made by Administrator

1. Parameter values

IV. ADMINISTRATION

The model is designed for the GE-265 Time Sharing System and is programmed in ALGOL. There is a seven-minute maximum wait between playing periods.

V. SOURCE

R. W. Newman, Consultant—Economic Division Models, Information Systems Service, General Electric Company, 570 Lexington Avenue, New York.

(*C*, 152, 209, 223)

General Electric Management Game (II)

I. DESCRIPTION

This game is basically marketing-oriented but does have manufacturing overtones. It is designed to have two competitive-interactive firms, each with six team members. (If necessary, it may be played with fewer members.) The country is divided into three districts in which each firm sets advertising budgets and selling price while estimating market growth so as to establish production capacity two periods ahead.

During the play the team can purchase such information as estimates of competitors' advertising expenses by district. Unexpected cost changes also occur during the play and it is difficult for either firm to profit if both use the same strategy.

II. TRAINING PURPOSE

The training purpose is to instill recognition in the team members that competition can, and will, react to their moves and strategies.

III. Decisions Made by Participants

1. Production capacity
2. Advertising budget for districts 1, 2, and 3
3. Price for districts 1, 2, and 3

Decision Made by Administrator

1. To inform (or not) the participants before the game that variable costs and delivery costs increase during the play

IV. Administration

The model is designed for the GE-265 Time Sharing System and is programmed in ALGOL. The printout of the play shows some of the features of the game, including the ability to purchase an estimate. The program listing shows where the model parameters are and implies how to change them.

V. Source

R. W. Newman, Consultant—Economic Division Models, Information Systems Service, General Electric Company, 570 Lexington Avenue, New York.

(C, 152, 223)

Industrial Sales Management Game

I. Description

This is an interactive game in which the players act as sales managers for a leading manufacturing company which has recently begun to market a small industrial power tool in competition with several other companies. The total market for each of the twelve periods is fixed, but a company's share of the market varies according to the way it uses its salesmen. When the game begins the manager has eight salesmen whom he can deploy in five market regions. Besides being able to add three more salesmen at specified times during the game, the manager can terminate, train his salesmen, or give them $100 bonuses. To help the manager determine total market potential an economic consultant forecasts regional sales trends with three economic indicators. The manager also receives information concerning total dollar sales volume, each salesman's sales, and his company's profit performance. Each player is evaluated by the profit his company earns. There is a 50 percent margin on sales. Costs are assessed for salesmen's salaries, commissions, and bonuses, as well as for training and termination.

II. Training Purpose

This game teaches the participant to effectively develop and utilize his sales force. It provides him with an opportunity to evaluate the utility of economic indicators and to estimate and react to his competitor's strategies.

III. Decisions Made by Participants

1. Salesmen retained, hired, and terminated
2. Salesmen trained
3. Bonuses granted
4. Allocation of salesmen to regions

IV. Administration

This game is administered by a referee who needs only a slide rule or small desk calculator. If four teams are playing, the referee should plan ten minutes to score the game.

V. Source

Jay R. Greene and Roger L. Sisson, *Dynamic Management Decision Games,* John Wiley & Sons, Inc., New York, 1959, pp. 46-57.

(*M*, 69, 109, 174)

International Operations Simulation
(INTOP)

I. DESCRIPTION

Four to twenty-five teams are formed (three to seven members per team), each to manage an international corporation which may have operations in Brazil, the European Economic Community, and the United States. For tax purposes, all corporations have their home office in Lichtenstein. Each team makes decisions regarding production, marketing, licensing, distribution channels, research and development, and financing of products in each area. Two products in two grades may be marketed in each area. Four possible grades may be produced. Decisions are made in light of economic and business conditions existent in each area. Intercompany transactions involving lending, licensing, and selling may be made. Marketing research information may be purchased. Long- and short-term borrowing and investment are possible. Intracompany transfer of capital and goods may be made. Timing and scheduling are very important. Performance is evaluated on the basis of quarterly income statements and balance sheets.

II. TRAINING PURPOSE

INTOP gives participants experience in making top management decisions regarding the handling of the international operations of a large corporation.

III. DECISIONS MADE BY PARTICIPANTS

1. Production level
2. Plant capacity
3. Product quality
4. Research and development
5. Borrowing
6. Dividends

7. Advertising
8. Markets
9. Marketing research
10. Price
11. Channels of distribution
12. Transfer of capital and goods
13. Product assortment
14. Negotiations between companies

DECISIONS MADE BY ADMINISTRATOR

1. Scheduling of costs, charges, and time lags
2. Running a control game

IV. ADMINISTRATION

Scoring is by computer, either IBM 709, 7090, or 7094, using FORTRAN II, or UNIVAC I-III, using a special language. The simulation is being converted for IBM 360 series and CDC 3300 series.

V. SOURCE

H. B. Thorelli, R. L. Grayes, and L. T. Howells, *International Operations Simulation,* The Free Press of Glencoe, Collier-Macmillan, London, 1964.

(*C,* 93, 174, 266, 267, 270)

International Trade

I. DESCRIPTION

This game simulates international trade between the United States and the Common Market. Participants decide the quantity of cotton and wine to be produced in their respective areas. Given the productive capacities and prices of these products in each area, the participants begin to trade between areas in an effort to improve the satisfaction in their respective home market as depicted by a set of indifference curves for each area.

The teams representing the same area (United States or Common Market) attempt to achieve the highest average indifference curve for their respective area.

II. TRAINING PURPOSE

The game seeks to put international trade in the proper perspective for businessmen. Emphasis is placed upon actions and motivations available to the importers and exporters. Also tariffs may be viewed in their proper setting.

III. DECISIONS MADE BY PARTICIPANTS

1. Combinations of cotton and wine quantities to be produced in the United States or in the Common Market
2. Quantities of these commodities to be exported from the United States or from the Common Market

DECISIONS MADE BY ADMINISTRATOR

1. Tariffs
2. Domestic production when prices exceed domestic costs

IV. ADMINISTRATION

This game is manual. It provides fact sheets containing the game facts and worksheets for recording decisions and their consequences. Indifference curves depicting the preferences of consumers for various combinations of wine and cotton quantities are included.

V. SOURCE

Erwin Rausch. Direct inquiries to Science Research Associates, Inc., 259 East Erie Street, Chicago, Illinois.

(*M*)

Joblot

I. Description

Joblot emphasizes the production aspects of management by using a simulated job shop environment. While most of the decisions are production-oriented, the players must consider problems of other functional areas. The players are given specifications for jobs and can bid on these jobs if they so choose. Job bids are modified by an index of past performance. Jobs are then awarded to the low bidder.

If awarded a job, the player must determine inventory policies, plant size and layout, and, most importantly, scheduling. Monthly decisions are made in which the players can alter any of their previous decisions for incomplete jobs and bid on new jobs. Performance is measured by total profit and job competition performance.

II. Training Purpose

This game offers the players experience in scheduling a job shop operation. It allows them to use specialized scheduling techniques such as PERT and CPM. It also teaches the relationship of production to other functional areas.

III. Decisions Made by Participants

1. Job bids
2. Inventory policies
3. Plant layout
4. Plant expansion
5. Machinery acquisition
6. Production schedule
7. Size of labor force

Decisions Made by Administrator

1. Team makeup
2. Size and complexity of firms

IV. ADMINISTRATION

This computer-scored game is programmed in FORTRAN IV. The game can be made more complex for larger computers or can be simplified for small computers. The game may also be changed to suit different educational and experience levels.

V. SOURCE

Geoffrey Churchill, *Prospectus-Joblot,* School of Business, University of Kansas, Lawrence, Kansas.

This game is not available for use at press time, but should be available shortly thereafter.

(*C*)

Low Bidder

I. DESCRIPTION

This game closely simulates the conditions that face executives in bidding for contracts in manufacturing, construction, and other industries. The participant learns how to select jobs in which there are few bidders, how to estimate the best markup, and how to protect the company against undesirable competition.

From two to twenty-five may play the game simultaneously (although three to eight is the recommended number). Each player begins with the same capital, has access to the same jobs, and is subject to the same operating costs. Each player chooses which job he wants to bid and how much he wants to bid so that he has a reasonable chance of getting enough work at a fair profit. Then the low bidders are determined for each job. One round of play represents an entire year's operation. Play may continue for any number of years or until bankruptcy.

II. Training Purpose

The game is designed to teach the participant to become adept at bidding low enough to get jobs with reasonable frequency, but high enough to cover operating costs and return a fair profit.

III. Decisions Made by Participants

1. Amount to bid on job
2. Amount of markup or profit on job

IV. Administration

This is a manually scored, player calculated game. The game kit includes necessary forms and instructions.

V. Source

Instructions Manual, William R. Park, *Low Bidder*, ENTELEK, Inc., 42 Pleasant Street, Newburyport, Massachusetts.

(*M*)

The Maintenance Game

I. Description

This game is probably best played by individuals, but a team approach may also be used. Each individual acts as the supervisor of the maintenance division of a company. He is responsible for the maintenance of certain major equipment and has at his disposal a preventive maintenance group and a breakdown maintenance group. The latter services equipment when it breaks down. The player's goal is to provide machine maintenance at minimum cost. This is accomplished by altering the size of the total workforce, either by hiring or laying off personnel, and by allocating personnel between the preventive and breakdown crews.

By increasing the preventive maintenance effort, machines run longer between breakdowns. Increasing the size of the breakdown maintenance crews means that a larger number of machines may be handled, but that there may also be more idle crews. If the number of breakdown crews is reduced, more overtime may be incurred to handle breakdowns. By continually analyzing the results of previous decisions and then modifying them, the participant should arrive at the optimal arrangement of work crews. It is suggested that 12 decision periods be used.

II. TRAINING PURPOSE

This game demonstrates several important ideas. The optimal solution to the problem is a "trade-off" situation, in which the cost of machine failure is balanced against the cost of maintenance. The participant learns about the formation of queues. He must use an iterative or trial-and-error method to solve the problem.

III. DECISIONS MADE BY PARTICIPANTS

1. Allocation of personnel between crews
2. Hiring and firing of personnel

IV. ADMINISTRATION

The game is scored by hand or with the assistance of a desk calculator. Five to ten minutes are required for each run of ten teams.

V. SOURCE

F. M. Campbell, *et al.,* "The Maintenance Game," *The Journal of Industrial Engineering,* Vol. XV, No. 1, January-February 1964, pp. 30-36.

(*M*, 35)

Manufacturing Management Laboratory

I. DESCRIPTION

The *Manufacturing Management Laboratory* is a computer-based simulation that is used to train individuals in making top management decisions for a firm involved in manufacturing. Four to ten teams of one to five individuals make up one industry; more than ten teams can be accommodated by forming multiple industries. Each team is placed in charge of a medium-to large-size manufacturing firm.

A single product is manufactured, inventoried, marketed, and sold by each team. Each team or firm competes for sales of the product in a segmented market while attempting to minimize production and marketing costs. The marketing, production, procurement, and finance decisions necessary for effective administration of the firm are all made in a framework of competition. Participants can improve their knowledge of competition and the economy by purchasing marketing research information.

Performance is demonstrated by (1) periodic income statements and balance sheets and (2) how well participants meet the market and growth objectives they set at the beginning of play.

The *Manufacturing Management Laboratory* has the option of allowing game complexity to be added in a stepwise fashion during a training application so that more complex analysis techniques can be employed as the game progresses. The game is of modular construction so that participant decisions can be added to a basic framework as more complexity is desired.

II. TRAINING PURPOSE

The game gives participants experience in making top management decisions in a manufacturing environment.

III. DECISIONS MADE BY PARTICIPANTS

1. Price
2. Production quantity
3. Raw materials purchases
4. Employees hired and fired

5. Plant investment
6. Shipments to zones
7. Advertising (national and zonal)
8. Product R&D
9. Plant maintenance
10. Market research
11. Borrowing
12. Dividends
13. Investment in bonds

DECISIONS MADE BY ADMINISTRATOR

1. Module selection
2. Relative influence of present and historical trends of price, product R&D, advertising on demand
3. Relative zonal demand potentials
4. Plant productivity
5. Labor productivity and wages
6. Productivity of new investments in plant
7. Rates paid on loans
8. Economic series shape
9. Range of expected deviation in accuracy of marketing research
10. Shape of demand curve

IV. ADMINISTRATION

The *Manufacturing Management Laboratory* is administered via remote terminal. All facilities required for play—the terminal and the computer, all materials, and the administrator—are provided by Simulated Environments, Inc. The site of administration is anywhere. The administrator's decisions are made to reflect the customer's situation.

V. SOURCE

Alfred P. West, Jr., Simulated Environments, Inc., University City Science Center, 3401 Market Street, Philadelphia, Pennsylvania.

(*C*)

Manufacturing Management Simulation

I. Description

This game concerns the manufacturing department of a firm which produces four hypothetical items (ambers, bells, clanks, and doodads). These items differ greatly in yearly sales volume, price, degree of seasonality in sales, and type of product sold, but all require the same raw materials (rods, slabs, and tacks).

In this noncompetitive game, the team attempts to effectively control production costs and maintain adequate production levels to meet demands. Participants make decisions concerning raw materials purchases, production levels, personnel matters, and the proper mix of "means" used to increase production efficiency in their modern plant. Each team is charged with the responsibility of minimizing production costs; this involves finding the balance between raw material discounts versus excessive raw material inventory, plant expenditure versus labor productivity, and sales service level versus finished goods inventory costs. Computer output provides profit and loss statements and reports on sales information, plant operations, and inventories.

II. Training Purpose

This game is designed to emphasize the need to balance inventory carrying costs with raw material discount, between finished goods inventory and variable sales demand, and between plant expenditures and labor productivity.

III. Decisions Made by Participants

1. Raw materials purchases
2. Production levels
3. Overtime
4. Hiring and termination of workers
5. Distribution policy
6. Plant and personnel expenditures

IV. ADMINISTRATION

This game is scored by a UNIVAC Solid-State 90 computer program which simulates the manufacturing environment.

V. SOURCE

Participant's and Player's Manual, *Manufacturing Management Simulation,* Remington Rand UNIVAC, Division of Sperry Rand Corporation, 315 Park Avenue South, New York, 1960. Direct inquiries to Director—Management Development, UNIVAC, Division of Sperry Rand Corporation, P.O. Box 8100, Philadelphia, Pennsylvania.

(C, 209)

The Market

I. DESCRIPTION

The participants, in groups of five, represent all the consumers of three products in a market. Each decides independently how to allocate the group's limited funds among the three products and how much money to retain for other needs. In their deliberations the groups are guided by tables which list the satisfactions they are assumed to derive from the consumption or possession of these articles in various quantities. The groups' demands, when added and aligned with the supply, determine market price. As they experiment to attain greatest satisfaction, price equilibrium is established. The price of one of the products is different in the next period of the game and the search for a new balance begins. Success of the individual and of the group is measured by the highest level of satisfaction achieved.

II. TRAINING PURPOSE

The game stresses the interaction of supply and demand, their influence on prices and quantities, and the principles of diminishing marginal utility.

The game demonstrates the effects of price changes in one product on the prices and sales volume of other products and also the equilibrium concept.

III. Decision Made by Participants

1. Quantity of each product to buy with budget

Decisions Made by Administrator

1. Size of budget
2. Supply curve (choice of three) for one of the products

IV. Administration

This is a manual game. Instructions are provided for the administrator. Fact sheets giving details of the game are furnished. The sheets supply curves for sweaters, records, and books; give the satisfaction (in utils) to be derived from owning various amounts of these products; and provide the satisfaction (in utils) derived from retaining various amounts of money. Also included are worksheets on which the student records decisions and computes results.

V. Source

Erwin Rausch. Direct inquiries to Science Research Associates, Inc., 259 East Erie Street, Chicago, Illinois.

(M)

Marketing in Action—A Decision Game

I. Description

The setting for this marketing game is the detergent industry. The industry includes three companies which compete for consumer sales by selling to supermarkets and wholesalers. The detergents sold are used for household laundry, dishwashing, and general purpose cleaning. Companies attempt to differentiate their product on the basis of factors which influence consumer preferences—cleaning power, suds quality, and gentleness. Companies have 25 product possibilities to choose from but may market only two brands at one time. It is possible to purchase information services—for example, brand preference tests and patterns of end-use of products. Each team is required to calculate income statements and balance sheets for its company in the fourth quarter of each year.

II. TRAINING PURPOSE

The primary purpose of the game is to stress the need for market objectives, market strategy formulation, and market strategy implementation. It also emphasizes the interrelationships and interactions of the basic marketing variables of price, product, and promotion.

III. DECISIONS MADE BY PARTICIPANTS

1. Sales forecast units
2. Production units
3. Advertising
4. Number of salesmen
5. Brand characteristics
6. Market research
7. Price
8. Loans

DECISIONS MADE BY ADMINISTRATOR

1. Economic index
2. Introduction of second brand

IV. ADMINISTRATION

Scoring can be done by hand or by computer; the differences in scoring are essentially procedural. The computer program is written in FORTRAN.

V. Source

Student Manual and Instructor's Manual, Ralph L. Day, *Marketing in Action—A Decision Game,* Richard D. Irwin, Homewood, Illinois, Revised, 1968.

(M, C)

Marketing Management Simulation

I. Description

This is a marketing game in which each company sells the same product in three regional markets, with each region having its own market patterns. The teams attempt to market a relatively new product in competitive markets where the major determinants of sales are product marketability and sales force effectiveness. Product marketability is dependent on advertising, selling price, and customer service records, while sales force effectiveness is dependent on ability of salesmen, incentives, and number of salesmen. Sales forecasting and inventory control are also important to company success since errors result in higher costs. Each team is required to keep a running record of its sales and profit for purposes of evaluating its decisions. Market research concerning competition, personnel, advertising, and performance is available to teams.

II. Training Purpose

This game emphasizes the functions and interrelationships of the marketing process. It demonstrates marketing principles and presents typical problems facing the marketing executive.

III. Decisions Made by Participants

1. Regional prices
2. Market research
3. Hiring, training, terminations, and transfers

4. Commissions
5. Advertising—type, dollars, and allocation
6. Production requests from factory
7. Transfers between regions—men and goods

IV. ADMINISTRATION

This computer simulation is programmed for Remington Rand UNIVAC computing systems.

V. SOURCE

Participant's Manual, *Marketing Management Simulation* (U 2007, Rev. 2A), Remington Rand UNIVAC, Division of Sperry Rand Corporation, 315 Park Avenue South, New York, 1960.

Direct inquiries to Director—Management Development, UNIVAC, Division of Sperry Rand Corporation, P.O. Box 8100, Philadelphia, Pennsylvania.

(C, 56, 174, 274)

Market Negotiation Management Game

I. DESCRIPTION

This competitive marketing game involves five companies—two manufacturers and three wholesalers. The manufacturers produce a single item to sell to the wholesalers at a negotiated price. The wholesalers, in turn, sell these items to retailers, who are represented by the referee. (Market information is provided to assist the decision makers in forecasting the retailers' needs.)

In order to gain a profit the manufacturer must cover fixed costs, inventory carrying costs, processing costs, and material costs. If he decides to borrow; he will also have interest charges. During the negotiating period, the manufacturers and wholesalers meet individually to work out short- or long-term agreements. The wholesalers submit forms to the referee listing the quantity of items they are willing to sell at specific prices. The referee merely accepts the least expensive goods to fill the retailers' needs. Wholesalers receive income from item sales and have fixed expenses and item costs. The performance of each team is evaluated in terms of profits gained.

II. TRAINING PURPOSE

This game provides valuable experience in business negotiation. Manufacturing and pricing decisions must be made in view of manufacturing costs and market trends.

III. DECISIONS MADE BY PARTICIPANTS

A. Manufacturers
   1. Raw material purchases
   2. Price to wholesalers
   3. Money borrowed
   4. Merger possibilities

B. Wholesalers
   1. Items purchased
   2. Price paid for items
   3. Price to retailers
   4. Money borrowed
   5. Merger possibilities

DECISIONS MADE BY ADMINISTRATOR

   1. Retailers' purchases
   2. Raw material costs
   3. Modification of game parameters

IV. ADMINISTRATION

Because most of the forms are completed by the players, this game is scored very easily. The administrator must indicate which wholesalers made sales and check the participants' forms.

V. Source

Jay R. Greene and Roger L. Sisson, *Dynamic Management Decision Games,* John Wiley & Sons, Inc., New York, 1959, pp. 70-83.

(M, 109)

Marketplan

I. Description

This is a noncomputerized game of total market planning which treats all the major product and promotional aspects of marketing management. The participants are faced with a large number of decisions to make in the areas of market analysis, product planning, sales, advertising management, research and development, and merger or acquisition. They must interpret economic trends and competitive information and develop an annual marketing plan based on four quarterly plans. Each quarterly plan must be flexible enough to cope with random variables introduced into the game.

The game is played with three teams of three to eighteen members. Each team, representing a company, starts with one-third of the market for either a consumer or industrial product—or both—and through its planning strives to create market leadership. Game time is usually one year. Quarterly operating statements and competitive information reports are furnished the teams; at the end of the four quarters the team with the most accumulated net profit is the winner. Real time can be either one or two consecutive days of seven or eight hours each.

II. Training Purpose

The training purpose is to integrate all the major product and promotional decisions of market planning into a realistic learning experience which will enable the participants to project the lessons into their real-life situations. Further purpose is to provide participants with experience in the group dynamics of decision making under pressure.

III. Decisions Made by Participants

1. Segmentation of a market
2. Marketing research and development, including use and interpretation of research reports
3. Interpretation of economic trends
4. Interpretation of competitive information
5. Product research and development
6. Product innovation
7. Product branding (brand naming, brand theming)
8. Pricing
9. Production forecasting
10. Product scheduling
11. Assignment of product sales features
12. Selection of advertising media (print, broadcast, collateral)
13. Selection of sales promotion media
14. Advertising to end-users, to the trade, and to manufacturers
15. Advertising planning over a campaign year
16. Advertising agency selection and integration
17. Assignment of advertising objectives
18. Selection, motivation, and compensation of a salesforce
19. Territorial and quota assignments for a salesforce
20. Integration of salesforce objectives with advertising objectives
21. Selection of sales services
22. Hiring, firing, and training of salesforce
23. Assignment of sales objectives
24. Merger and acquisition

IV. Administration

The model design, necessary forms, and scoring are all furnished by the game source in a personal presentation of the game, followed by professional evaluation and critique. The game is available through personal presentation only.

V. Source

Hanan & Son, Management Consultants, P. O. Box 1234, Grand Central Station, New York.

(M)

MARKSIM
A Marketing Decision Simulation

I. Description

Each participant operates as the manager of a manufacturing firm which competes with two other firms in the industry. The participant must make decisions as to price and quality of product, shipment to distribution centers, level of production, national advertising expenditures, and advertising allowances to retailers. Goods manufactured by the firm are distributed either through the company's own distribution centers or through wholesalers to the retailers. The manager may vary the amount of quality built into his products in order to supply the demands of three different market segments—low, medium, and high quality products. Performance is evaluated on the basis of quarterly income statements and balance sheets.

MARKSIM is designed to be used in conjunction with a text which discusses various aspects of marketing management. In the later chapters, the text provides discussions on various topics pertaining to the game such as market segmentation, quality, advertising, and distribution channel management.

II. Training Purpose

MARKSIM provides experience in making marketing decisions in a competitive situation. The participants are forced to anticipate demand and to vary their marketing mix accordingly.

III. Decisions Made by Participants

1. Production level
2. Product quality
3. Shipment to new distribution
4. Advertising
5. Marketing research
6. Retail list price
7. Repayment of debt and loans

Decisions Made by Administrator

1. Number of industries
2. Number of participants per firm
3. Number of periods of play
4. Changing model parameters if desired (for example, market potentials)

IV. Administration

MARKSIM is programmed for use on the IBM 1620, 700/7000 series, and 360 series. Upon adoption, the Publishing Department of the International Textbook Company will provide these programmed computer decks free of charge. MARKSIM has also been programmed for CDC 3300/6400 and IBM 1130 computers. The basic program language is FORTRAN.

V. Source

Participant's Manual, Paul S. Greenlaw and Fred W. Kniffin, *MARKSIM, A Marketing Decision Simulation*, International Textbook Company, Scranton, Pennsylvania, 1964.

(C, 112)

Materials Inventory Management Game

I. DESCRIPTION

The game is designed to create in the participant an awareness of the key inventory costs and to illustrate the use of the basic economic order quantity (EOQ) formula and sales forecasting. The simulation assumes the participant has little or no knowledge of EOQ formulas or forecasting techniques. A single item, which is representative of the other items in stock, is controlled by the participant.

In the first pass, the participant runs the materials department without exposure to analytical techniques. After this pass, the instructor discusses EOQ formulas and sales forecasting techniques. The participant is then ready for Pass 2 in which he uses an EOQ formula and a moving average forecasting technique. The total costs for Passes 1 and 2 are compared to demonstrate the advantages of EOQ formulas and the lag of moving average forecasting. Each decision requires 10-15 minutes.

II. TRAINING PURPOSE

The training purpose of this inventory game is to demonstrate to the participant the necessity of balancing order costs, carrying costs, and stockout costs.

III. DECISION MADE BY PARTICIPANTS

    1. Order quantity

DECISIONS MADE BY ADMINISTRATOR

    1. Economic index
    2. All costs can be changed to change the game setting

IV. ADMINISTRATION

The game is manual and costs are computed by the administrator.

V. Source

Jay R. Greene and Roger L. Sisson, *Dynamic Management Decision Games,* John Wiley & Sons, Inc., New York, 1959, pp. 11-17.

(M, 109)

Materials Management Simulation

I. Description

This is a competitive-interactive materials management game which can be played by up to ten teams or individuals. The ideal number of participants on a team is five. These persons take the part of the president, controller, sales manager, purchasing agent, and warehouse manager. The team simulates the operation of a distribution company which buys and sells three products; the products are purchased in large lots and sold in smaller lots. The major activities of the simulated company are purchasing, warehousing, and marketing. All teams begin operations under the same conditions. They are furnished with purchasing and sales volume for the previous year. Each period of play represents one month.

II. Training Purpose

The training purpose is to give participants practice in using analytical methods, operations research, and scientific management in a realistic environment.

III. Decisions Made by Participants

1. Number of advertising programs per product
2. Purchase and selling price for each product
3. Amount of funds borrowed
4. Funds paid back
5. Quantities of each product ordered

6. Number of salesmen hired and released
7. Operations improvement
8. Units dumped

IV. Administration

This game may be either manually or electronically computed. A computer program in FORTRAN for use on an IBM 1620 is included with the game.

A list of purchasing and sales potential for the 12 periods is supplied in the Player's Manual.

V. Source

Participant's Manual, William M. Hawkins and Ronald W. Boling, *Materials Management Simulation,* 1963, Bureau of Business and Economic Research, College of Business Administration, University of Tennessee, Knoxville, Tennessee.

(M, C)

M.I.T. Marketing Game

I. Description

This is a competitive marketing game in which management teams of three to five players sell floor polishers to retailers in nine census regions of the United States. Four companies compete in a market which, although highly unstable, seems to be a function of shifts in personal disposable income. Many of these sales are made through independent distributors who may process and generate orders, maintain inventories, handle payments, and deploy their own sales force. Other sales are made directly to retailers by the company's own salesmen. These salesmen also provide information to the retailers to assist them in making sales to the final consumer.

The product quality, as defined by characteristics, has a great effect on final sales to consumers. Besides being more desirable to the customer, high quality products induce greater sales efforts by the distributors and retailers. Sales are affected by advertising in trade and consumer magazines, promotional campaigns, price, and retail credit.

In addition to these decisions, which are concerned primarily with marketing, the companies must make decisions as to the volume and quality of product to produce, the means of finance, and other general management decisions.

II. Training Purpose

The game allows its players to make decisions in a complex situation surrounded by uncertainty. It improves skills in analysis, decision making, communications, and human relations.

III. Decisions Made by Participants

1. Production volume
2. Product characteristics
3. Advertising
4. Financing
5. Distributors and/or allocation, salary, and commissions of salesmen
6. Communications to distributor
7. Dividends
8. Pricing
9. Introduction of new brands
10. Information purchases

Decisions Made by Administrator

1. Actions of distributors
2. Actions of retailers
3. Actions of consumers

IV. Administration

This computer-scored game is coded in FORTRAN II FAP for the IBM 7094 with a running time of about 20 minutes excluding I/0 and coded in FORTRAN IV for the IBM 360.

V. SOURCE

Player's Manual, *M.I.T. Marketing Game,* Massachusetts Institute of Technology, Alfred P. Sloan School of Management, 50 Memorial Drive, Cambridge, Massachusetts.

(C, 183, 259)

Monopologs

I. DESCRIPTION

The individual participant or team manages an Air Force supply system. The system includes one depot and five air bases in a hypothetical logistics system. Although the game setting is an Air Force logistics system, the game applies equally well to industry—for example, the depot could be a wholesaler or toolroom, and the bases could be the customers. The key problem is the uncertainty associated with the demand for spare parts. In view of this variable demand, the game manager selects a strategy designed to minimize total cost by balancing the cost of carrying stock, cost of running out of stock, and costs of ordering parts. The participant must consider specific costs such as part costs, setup costs, expediting costs, and others.

The game begins with one base in operation; others are added later as play progresses. The manager computes his own costs and is able to compare them with the total costs of others who have played the game. Demand is developed by random numbers or a spinner similar to a roulette wheel to dramatize the randomness of requests for spare parts. This approach allows the participant to play the game again and not repeat the same conditions.

II. TRAINING PURPOSE

The purpose of this simulation is to provide an inventory management situation in which the participant will gain insight into various inventory problems and become familiarized with interaction of a supply system. It also stresses the effect of management decisions on cost.

III. Decisions Made by Participants

    1. Procurement of new parts
    2. Repair of parts
    3. Distribution of parts to bases

IV. Administration

The game is manual. It can be administered by the participant or a game administrator.

V. Source

Manual, Jean R. Renshaw and Annette Heuston, *The Game Monopologs* (RM-1917-1), The RAND Corporation, Attention: Reports Department, 1700 Main Street, Santa Monica, California. Revised ed., 1960.

(M, 34)

Monopologs: Toolroom Management Game

I. Description

This game is an adaptation of the original *Monopologs* game developed by the RAND Corporation. The authors of this game have substituted a toolroom and four production departments for an Air Force depot and four bases. This adaptation demonstrates how the game can be adjusted for industrial use if desired. Except for the game setting, the games are similar.

In this game the players, who act as toolroom managers, are given the responsibility of supplying dies to the four production departments of their firm. They are given the choice of purchasing new dies from a supplier, constructing the dies from steel stock, or repairing used dies of the firm. Lead times and costs are assigned to each of the options, including extra set-up costs for each method. There are also costs for storing and transporting the dies within the plant. A severe penalty cost is assessed to the toolroom department if any of the production departments depletes its supply of dies. The player's object is to minimize his costs over a 30-week period.

The demand for the dies by the production departments is generated manually, based on past probabilities of need. This same method is used to determine which of the replaced dies are repairable and which are not.

II. Training Purpose

This game dramatizes to the players the need to develop a systematic, coordinated plan to equate the need for dies with the cost of carrying dies.

III. Decisions Made by Participants

1. Number of dies produced
2. Means of obtaining dies

Decisions Made by Administrator

1. Number of dies needed by each department
2. Number of repairable and nonrepairable dies

IV. Administration

Monopologs is manually scored, using specially designed forms for computing costs. The scoring of the 30-week period can generally be done in 15 minutes.

V. Source

Forrest M. Campbell and E. Robert Ashworth, "Monopologs: Management Decision Making Game Applied to Toolroom Management," *Journal of Industrial Engineering*, Vol. XI, No. 5 (September-October 1960), pp. 372-377.

For the original *Monopologs* game see Manual, Jean R. Renshaw and Annette Heuston, *The Game Monopologs* (RM-1917-1), The RAND Corporation, Attention: Reports Department, 1700 Main Street, Santa Monica, California. Revised ed. 1960.

(M, 34)

MSU Investment Game

I. DESCRIPTION

This game, which is used in conjunction with a total enterprise game such as *MSU Management Game,* emphasizes investment problems in a competitive environment. Before the investment game is begun the players play the general management game for four quarters.

The participants are then divided into three groups: promoters, over-the-counter dealers, and investors. The promoters are further divided into teams of three to five persons. Each of these teams manages a company in the total enterprise game. They begin with a specified amount of cash on hand, but may advantageously gain additional funds by financing. The over-the-counter dealers are assigned to specialize in the securities of a specific company. At the beginning of the game investors are assigned to dealers, but they are free to change dealers at any time.

The objective of the participants, each of whom begins the game with equal amounts of cash, is to maximize their own income from dealing with stocks and bonds. The promoters must necessarily be concerned with the performance of their company. The game is played in eight quarterly decisions.

II. TRAINING PURPOSE

This game is designed to allow the participants to become familiar with the problems of starting and operating a small business.

III. DECISIONS MADE BY PARTICIPANTS

Promoters
  1. Company operations
  2. Company financing
  3. Personal investments

Over-the-counter dealers
   1. Government bond purchases
   2. Securities prices
   3. Personal investments
Investors
   1. Personal investments

DECISIONS MADE BY ADMINISTRATOR

   1. Total enterprise game
   2. Participant assignments
   3. Cash on hand

IV. ADMINISTRATION

This game can be scored either manually or by a computer. The author warns that about 20 hours of clerical assistance per period are necessary to administer the game.

V. SOURCE

Richard C. Henshaw, Jr., *MSU Investment Game,* Michigan State University, East Lansing, Michigan, 1961.

(M, C)

The National Economy

I. DESCRIPTION

Participants are divided into teams representing the consumer goods industry, luxury goods industry, and producers goods industry. These three industries make decisions on how to run the economy. The industries face an increasing population requiring more industrial capacity, more income, and more jobs. For these goals to be achieved the participants must overcome such restrictions as inadequate investment or reduced employment when there is excess industrial capacity. Success is measured by the average employment level and by the stability of the economic growth that is achieved.

II. TRAINING PURPOSE

The game is designed to enable the participants to understand more clearly some of the forces that influence the national economy—consumption, investment, inflation, unemployment levels, savings, and the role of the government.

III. DECISION MADE BY PARTICIPANTS

1. Investment by each industry

IV. ADMINISTRATION

The game includes various worksheets on which to record decisions and their consequences and fact sheets. Game instructions are provided along with a sample to follow.

V. SOURCE

Participant's Manual, Erwin Rausch, *The National Economy,* Science Research Associates, 259 East Erie Street, Chicago, Illinois, 1968.

(M)

One-Page Retailing Game

I. DESCRIPTION

This very simple game is designed to show the effects of price in a competitive situation under varying conditions. Two players have franchises to sell baseball figures at a baseball game. Each sets his price separately, the only variable in the game. A competitive price index is figured for each, using a prescribed formula and multiplied by a noncompetitive price index which varies inversely with price. This number is multiplied by a base demand to determine units sold. Fixed and variable expenses are subtracted from sales income to determine net profit. The players compete for ten games; the player showing the highest total profit (net) is the winner.

II. TRAINING PURPOSE

This game is designed to show the effects of price on sales under varying conditions, such as variation in the elasticity and importance of competitive price differences.

III. DECISION MADE BY PARTICIPANTS

1. Price

DECISIONS MADE BY ADMINISTRATOR

1. Competitive price index formula
2. Noncompetitive price index table

IV. ADMINISTRATION

This hand-scored game can be played with pencil and paper by two participants with no assistance from the administrator once the competitive price index formula and the noncompetitive price index table are prepared. These two factors can be varied easily by the administrator to show differing effects of price and elasticity.

V. SOURCE

Robert E. Schellenberger, "A Computerized Multipurpose Management Game Applied to Retailing," *Journal of Retailing*, Vol. 41, No. 4, Winter 1965-1966, pp. 10-20.

(M)

Operation Suburbia

I. Description

This planning game is a highly interactive game involving five companies which own a total of 16 plots of land. These five companies are very different in their business orientations and general goals. They are involved in five different types of businesses: shopping center development, investment, manufacturing, land holding, and home construction. All the teams, except the investment company, own a certain combination of the plots and desire another combination. The investment company wants to sell its three plots at the highest possible prices. All but the home building and the investment companies begin with cash on hand.

During the playing period each team may send one member to confer with a single member of another team. Through these conferences, each team can buy and sell land and options to buy land in order to meet its general goals. Each conferee must try to strike the best possible bargain to fulfill the specific needs of his team. Because the teams are constantly buying and selling land, the interaction takes place in an ever-changing environment.

II. Training Purpose

Operation Suburbia is an interaction game which stresses the necessity for communication within and among groups in the planning and organizing of work to reach objectives. The participants learn to develop alternative solutions to their problems in a complex and changing environment.

III. Decisions Made by Participants

1. Land bought and sold
2. Land prices
3. Options bought, sold, and executed

DECISIONS MADE BY ADMINISTRATOR

1. Beginning situation
2. General goals
3. Time available

IV. ADMINISTRATION

This game is administered by observers who take notes on the actions of each team and evaluate their performance. They note such things as how well each group organizes itself, states its problem, explores the alternatives, gathers and analyzes facts, and decides and follows its best alternative. The game requires about one hour to administer.

V. SOURCE

Allen A. Zoll, 3rd, *Dynamic Management Education,* 120 Bell Street, Seattle, Washington.

(M)

Personnel Assignment Management Game

I. DESCRIPTION

This is a noncompetitive game in which the players act as regional branch managers for an accounting firm. Their most important job is to assign audit teams to jobs in their area. A great deal of variation exists in the abilities of the teams to perform various types of jobs. The player is given a form assigning efficiency ratings for each of the teams for the various job types. The objective of each player is to maximize the efficiency with which his teams are deployed. The number of jobs may be greater or less than the number of teams, but the objective remains the same.

After the players have gone through three or four periods, the game is stopped. The instructor then presents some basic techniques of linear programming. After this interim, play is again continued with a few more allocation problems of increasing difficulty. Hopefully, both the quality of the solutions and the ease with which they are completed will improve.

II. Training Purpose

This game shows how linear programming can be used to find an optimum solution to a problem involving assignment of men to jobs.

III. Decision Made by Participants

    1. Allocation of teams

Decisions Made by Administrator

    1. Team efficiencies
    2. Jobs to be fulfilled
    3. Teams available
    4. Time available

IV. Administration

This game is scored by comparing each player's allocation of his auditing teams with the optimum allocation given by the linear programming solution.

V. Source

Jay R. Greene and Roger L. Sisson, *Dynamic Management Decision Games*, John Wiley & Sons, Inc., New York, 1959, pp. 18-24.

(M, 109)

PERTSIM

I. DESCRIPTION

In this game the players place bids for a road construction project and supervise its completion. For every bid the player is assigned a probability of getting the bid, based on the rank order of his bid and the actual dollar differences between his bid and the other bids. Total expected profit is computed by multiplying this probability to obtain and supervise every construction project.

Supervision consists of deciding when to begin certain activities and the speed with which they are expedited. This information is the input data for the computer which prints out the time and costs for each activity. Additional information can be purchased to assist the players in making decisions. After each output is received, the player makes new decisions concerning the activities to be started and expedited. Total expected profit is the sole measure of performance.

II. TRAINING PURPOSE

PERTSIM allows the players to use PERT and CPM techniques in a simulated environment. The computer output and subsequent decisions allow the players to analyze their position and make new decisions.

III. DECISIONS MADE BY PARTICIPANTS

1. Cost and time bids
2. Activities begun and expedited
3. Information purchased

DECISION MADE BY ADMINISTRATOR

1. Parameters

IV. Administration

This is a computer scored game. A small manual simulator is provided in the PERTSIM text to allow the players to learn the important aspects of the game. The game is first played using this hand simulator. The administrator need not make any decisions, but may change the parameters if he wishes.

V. Source

Lloyd A. Swanson and Harold L. Pazer, *PERTSIM*, International Textbook Company, Scranton, Pennsylvania, 1969.

(C)

Portfolio Management Game

I. Description

This is a noncompetitive game in which the players act as investment managers for four clients with different needs, backgrounds, and money available for investment purposes. The objective for the players is to tailor an investment program for each client, choosing from a listing of 14 common stocks and 16 corporate bonds.

The players are provided with specific information about each client, concerning such things as occupation, age, yearly income, present and future cash needs, and marital and family status. Financial information for the past three years is also provided for each of the corporations in which the players can buy stock or bonds. The players are also given ten indices of the state of the economy for the preceding three years.

All sales and purchases of bonds are made on January 1. The client must pay all the fees normally included with such investments, such as odd lot fees, state and federal taxes, and SEC fees. All bonds, which must be traded in $1,000 units, have a constant maturity date of 30 years. Stock dividends and splits are assumed to take place on January 2. Using such information the players build a portfolio to suit the needs and desires of each client.

II. Training Purpose

The *Portfolio Management Game* teaches the player to fit the needs and desires of specific clients with the available corporate stocks and bonds.

III. Decisions Made by Participants

1. Stocks and bonds bought
2. Stocks and bonds sold

Decision Made by Administrator

1. Number of periods played

IV. Administration

This game requires a subjective judgment by the administrator who evaluates the investment policies the players have made for each client. No single measure such as cash flow, income, or market value is of overriding importance.

V. Source

Player's Manual, R. Bruce Ricks, *Portfolio Management Game,* Prentice-Hall, Inc., Englewood Cliffs, New Jersey, 1965.

(M)

Production

I. Description

Production employs a game board which depicts a factory production line and a toy model which represents a product to be assembled by the competing teams. Each team consists of a director of personnel, a plant foreman, and six "skilled workers." The model is moved from assembly station to assembly station on the game board, each player participating in the assembly of the product. The object of the game is for each team to meet a production quota by learning to assemble the model quickly, without making mistakes. Each mistake represents a defect in the product and slows the production process. The team which can reduce defects and increase productivity most effectively is the winner.

Each player is paid on a piece-rate basis. If total productivity increases, individual earnings rise. The director of personnel may change the position of players in the production line. At the conclusion of the game, each player decides whether or not he would like to have the same player next to him in the future. An individual winner is selected on the basis of income generated and his acceptance by other workers.

II. Training Purpose

The training purpose of the game is to illustrate the importance of good teamwork in increasing production efficiency and to show the human relations problems involved in establishing this teamwork. It emphasizes the idea that high productivity with low defects benefits both labor and management.

III. Decisions Made by Participants

None is recorded; however, each participant does his best to contribute to "zero defects."

IV. Administration

The administrator, in this manually scored game, scores the teams on their ability to increase productivity and decrease defects. He also distributes points to individuals based on the number of units they produce.

V. Source

Production: A Management Training Game, Abt Associates, Inc., 55 Wheeler Street, Cambridge, Massachusetts.

(*M*)

Production-Manpower Game

I. DESCRIPTION

This production scheduling game simulates a paint factory. Two management teams are presented with identical situations and information. They attempt to minimize total variable costs related to production—given a forecast of demand, current manpower, and current inventory. In general, inventory and overtime are used as cushions to absorb forecasting errors. The game is based on the model developed by Holt, Modigliani, Muth, and Simon in their book *Planning Production, Inventories, and Work Force* (Prentice-Hall, Inc., Englewood Cliffs, New Jersey, 1960). The computer calculates costs, forecast and actual orders, production, inventory, and labor force for both teams; it also calculates the optimal production and manpower quantities based on the HMMS model along with the optimal costs that can be compared with the two teams' performances.

II. TRAINING PURPOSE

The game model is designed to stress the factors relevant to scheduling decisions and to demonstrate how the computer can aid the decision maker in arriving at sound decisions.

III. DECISIONS MADE BY PARTICIPANTS

1. Number of gallons of paints to produce
2. Size of workforce

DECISIONS MADE BY ADMINISTRATOR

1. Initial inventory
2. Initial manpower
3. Forecast orders

IV. ADMINISTRATION

The game is programmed in FORTRAN for the IBM 1620 computer.

V. SOURCE

John J. Bachhuber, *Production-Manpower Game,* 1620 General Program Library (10.2.009), 1958. Requests for manuals and computer documentation should be directed to Program Information Department, Program Distribution Center, International Business Machines Corp., 40 Saw Mill Road, Hawthorne, New York.

(*C*)

PRODUCTPLAN

I. DESCRIPTION

This is a noncomputerized game of product planning which treats all the major product and promotional aspects of new-product planning. The participants are faced with a large number of decisions to make in the areas of market analysis, product technology, costing and price feasibility, research and development, acquisition of supplementary capabilities, and test marketing. They must interpret economic trends and competitive information and develop a new-product plan based on four quarterly plans. Each quarterly plan must be flexible enough to cope with random variables introduced into the game.

The game is played with three teams of three to eighteen members. Each team, representing a company, tries to develop a new consumer or industrial product—or both—and to create a market for it. Game time is usually one year. Quarterly operating statements and competitive information reports are furnished the teams; at the end of four quarters the team whose product has earned the most accumulated net profit is the winner. Real time is one day of seven to eight hours.

II. TRAINING PURPOSE

The training purpose is to integrate all the major product and promotional decisions of new-product planning into a realistic learning experience which will enable the participants to project the lessons into their real-life situations. Further purpose is to provide participants with experience in the group dynamics of decision making under pressure.

III. DECISIONS MADE BY PARTICIPANTS

1. Segmentation of a market
2. Product research and development
3. Product creation and innovation
4. Product branding (brand naming, brand theming)
5. Pricing-feasibility testing
6. Production forecasting for test marketing
7. Product scheduling
8. Marketing research and development, including use and interpretation of research reports
9. Interpretation of economic trends
10. Interpretation of competitive information
11. Acquisition of supplementary capabilities
12. Test market advertising and sales promotion

IV. ADMINISTRATION

The model design, necessary forms, and scoring are all furnished by the game source in personal presentation of the game, followed by professional evaluation and critique. The game is available through personal presentation only. This game has been adapted for play as a correspondence course through the mail, entitled *Product Game*. Decisions are mailed periodically by players for scoring and critique.

V. Source

Hanan & Son, Management Consultants, P.O. Box 1234, Grand Central Station, New York.

(M)

Production Scheduling Management Game

I. Description

This noncompetitive production control game requires that the players schedule jobs on three machines in a production department. Machines A, B, and C run on an eight-hour per day basis with different costs for each of the machines. Overtime work allows the player to schedule the machines an additional eight hours a day at higher costs. At the beginning of each simulated three-day period, forms are provided which show the jobs available, revenue for each job completed on schedule, material costs, and the time and sequence of the necessary production. The participant must decide which jobs to accept and the exact production schedule he wishes to implement. Production of the jobs is such that operations must be completed once they are begun, operations must follow in sequence, and no machine can handle more than one job at a time. Costs are assessed for machine usage, materials, labor, sales expense, and overhead. An income statement is provided to evaluate the players' profit performance.

II. Training Purpose

This game stresses the problems encountered in scheduling production facilities. The desired objective is that the players will develop systematic procedures, such as Gantt charts and other tools, for solving their scheduling problems and will realize the value of such procedures.

III. Decisions Made by Participants

1. Jobs accepted
2. Production schedules

Decisions Made by Administrator

1. Jobs available
2. Decision time available

IV. Administration

The referee scores this game manually, using forms provided, to derive the player's income statement.

V. Source

Jay R. Greene and Roger L. Sisson, *Dynamic Management Decision Games,* John Wiley & Sons, Inc., New York, 1959, pp. 38-45.

(*M*, 109)

Production Scheduling Simulation

I. Description

This management game is designed to simulate the scheduling of production facilities in a company where three different products are being manufactured. Several of the production steps or operations involved are common to the processing of two or even all three of the products. The game deals with one area of a company's operation and can be played by either individuals or teams.

Based upon usage histories, decisions are made regarding what quantities of each product to produce weekly and how to go about production of these quantities in order to meet shipping deadlines as established by the game umpire. The establishment of a deadline (which may vary with the product, and be set for any day of the week) introduces the element of time. The time factor allows the introduction of an option: production at minimum costs or production in minimum time.

Production schedules are required to be flexible enough to allow time for unforeseen machine breakdowns. The game umpire or a computer determines which machines suffer mechanical failures and how much time is required for subsequent repairs.

The game is not competitive in the sense that the decisions of one team will affect the condition of the other teams. However, the teams play against an environment, and a rivalry can be introduced between teams by comparing intermediate and final results. The framework of the game is such that the basis for comparison can be established as any of several criteria. Changing certain parameters will allow for the establishment of new criteria at any time. The criterion for comparison could be minimization of manufacturing costs or the minimization of delivery times or a combination of the two.

II. Training Purpose

This game is designed to teach the fundamental techniques involved in the functioning of a specific industrial area; to provide a problem situation such that the consequences of the decisions made influence many subsequent decisions; to demonstrate the value of careful planning; to encourage discovery and analysis of advantages and disadvantages of alternative strategies; to provide a dynamic situation for learning various management skills; and to provide future managers with practice, insight into, and improvement of their main function—decision making.

III. Decisions Made by Participants

1. What quantity to produce of the three products
2. Production at minimum cost (or)
3. Production in minimum time

4. Labor force changes and assignments
5. Number of shifts
6. Scheduling of overtime

DECISIONS MADE BY ADMINISTRATOR

1. Which machines suffer mechanical failure
2. How long for repair time
3. Production deadlines

IV. ADMINISTRATION

The game may be hand scored or scored by a computer. The game is written in FORTRAN and is adaptable to any computer system with either a FORTRAN II or FORTRAN IV compiler.

V. SOURCE

Gray J. Arnold, S. Kyle Reed, and Robert S. Hoeke, *Production Scheduling Simulation,* Center for Business and Economic Research, Knoxville, Tennessee, 1964. Copies of the manual may be obtained through Center for Business and Economic Research, University of Tennessee, Knoxville, Tennessee.

(*M, C*)

Production Simulation Project

I. DESCRIPTION

This production model simulates the operation of a factory which consists of three departments, four types of inventory, and fifteen final products. The entire simulation is computer controlled; the participants submit decisions (or subroutines) to the computer, which calculates results and provides other needed information. Participants attempt to minimize total relevant costs—

regular payroll, hiring and layoff, overtime, and inventory—by properly scheduling production and labor force. The main program includes the model from Holt, Modigliani, Muth, and Simon, *Linear Decision Rule for Production and Employment Scheduling* (Prentice-Hall, Inc., Englewood Cliffs, New Jersey, 1960), and uses it to calculate suggested workforce and production for the next decision period. The computer output includes information about demand, inventory levels, overtime, regular time, costs, production units, and other information.

II. Training Purpose

The objective of this simulation is to allow the participant to find the decision processes which reduce costs by better production and workforce scheduling.

III. Decisions Made by Participants

1. Quantity to produce of each of the 15 final products
2. Quantity to produce in the subassembly and parts departments
3. Quantity of each of the eight raw materials to order
4. Size of workforce in each of the departments

IV. Administration

The exercise is completely computer controlled. The model is programmed in FORTRAN IV and presently used on the IBM-7090.

V. Source

Student's Manual, Production Simulation Project, Graduate School of Business, Stanford University, Stanford, California. Direct inquiries to Peter R. Winters.

(C)

Project SOBIG

I. Description

This is a stock market game in which each team, comprised of three members, is involved in buying, selling, and holding shares in four corporations. The teams in the game are acting as investment committees of banks and as such will invest in the stock market. Each team will start with a portfolio of stocks held as well as a cash account. As in an actual stock market, characteristics of the stock and its activity are reflected in the stock's value.

Teams will be given their financial status at the beginning of each period; the net accumulated gain or loss will indicate how well the team has done. Each day of real time equals one year of game time.

II. Training Purpose

The game is designed to teach the functional relationships of the stock market and the transactions involved in these relationships.

III. Decisions Made by Participants

1. Allocation of funds to 11-month bonds rather than stocks (if desired)
2. Cash balance
3. Stocks traded
4. Stocks held
5. Use of limit orders
6. Purchase of information from security analyst

Decision Made by Administrator

1. Adjustment of team account

IV. Administration

Official game forms include balance sheets, financial reports, and annual summaries of account. The game time is one year. There are three 12-minute trading sessions per quarter. The game is manually computed.

V. Source

John L. Kennedy, Department of Psychology, Princeton University, Princeton, New Jersey. Direct inquiries to Robert Graham, School of Business and Technology, Oregon State University, Corvallis, Oregon.

(*M*)

PROSIM: A Production Management Simulation

I. Description

Any number of companies may be formed, each to manage the production operations of a firm. For each decision period, which represents one day's operations, the firm makes production-oriented decisions for three products, each of which is processed on two sequential production lines. Fluctuating three-day demand schedules for each product must be met, or back-ordering costs are incurred. Each day, the firm may make expenditures both for quality control, in an effort to reduce its reject rate, and for plant maintenance, to decrease the probabilities of incurring machine breakdowns. Four machines are available on each of the company's two production lines. Each day decisions must be made as to which worker (from a pool of available operators) should be assigned to each machine, whether each worker should be trained to increase his proficiency, and how many hours and which product should be scheduled on each machine.

The firm has the option of placing regular and/or expedited raw materials orders each day, incurs inventory carrying costs, and is subject to set-up costs when products are shifted from one machine to another from one day to the next. Additionally, present workers may be laid off or terminated and new operators hired. The basic objective of each firm is to maximize its efficiency by minimizing its actual costs relative to a standard cost/unit structure provided the firm.

II. Training Purpose

PROSIM is designed to be used in conjunction with a text which discusses various aspects of production management. It gives participants experience in making a number of interrelated production management decisions in a dynamic setting. The PROSIM text contains chapters illustrating how various production management concepts and analytical tools (e.g., inventory control models) may be applied by the participants in managing their firms.

III. Decisions Made by Participants

1. Quality control expenditures
2. Plant maintenance expenditures
3. Regular raw material orders
4. Expedited raw material orders
5-36. Operator to be scheduled; to simply work or be trained; hours scheduled; and product scheduled on each of four machines on each of two production lines

Decisions Made by Administrator

1. Number of firms
2. Number of participants per firm
3. Number of periods of play
4. Changing model parameters if desired (for example, demand levels)

IV. Administration

PROSIM is designed explicitly for use on IBM 700/7000 and 360 series computer systems. It has also been run on other computers. The basic program language for the game is FORTRAN.

V. Source

Paul S. Greenlaw and Michael P. Hottenstein, *PROSIM: A Production Management Simulation,* International Textbook Company, Scranton, Pennsylvania, 1968.

Upon adoption, the Publishing Department of the International Textbook Company will provide these programmed computer decks free of charge.

(C)

Prospectville

I. Description

This game is a competitive and interactive simulation of field sales work in a company with three broad categories of products with nine items in each category. The game play time is set at four days with no time compression. Each team has as its goal the maximization of market share.

Each team is supplied with a list of prospects. The team determines which of these prospects it will contact for an appointment, which it will call on without an appointment, and what products will be presented. The time utilization for presentations is set by the game rules. The team keeps track of the time taken for travel, lunch, and presentations. At the end of each day, each team receives a score sheet indicating the gross profits on the products it has sold, penalties for not making appointments, and details such as potential business and share obtained on the calls made.

The team with the highest gross profit at the end of four days wins.

II. Training Purpose

The game is designed to train salesmen to budget their time, determine whether to call or visit prospects (or both), choose the most advantageous itineraries, and what products to sell.

III. Decisions Made by Participants

1. Which prospects to visit
2. What products to present
3. Determine itinerary
4. Make appointment or call cold

Decisions Made by Administrator

1. Whether or not salesmen make an appointment
2. Determine share of business obtained by each team
3. To penalize salesmen for failing to make phone appointment

IV. Administration

This game is manually scored and can be played by mail. The game administrator assigns factors to presentation and also has a master list of prospects which indicates all products that can be sold and the gross margin on these.

V. Source

R. C. Long, Manager, Marketing Research Division, Handy and Harman, Inc., 850 Third Avenue, New York.

(*M*, 174)

The Public Sector

I. Description

In this game the participants first represent those people in local industries who decide on wage levels for the coming year and then represent the community's elected officials who are concerned with tax decisions and the allocation of public revenues. They are faced with an environment in which business revenues as well as the costs of governmental services are gradually rising with time, the latter steadily and the former interrupted by periods of low activity. If, as a result of adverse combinations of business conditions, wage decisions, and high tax rates, one or more of the industries does not produce the return on investment specified by the administrator, operations must be discontinued until conditions are again more favorable. While the industry is idle, the community loses revenue and incurs additional welfare costs.

Success is measured by community income and services provided for citizens; the best group is the one that provides the widest range of public services coupled with good income improvement.

II. Training Purpose

The training purpose is to familiarize the participants with the public sector of the economy, the services which are provided, where and how funds are raised, and what considerations influence the determination of tax rates.

III. Decisions Made by Participants

1. The local tax rate
2. What new improvements in public services to provide
3. Wage level
4. When to provide the improvements in public service

Decisions Made by Administrator

1. The level of business activity
2. Minimum rate of return below which an industry must close

IV. Administration

All computations are manual. Worksheets for participants' decisions and computations and the effects of these decisions on the environment are provided. Fact sheets are included which give details pertaining to the game and the limits within which the participant may decide upon specific values for independent variables.

V. Source

Erwin Rausch. Direct inquiries to Science Research Associates, Inc., 259 East Erie Street, Chicago, Illinois.

(*M*)

Purchasing

I. Description

This is a competitive game played by teams of three to five members (the number of teams is unlimited). Competition is between teams and among members of each team.

Participants play the role of purchasing agents for a financially stable company whose annual purchases run upwards of $2 million. They attempt to purchase at the lowest overall cost when considering production needs, order costs, and inventory charges while maintaining the highest possible quality and reliability of vendor performance.

Questions are referred to participants as teams and as individuals for decisions. The game gives instant feedback to provide participants with results of their decisions. Interchanging ideas and judgments of performance between team members provides additional feedback.

II. Training Purpose

This game attempts to highlight the major features of purchasing for a new employee, as well as to help sharpen the skills of experienced purchasers.

III. Decisions Made by Participants

1. Quantity discounts (quantity discounts versus cost of carrying inventory)

2. Risk evaluations
3. Human relations
4. Standard of performance
5. Reducing cost of purchasing function itself

IV. Administration

The game is manually scored. An administrative guide booklet is provided. The administrator leads pregame and postgame discussion. Playing time is approximately one and one-half hours.

V. Source

Erwin Rausch. Direct inquiries to Science Research Associates, Inc., 259 East Erie Street, Chicago, Illinois.

(*M*)

Region

I. Description

In this game eight teams (three to five members per team) own parts of a bicounty regional area. At the beginning of play, three teams own and operate farms and the other five teams own and operate urban land use sectors (basic industry, wholesaling, nonpersonal services, personal goods and services, and residences of three socioeconomic classes). The playing board contains 900 squares (30 x 30), each square representing a square mile of land. All land use is on a square mile basis: that is, only one land use is allowed per square mile.

Teams may set their own objectives, which may include maximizing the economic return of their land holdings, acquiring political power, or building a "good city" (using whatever definition they assign to "good"). To accomplish their objectives, teams may vote for political officials (a mayor, a zoning commissioner, and a county commissioner from each county), purchase and trade land, develop their land, make bargains, and create alliances. Each round simulates a year and lasts about an hour.

All team economic and political actions are fed through a computer which prints out the status of each team at the end of the round and shows the consequences of each team's actions and their effects on all other teams. Likewise, the political actions of the mayor and county commissioner (setting tax rates, building municipal services and roads, providing utility service, and constructing new terminals and utility plants) and of the zoning commissioner affect the development of private land use.

Region is not a "zero-sum" game. Thus, even though conflicts develop between rural and urban interests and between owners of competing businesses, teams often find that cooperation and planning with other teams will best further their own objectives.

II. Training Purpose

This game gives participants an overall view of urban growth and development within a regional context. Teams are free to follow a wide range of objectives and strategies within a socioeconomic system, which they are able to change in a democratic process. During the play participants are made aware of the complex interspacial and intertemporal ramifications of their actions. The model offers an interdisciplinary approach to urban problems which makes it an innovative teaching tool.

III. Decisions Made by Participants

1. Vote for political officers
2. Acquire land
3. Sell and trade land
4. Build eight types of land-use developments
5. Operate businesses
6. Set prices for commercial establishments
7. Set wages for businesses
8. Operate residences
9. Maintain or demolish land-use sectors
10. Expand density of land-use development
11. Set local tax rates

12. Use federal-state aid
13. Balance local budget
14. Build roads
15. Supply municipal services
16. Provide utility service
17. Build terminal facilities
18. Annex land
19. Incorporate new cities
20. Zone land use

IV. ADMINISTRATION

There is no formal scoring system, but an IBM 1130 computer (using FORTRAN IV) provides an up-to-date account of team holdings and an income statement at the end of each round.

V. SOURCE

Peter House, Director, Urban Systems Simulations, Washington Center for Metropolitan Studies, 1717 Massachusetts Avenue, N.W., Washington, D.C.

(*C*)

Rolling Doughnut Metal Truck Company

I. DESCRIPTION

Two teams of three to twelve participants each act as bargainers, for either union or management, who must negotiate for a new labor contract. Each team attempts to obtain the best contract for its side. The issues involved are wages and salaries, fringe benefits, holidays, terms of contract, union shop, and grievance procedure. The two teams caucus to determine strategy, meet together to negotiate, return to caucus, etc. The administrator may determine the timing of the negotiating sessions. The game may be played over a period of several hours or extended to several days.

II. Training Purpose

To develop the ability of the participants to communicate and negotiate effectively.

III. Decisions Made by Participants

The two teams must reach agreement on the following:

1. Wages and salaries
2. Fringe benefits
3. Holidays
4. Terms of contract
5. Union shop
6. Grievance procedure

Decisions Made by Administrator

1. Time
2. Time factors

IV. Administration

Scoring is manual, and the winners are evaluated on the basis of an optimal point system.

V. Source

Participant's Manual, John W. Keltner, Milton Valentine, and Charles Goetzinger, *The Rolling Doughnut Metal Truck Company,* Oregon State University, Corvallis, Oregon. Direct inquiries to John Keltner, 165 De-Armond Way, Corvallis, Oregon.

(*M*)

Sales Environment Learning Laboratory
(SELL)

I. Description

The *Sales Environment Learning Laboratory* (SELL) is a computer-based market simulation that is used to train individuals in making sales and marketing decisions. Four to ten teams of one to five individuals make up one industry; more than ten teams can be accommodated by forming multiple industries. Each team is placed in charge of the sales or marketing department of a medium- to large-size company.

The market environment is characterized by a single product being marketed to three to fifteen customers. The customers are divided into at most six market segments. The game participants, as department heads, have up to ten different appeals such as price, national advertising, zonal advertising, service, and salesmen's calling time to attract the customer to their product offerings. While marketing their products, game participants must also marshal their finished goods inventory and cash. The marketing, inventory, and finance decisions are all made in a framework of competition. Participants can improve their knowledge of competition and the economy by purchasing marketing research information.

Performance is demonstrated by (1) periodic income statements and balance sheets and (2) how well participants meet the market and growth objectives they set at the beginning of play.

II. Training Purpose

The game gives participants experience in making management decisions in the functional area of sales or marketing.

III. Decisions Made by Participants

1. Price
2. Advertising

3. Allocation of other appeals such as service, salesmen's hours, etc.
4. Market research
5. Forecast demand
6. Borrowing
7. Production level
8. Investment

DECISIONS MADE BY ADMINISTRATOR

1. The number of teams
2. The number of customers of each type
3. The number of types of customers (market segments)
4. The number of different appeals (advertising, salesmen's hours, price, service, etc.)
5. The initial asset position of the teams
6. The relative attractiveness of the different appeals to each type of customer
7. The shape of the demand curve for the total market as a function of the various appeals
8. The manner in which demand is divided among the types of customers (market segments)
9. The relative severity of overordering goods or stocking out of goods
10. The performance of the general economic index (nationally and by market segment)
11. The relative amount of buyer brand loyalty for each type of customer
12. The range of expected deviation in the accuracy of marketing research
13. The rate of interest on borrowed funds
14. The willingness of various customers to split orders
15. The relative amount of carryover of appeal between periods

IV. ADMINISTRATION

SELL is administered via remote terminal. All facilities required for play —the terminal and the computer, all materials, and the administrator—are provided by Simulated Environments, Inc. The site of administration is anywhere. The administrator's decisions are made to reflect the customer's situation.

V. SOURCE

Alfred P. West, Jr., Simulated Environments, Inc., University City Science Center, 3401 Market Street, Philadelphia, Pennsylvania.

(C)

SALESPLAN

I. DESCRIPTION

This noncomputerized game of sales planning treats all the major product and promotional aspects of sales management. The participants are faced with a large number of decisions to make in all areas of sales management plus the related areas of market analysis, product planning, advertising and sales promotion, research and development, and merger and acquisition. They must interpret economic trends and competitive information and develop an annual sales plan based on four quarterly plans. Each quarterly plan must be flexible enough to cope with random variables introduced into the game.

The game is played with three teams of three to eighteen members. Each team, representing a company, starts with one-third of the market for either a consumer or industrial product—or both—and through its sales planning strives to create market leadership. Game time is usually one year. Quarterly operating statements and competitive information reports are furnished the teams; at the end of four quarters the team with the most accumulated net profit is the winner. Real time is one day of seven to eight hours.

II. TRAINING PURPOSE

The training purpose is to integrate all the major product and promotional decisions of sales planning into a realistic learning experience which will enable the participants to project the lessons into their real-life situations. Further purposes are to provide participants with experience in the group dynamics of decision making under pressure.

III. Decisions Made by Participants

1. Segmentation of a market
2. Selection, motivation, and compensation of a salesforce
3. Territorial assignment of a salesforce
4. Quota assignment for a salesforce
5. Integration of salesforce objectives with advertising objectives
6. Selection of sales services to support salesforce in the field
7. Hiring, firing, and training of a salesforce
8. Assignment of sales objectives
9. Product research and development
10. Product innovation
11. Product branding (brand naming, brand theming)
12. Pricing
13. Production forecasting
14. Product scheduling
15. Assignment of product sales features
16. Selection of advertising media (print, broadcast, collateral)
17. Selection of sales promotion media
18. Advertising to end-users, to the trade, and to manufacturers
19. Advertising planning over a campaign year
20. Advertising agency selection and integration
21. Assignment of advertising objectives
22. Merger and acquisition
23. Marketing research and development, including use and interpretation of research reports
24. Interpretation of economic trends
25. Interpretation of competitive information

IV. Administration

The model design, necessary forms, and scoring are all furnished by the game source in personal presentation of the game, followed by professional evaluation and critique. This game is available through personal presentation only. The game has been adapted for play as a correspondence course through the mail, entitled *Sales Game*. Decisions are mailed periodically by players for scoring and critique.

V. SOURCE

Hanan & Son, Management Consultants, P.O. Box 1234, Grand Central Station, New York.

(*M*, 224, 225)

Sales Strategy

I. DESCRIPTION

In this interactive game the participants compete with each other as well as with other teams. Each team is composed of from three to five members with no limit on the number of teams. The participants' role is to play district managers of a consumer product manufacturer, and they must make both team and individual decisions. Participants receive immediate feedback on these decisions. Resulting team decisions are compared with other team decisions. Playing time is about one and one-half hours.

II. TRAINING PURPOSE

The game is designed to draw attention to problem areas which field sales managers must deal with, such as assigning priorities in a changing market, planning new product introduction, and improving performance. The game also highlights basic opportunities in sales management.

III. DECISIONS MADE BY PARTICIPANTS

1. Assignment of priority to various selling activities (that is, time, competitors, activities of company)

2. Personnel selection
3. New product introduction
4. Performance improvement

IV. ADMINISTRATION

An administrator's manual is furnished for instruction on game process administration.

V. SOURCE

The Didactic Game Company, Box 500, Westbury, Long Island, New York.

(*M*, 226)

Scheduling Game

I. DESCRIPTION

This production scheduling game can be played by any number of participants, each of whom operates his own department. The game is played in four daily sessions which range from an hour to two and one-half hours. Since this game is designed as a training device for newly hired personnel and summer employees, part of each session is devoted to discussion of scheduling problems and techniques.

As the problems are discussed and techniques are developed, the game becomes more complex. Participants must make their decisions in the total environment of the firm, with a close watch on raw materials and scheduled requirements. The players must set the original production level and the weekly amounts of Products A and B to make throughout the game to meet variable demands, which are determined from a random number table based on a normal curve. They must concern themselves with the trade-off between stockout costs and inventory carrying costs. They must consider the costs of changing production levels of the specific product produced. Each player's objective is to meet demand at the lowest possible cost.

II. TRAINING PURPOSE

The game is designed to show the basic problems of production control and to increase the player's understanding of the relationship of production scheduling to other areas of the firm.

III. DECISIONS MADE BY PARTICIPANTS

1. Beginning production level
2. Amounts of Products A and B scheduled
3. Changes in production level

IV. ADMINISTRATION

Although most of the calculations are carried out by the players in this manually scored game, the umpire may need some clerical assistance. Because the umpire leads the discussion sessions and explains some of the scheduling techniques, it is desirable that he have practical production experience. All materials for play are included in the game kit.

V. SOURCE

Philip H. Williams, Industrial Engineering Division, The Procter & Gamble Company, Ivorydol Technical Center, Cincinnati, Ohio.

(*M*)

Stanford Business Logistics Game (Mark V)

I. DESCRIPTION

The hypothetical firm in this business game manufactures eucalyptus oil in California and sells it through its New York warehouse. Six modes of transportation are available to the game players with differences in time, quality, and cost rates for each mode. This logistics game allows the participant to seek the elusive, delicate balance between cost of carrying inventory versus cost of stockouts. The proper "mix" of transportation modes under varying economic conditions stresses the importance of sound transportation management. The computer output includes current shipment status, inventory position, profit and loss statements, and economic forecasts.

II. TRAINING PURPOSE

The purpose of the *Stanford Business Logistics Game* is to direct attention to the key problems of handling the logistics functions of a large manufacturing firm and to emphasize the importance of careful selection of distribution strategies so as to minimize long-run total cost. The game provides decision-making experience in scheduling and dispatching shipments, selecting transportation modes on the basis of total costs, and balancing inventories.

III. DECISIONS MADE BY PARTICIPANTS

1. Mode of transportation
   a. Airlines (2)
   b. Truck (4)
   c. Railroad
   d. Forwarder
   e. Cooperative
   f. Ship
2. Shipment quantities by mode
3. Airline-blocked space option
4. Lease warehouse option

DECISIONS MADE BY ADMINISTRATOR

1. Economic index
2. Environment changes

IV. Administration

The game is programmed in FORTRAN H for the IBM 360/67 and in FORTRAN IV for the IBM 7090/94 and CDC 6500.

V. Source

Karl M. Ruppenthal, D. Clay Whybark, and Henry A. McKinnell, Jr., *Stanford Business Logistics Game,* Graduate School of Business, Stanford University, Stanford, California, 1967.

(C)

Supervisory Skills

I. Description

Participants are divided into teams of three to five players. Teams compete as do members within each team. The participants play roles of supervisors in an assembly department with its own stockroom, materials handling, and clerical staff. Questions for decisions are referred to the participants one at a time; decisions are made individually and in groups. The game gives instant feedback so that participants know immediately the results of their decisions. Later, team decisions are evaluated against those of other teams. Ideas and judgments of performance are interchanged between team members to provide additional feedback.

II. Training Purpose

This game's purpose is to help sharpen managerial skills of supervisors and to instill appreciation for benefits of detailed planning, specific goal setting, acceptance of responsibility, selection of priorities, and communications (upward and downward).

III. Decisions Made by Participants

1. Goals to set for specific improvements
2. Order in which improvements should be made
3. Preparation of reports to superiors

IV. Administration

A guidance booklet is provided for administering the game. Pregame and postgame discussions are led by the administrator. Game time is approximately one and one-half hours.

V. Source

Erwin Rausch. Direct inquiries to Science Research Associates, Inc., 259 East Erie Street, Chicago, Illinois.

(M)

Transaction

I. Description

This investment game emphasizes the concepts and operations of buying and selling stock. The game can be played alone or with groups. The participant is provided with several years of history of a real-life firm; as the game progresses, more information is provided—such as financial statements, expansion plans, new product announcements, and the stock market price. The latter is provided with a simulated tickertape. The game manager attempts to maximize profit by requesting stop, limit, and buy orders and by requesting sell short, cover, and sell orders. The game also teaches the role of the stockholder and how corporations borrow money by issuing debentures, withhold a portion of income for expansion, and pay a portion of the income to their stockholders for use of their capital.

II. Training Purpose

The game is designed to demonstrate operations of the stock market and to allow the participants an opportunity to sharpen their skills of buying and selling in a changing market.

III. Decisions Made by Participants

1. Buy order
2. Limit order
3. Stop order
4. Sell order
5. Sell short order

IV. Administration

The game is administered by the players. All forms, charts, and necessary instructions are enclosed in the game kit.

V. Source

Entelek Inc., 42 Pleasant Street, Newburyport, Massachusetts.

(*M*)

Uniproduct

I. Description

This is a functional inventory-production game which emphasizes decision variables involved in manufacturing a single product from a single raw material. The participant's objective is to minimize the average monthly cost by making decisions concerning finished goods inventories, varying production rates and operating levels, special ordering, and purchasing raw materials at varying costs.

The participant starts with a record of past sales and future sales forecasts. The simulator then furnishes the number of the current month, raw material and finished goods inventory levels, current month raw materials arrival schedule, previous months' scheduled production, and a complete history of past demand.

II. Training Purpose

The training purpose is to expose and involve the participant in a system which cannot be analyzed deterministically for optimal policies. By identifying crucial elements, estimating parameters, studying the distributive nature of stochastic variables, and analyzing experience, the participant should learn heuristic reasoning.

III. Decisions Made by Participants

1. The quantity of product to be manufactured the next month
2. The quantity of raw material to be ordered on a request basis for delivery in two months
3. The quantity of raw material to be special ordered for rush delivery the next month

Decisions Made by Administrator

1. Number of months to be simulated
2. The demand function in terms of the trend and seasonality
3. The constraints of product capacity and material purchases
4. The cost of procurement, production, and invention

IV. Administration

Simulation programs exist in FORTRAN for IBM 7094 and 1620, and in BASIC for the GE 255 and 625 time-sharing computers. Fifteen years of monthly operations can be simulated in about two seconds on the IBM 7094.

V. Source

Robert B. Andrews and Thomas E. Vollmann, "Uniproduct: A Pedagogical Device," *California Management Review,* Winter 1967, pp. 65-70.

(*C*, 11)

UNITEX

I. Description

Unitex is a production scheduling and inventory game in which the participants manage a company making a single product for stock. A single unit of raw material is needed for the finished product. The participants must set plant capacity and plant production and determine regular and expedited raw material orders in their monthly decisions.

The participants in this game must write a decision rule subprogram containing the previous decisions. Their objective throughout the game is to set decision rules which minimize total costs while meeting demands.

II. Training Purpose

This game is to teach the participants to set better decision rules to reduce costs in a manufacturing company. They must achieve a balance between various production and inventory costs.

III. Decisions Made by Participants

1. Plant capacity
2. Production scheduled

3. Regular raw materials orders
4. Special raw materials orders

1. Product demand
2. Parameter values

IV. Administration

This computer-scored game is written in FORTRAN IV. It may be run in either of two models, single runs or student batches. Extensive programming instructions are given in the source manual.

V. Source

Howard E. Johnson, *Unitex—A Production-Inventory Computer Model for Classroom Use,* College of Business Administration, University of Texas, Austin, Texas, 1967.

(C)

Using Financial Data in Business Decisions

I. Description

This is an accounting-oriented, hand-simulated business game. Individuals or teams submit basic decisions on price, advertising, borrowing, and merchandise purchases to the administrator, who in turn calculates the final sales for the simulated business firm. Participants are then required to complete profit and loss, cash flow, and balance sheet statements for the accounting period. The final assignment is to determine the selling price for the business based on the present value of net assets and the value of the future income stream. The final assignment also includes evaluating a competitor for purposes of making an offer to buy.

II. Training Purpose

The purpose of the game is to provide experience in preparing financial statements for a firm—balance sheets, profit and loss, and cash-flow statements—and to stress the use of financial statements for management decision making.

III. Decisions Made by Participants

1. Sales price
2. Units of merchandise to purchase
3. Advertising expenditure
4. Borrowing if necessary

Decision Made by Administrator

1. Industry sales index

IV. Administration

The calculations are manual. The administrator determines final sales by completing a few simple calculations.

V. Source

Participant's Manual, Robert E. Seiler, *Using Financial Data in Business Decisions,* Charles E. Merrill Books, Inc., Columbus, Ohio, 1965.

(*M*)

Industry Games

A separate classification for industry games might be tenuous, for industry games include both general purpose and special purpose and functional games. However, we justify this classification because the structure of the model is similar to that found in a specific industry—not like that of a general purpose game such as the AMA game. Additionally, data in the model reflect the everyday operation of a business. For example, in the *Pitt-Amstan Game,* profiles based on 1,200 actual and potential Pitt-Amstan customers were programmed into the computer, thereby very definitely tailoring the game not only, in this case, to a specific industry but also to a specific company. We feel this specificity also holds for other games which we have classified as industry games.

ADVERTISING

Adman

I. DESCRIPTION

This game is designed to introduce some of the problems involved in buying and selling advertising. A number of players represent banks, whose object is to select the most cost-effective type of advertising from among five advertising media. Other players represent the advertising media, either newspaper, television, radio, direct mail, or outdoor advertising, attempting to sell as much advertising as possible. Each of the players is given a profile describing his bank or medium and any pressures which he may be under as an individual. Each of the media also has deposits in each of the banks, which may be moved at will. A second objective of the bank players is to improve these deposits. The problems faced by the bank players are primarily human relations and resource allocation, while the media players try to increase their share of the banks' advertising budgets. The game may be played by six to twenty persons.

II. Training Purpose

The training purpose of *Adman* is to present to the student some of the problems in selecting efficient advertising and to acquaint him with advertising prices and terms and the advantages of different advertising media.

III. Administration

The game is manually scored. It requires about three hours to complete, allowing 20 minutes for explanations, one and one-half hours for play, and at least one hour for discussion and evaluation.

IV. Source

Manual, *Adman,* Abt Associates, Inc., 55 Wheeler Street, Cambridge, Massachusetts. The game is proprietary.

(*M*)

ADPLAN

I. Description

This is a noncomputerized game of advertising planning which treats all the major product and promotional aspects of advertising management. The participants are faced with a large number of decisions to make in all areas of advertising planning plus the related areas of market analysis, product planning, sales management, research and development, and merger and acquisition. They must interpret economic trends and competitive information and develop an annual advertising plan based on four quarterly plans. Each quarterly plan must be flexible enough to cope with random variables introduced into the game.

The game is played with three teams of three to eighteen members. Each team, representing a company, starts with one-third of the market for either a consumer or industrial product—or both—and through its advertising planning strives to create market leadership. Game time is usually one year. Quarterly operating statements and competitive information reports are furnished the teams; at the end of four quarters the team with the most accumulated net profits is the winner. Real time is one day of seven to eight hours.

II. Training Purpose

The training purpose is to integrate all the major product and promotional decisions of advertising planning into a realistic learning experience which will enable the participants to project the lessons into their real-life situations. Further purposes are to provide participants with experience in the group dynamics of decision making under pressure.

III. Decisions Made by Participants

1. Segmentation of a market
2. Advertising planning over a campaign year, including multiple media integration, budgeting, and theming
3. Assignment of advertising objectives
4. Advertising to end-users, to the trade, and to manufacturers
5. Assignment of product sales features
6. Selection of advertising media
    a. print media
    b. broadcast media
    c. collateral media
7. Selection of sales promotion media
8. Advertising agency selection and integration
9. Integration of salesforce objectives with advertising objectives
10. Product research and development
11. Product innovation

12. Product branding (brand naming, brand theming)
13. Pricing and advertising correlation
14. Production forecasting and advertising correlation
15. Product scheduling
16. Marketing research and development, including use and interpretation of research reports
17. Interpretation of economic trends
18. Interpretation of competitive information
19. Role of advertising in merger and acquisition

IV. ADMINISTRATION

The model design, necessary forms, and scoring are all furnished by the game source in personal presentation of the game, followed by professional evaluation and critique. The game is available through personal presentation only. The game has been adapted for play as a correspondence course through the mail, entitled *Ad Game*. Decisions are mailed periodically by players for scoring and critique.

V. SOURCE

Hanan & Son, Management Consultants, P.O. Box 1234, Grand Central Station, New York.

(*M*)

AEROSPACE

Aerospace Business Environment Simulator

I. DESCRIPTION

This is a research and development/production game concerned with space and missile systems. It is designed to involve participants with decision problems confronting aerospace and other defense company managers.

Each of up to five competing management teams composed of five members (this may vary from three to six) will organize its own company and formulate policies in the functional areas of planning, organizing, directing, and controlling. The teams will then make decisions on procurement, operations, and bidding. The decision results are fed back to the teams in the form of operating reports, requests for bids, and contract awards.

The game is played in ten periods varying from one to three hours.

II. TRAINING PURPOSE

The training purpose is to give participants laboratory training in defining objectives and policies, establishing organizations, and in making decisions and problem analysis.

III. DECISIONS MADE BY PARTICIPANTS

1. Number of men hired and fired
2. Facilities built
3. Facilities sold
4. Amounts for education and training expense
5. Regular time and overtime man-hours
6. Subcontracted man-hours
7. Wage rate
8. Debt added or retired
9. Total dollar and per hour bids

DECISIONS MADE BY ADMINISTRATOR

1. Determine number of contracts to be offered
2. Introduction of prosperity and depression
3. Wage rates
4. Contract rates
5. Interest rates
6. Income tax rates

IV. Administration

The game is programmed in FORTRAN and will operate under most FORTRAN Monitor Systems including FORTRAN II IBSYS. It is structured in the form of a main execution routine and 11 major subroutines. Results may be rerun at any time. The program requires only about one minute in an IBM 7094, but the complete processing cycle takes about two hours.

V. Source

Roger K. Summit, *Aerospace Business Environment Simulator,* Lockheed Missiles and Space Company, 3251 Hanover Street, Palo Alto, California, revised ed., 1963. For copies of game direct inquiries to Peter Melitz, IBM Corporation, 3224 Wilshire Boulevard, Los Angeles, California.

(*C*)

Dynamo Aerospace Simulation Workshop

I. Description

This game simulates top management decision making regarding contracts. The participating teams represent different companies. Each company has two products: space systems and aircraft systems. Each company also has two primary functional areas, production and research development. The teams are required to make three types of decisions for each functional area: (1) resource changes, (2) contract performance, and (3) contract bidding. A computer reports the results of the decisions made—financial results, requests for new bids, and contract awards.

II. Training Purpose

The simulation provides a realistic and dynamic environment within which to make top management decisions related to contract work.

III. Decisions Made by Participants

1. Personnel hiring and firing
2. Education and training expenditures
3. Wage rates
4. Facility expansion or contraction
5. Financial needs (cash, debt)
6. Scheduling man-hours per contract (also overtime scheduling)
7. Subcontracting
8. Contract bid price
9. Proposal expenses

IV. Administration

Decision sheets are provided for each participating team. The model is programmed in FORTRAN for the IBM 7094.

V. Source

Lockheed Management Development Seminars Manual, *Dynamo Aerospace Simulation Workshop,* Lockheed California Company, Lockheed, California.

This game is proprietary and not available outside the Lockheed Company.

(C)

Materiel Management Game

I. Description

This is a total enterprise game with special emphasis on the purchasing function. Each participant studies the "daily" input alone, and then meets with other team members to make team decisions as director of materiel. The daily problems presented to the participant involve problems in such areas as organization, administration, and relationships with suppliers, organization units, and the public. These problems can total 40 or more. The setting is a competitive one with five teams competing.

The materiel division is presently phasing out an air-to-air missile project, but has recently won a $50,000 contract for the Rin-Tin-Tin Missile. Bids are being received on the various components of this missile. The materiel director's subordinates have been instructed to complete every possible contract by accepting the low bid. Any exceptions to this rule are to be ratified by the director. Nearly all of the decisions reached by the players will involve communications from their superiors, their subordinates, or those outside their company. The director of materiel may choose one of the general alternatives accompanying the correspondence or may make any other decision he desires. He may also make decisions concerning the organizational structure of his division, utilization of personnel, or changes in division policy.

II. Training Purpose

The purpose of this game is to provide an understanding of the purchasing function as an on-going process and to teach the general administrative skills required by top level management. It forces the participants to evaluate the procedures and practices carried out in their purchasing division and to react to problems as they arrive.

III. Decisions Made by Participants

Specific decisions to problems under the following titles:
1. Organization
2. Administration
3. Relationships
   a. With suppliers
   b. With organizational units
   c. With the public

Decisions Made by Administrator

Decisions Made by Administrator

1. Specific problems

IV. Administration

In order to satisfy the competitive appetites of the participants, the administrator manually rates each of their decisions on a three-point scale (above average, average, and below average). Although those who do best on this point system are judged the "winners," the real winners are those who learn to evaluate and improve their administrative skills. At the end of the game the players also evaluate themselves.

V. Source

Allen A. Zoll, 3rd, *Dynamic Management Education,* United Business Supply, 120 Bell Street, Seattle, Washington.

(*M*)

Operation Interlock

I. Description

Operation Interlock is a total enterprise game involving five teams which produce a high-priced product used in the aerospace industries. These five teams are the sole producers of the item, which is sold to both civilian and Air Force buyers. Sales are made directly to the civilian market, while the Air Force accepts quarterly bids to fill its needs.

During the period of the ten quarterly decisions the economy moves through various levels of prosperity—through boom and recession. Management must coordinate production levels and marketing expenditures, while simultaneously reacting to the various changes in the external economy. After this game is completed each team rates itself on various aspects of its company's performance to bring about a self-evaluation.

II. Training Purpose

This general management game shows the effects of both internal and external factors upon a company's performance. It focuses attention on the interlocking nature of business decisions.

III. Decisions Made by Participants

1. Production levels
2. Marketing expenditure
3. Research and development
4. Military and commercial unit prices
5. Plant size
6. Loans
7. Dividends

Decisions Made by Administrator

1. Economy level and market environment
2. Air Force requirements
3. Dumping in a foreign market

IV. Administration

This game is usually scored manually by the administrator, but it can be scored with a program written for the IBM 7090. Manual tabulation of the results of the five teams requires approximately 35 minutes.

V. Source

Allen A. Zoll, 3rd, *Dynamic Management Education,* United Business Supply, 120 Bell Street, Seattle, Washington.

(*M, C*)

Staff Training Exercise for Programming Supervisors
(STEPS)

I. DESCRIPTION

In this game the three-man teams are charged with effectively utilizing programmers to carry out a contract they have been awarded for the space-man missile control system. Each of these men is the head of one of the three sections: control, processing, and INPUT/OUTPUT. Each player is assigned specific tasks which lead to completion of the programs for the contracted system. The objective of the team is to complete the programs by the specified date and within the $300,000 budget allocation.

Six personnel categories are provided with known costs and capabilities. All men within a category are assumed to be of equal ability, with the exception that programmers who are transferred to jobs similar to others they have worked on are more efficient. Each man must be assigned to a specific phase of a particular program. During the 20 periods of the game the three section heads are seated near each other to facilitate communication. These three section heads can hire, fire, transfer, or promote programmers to fit their specific needs. After a two-week period of simulated activity, four reports are prepared for the section heads to assist them in making future decisions.

II. TRAINING PURPOSE

STEPS was designed to train supervisors of a programming effort. The work environment seeks to simulate production and personnel problems and to develop decision-making competence.

III. DECISIONS MADE BY PARTICIPANTS

1. Hire personnel
2. Assign personnel
3. Transfer personnel

4. Promote personnel

5. Terminate personnel

IV. Administration

This game has been programmed for the Philco 2000. The computer prints out four kinds of information for the players: (1) personnel rosters, (2) progress reports, (3) personnel change reports, and (4) financial reports.

V. Source

Richard J. Gilinsky, *STEPS Player's Manual,* System Development Corporation, 2500 Colorado Avenue, Santa Monica, California.

(*C*, 26, 209)

AGRI-BUSINESS

The California Farm Management Game, Southern San Joaquin Valley Farms

I. Description

This game simulates the operation of a San Joaquin Valley farm. Changes in data, parameters, and variables may be made to study various conditions, and some decisions may be eliminated to increase emphasis on particular problems. Any number of teams may play the game.

Six crops are included in the game and a number of new crops, up to a total of ten, may be added. Joint crops, with yields of the principal product determined stochastically and the subsidiary product as a percent of the main crop, may be considered. Double cropping for certain crops is included and some choices are possible as to the double crops.

Exceptionally complete details are provided participants with regard to crops, yields, prices, and fluctuations; for irrigation by crops; machinery requirements and performance rates; initial or starting conditions; and so forth.

Many reports are provided the participating teams—e.g., fertilizer costs, labor costs, etc.; loan payments, interest, and balances; cash purchases and sales; net farm income, cash balances; financial position and net worth.

Net worth at the end of the period is the criterion used to determine the success of the teams' strategy. The simulation may run for any number of years; each run of the game represents one year's operation.

II. Training Purpose

The game attempts to simulate the conditions under which farm operating decisions are made.

III. Decisions Made by Participants

1. Crops and field usage
2. Land purchase
3. Fertilization rates
4. Irrigation systems
5. Machinery combinations
6. Credit, loans, and repayment schedules

Decisions Made by Administrator

1. The decision areas which are to be included (or deleted)
2. Specified levels of fertilizer (if this decision is to be deleted)
3. Credit levels, which are not set by the program
4. Parameter and variable changes

IV. Administration

The game is programmed in FORTRAN IV for the IBM 7040 or 7044. Help of an experienced programmer will be required to adapt the game for other computers. Changes in the game can be easily made with a minimum of program change. Decisions not to be included may have specified levels set by the administrator and credit controls will have to be exercised by the administrator himself.

The complete computer program is reproduced in the *Administrator's Manual,* along with detailed instructions for tailoring the program to local conditions or to simulated specific farm conditions.

V. SOURCE

Participant's Manual, J. Edwin Faris, John Wildermath, and Allen M. Pratt, Jr., *The California Farm Management Game,* College of Agriculture, University of California, Davis, California. Published in 1966 by the Giannini Foundation of Agricultural Economics.

(C)

A General Agricultural Firm Simulator

I. DESCRIPTION

This firm simulator is not a management game in the usual sense, but could provide the computer programming procedure for the common components of a wide variety of agricultural firm simulations. The numerical data used by the model are modified by means of records of a single format.

Detailed instructions are given to enable any person interested in simulating an agricultural (or similar) firm to describe the situation which he wishes to simulate. For example, instructions are given for input and product identification; activity identification; output; product price, trend, and variability; input service purchase and sale; capital goods purchase, sale, and inventory; capital gains; financial capital; maintenance; insurance; taxes; cash flows. The user enters the details which describe the firm he wishes to study. He then tests several courses of action by use of the model and additional data regarding the specific problem to be run.

Any of the many simulations can be used as a farm management game to compare strategies of competing teams.

II. Training Purpose

The booklet contains detailed instructions intended to promote the use of simulation as a learning tool by reducing the cost of programming those components of a simulation which are applicable to a wide range of problems.

III. Decisions Made by Participants

The decisions made by participants will depend on the data programmed into the simulation. The data of the model can be modified by means of records of a single format. All kinds of agricultural firms may be simulated; decisions made depend upon the problem presented.

Decisions Made by Administrator

1. Physical resources controlled by the firm
2. Physical resources bought, sold, etc.
3. Financial capital and its use
4. Input services required and outputs produced
5. Prices and inventories
6. Taxes, insurance, and other costs

IV. Administration

Instructions are rather complex but are intended for the person familiar with a computer and faced with the problem of simulating several different types of agricultural firms. The user of this material may describe any agricultural firm which he wishes to simulate. Data must be entered in prescribed formats; additional subroutines may be required to meet the user's specifications. Source programs are available.

V. Source

R. F. Hutton and H. R. Hinman, *A General Agricultural Firm Simulator,* A.E. & R.S. #72, Department of Agricultural Economics and Rural Sociology, Agricultural Experiment Station, The Pennsylvania State University, University Park, Pennsylvania. Published in May 1968.

(C)

Farm Organization and Investment Game

I. Description

The game may be used for individual or small group decision making, to make year-to-year planning decisions for an irrigated farm on the southern high plains of Texas. The players may choose among five crops, with one to four intensity levels for each crop. The players are operating under a restrictive level of capital availability and must meet fixed levels of living expenses, overhead expenses, and mortgage payments.

After the student has made out his cropping plan for the year, he (or the supervisor) selects a price-cost-yield combination by a random process from a "pool" of 50 combinations. The student then determines his costs for the year and his sources of operating capital. If he cannot raise enough capital for his expenses he is declared bankrupt. If he has adequate capital available he continues the game by determining his income, making a decision on disposal of farm income, and completing the worksheet.

The problem has a "savings account" option which pays 5 percent interest and a growth opportunity in the form of the option to add a second irrigation well at the beginning of any year at the cost of $20,000. Although the budgeting exercise on the same farm may indicate the second well would be worth more than $60,000 under "average conditions," many of the attempts to add the well in the game force the farm into bankruptcy.

II. Training Purpose

The students have previously made farm plans for the assumed farm under static, perfect knowledge conditions. The simulation exercise is designed to illustrate some of the contingencies that one must be prepared for when making plans for the "average" conditions.

III. Decisions Made by Participants

1. The cropping plan for each year
2. Whether to invest in the second irrigation well
3. Source of funds and disposition of excess funds

IV. Administration

Students are given the mimeographed laboratory exercise material, and a supply of extra worksheets is available. The game may be used either as a supervised lab exercise or as "homework." Students are instructed to work as many years as possible.

V. Source

James S. Wehrly, Department of Agricultural Economics and Sociology, Texas A&M University, College Station, Texas.

(*M*)

Illini Egg-Handler Simulation

I. Description

In this total enterprise game four management teams operate four egg-handling plants in Midland, Illinois. They all begin the game in the same market areas. They buy eggs from the producers and sell them to both retailers and brokers. The teams must decide the prices at which they will buy and sell relative to competition. Since the market prices vary and are unknown to the players, they set their prices within a six cent range (+3¢ to −3¢) around the market price in their monthly decisions. They may also set limits on the number of eggs they wish to purchase in a month. They determine inventory levels, plant size, truck purchases, advertising, and labor utilization, and they make investment decisions. The game winner is determined by net profits before taxes.

II. TRAINING PURPOSE

This general business game is designed to emphasize the relationships between a firm and its environment. The seasonal and long-term trends are important in the egg industry. The game also teaches general business management principles.

III. DECISIONS MADE BY PARTICIPANTS

1. Relative price to producers
2. Maximum monthly purchases
3. Relative selling prices to retailers and institutions
4. Truck purchases
5. Inventory level
6. Advertising expenditure
7. Labor utilization
8. Additions to plant capacity
9. Outside investments
10. Bank loan reduction

IV. ADMINISTRATION

This game has been programmed for the IBM 7094 computer and could easily be adapted to other large computers. The computer prints out income statements, balance sheets, and statements of general information. The source deck can be obtained from the authors.

V. SOURCE

Participants' Instructions, R. P. Bentz and R. J. Williams, *Illini Egg-Handler Simulation,* University of Illinois, Urbana, Illinois, 1965.

(C)

Oklahoma Farm Management Decision Game No. II

I. Description

This game is the result of a study of farm decision problems in the Great Plains area. The participant is faced with the problem of operating a 200-acre farm on which the only crop is corn. Data with regard to yield per acre and probabilities of various yields are given. Corn grown or purchased may be used to raise steers or hogs. Equipment and buildings are available for 100 steers per year, but pasture for 200 steers is available. Data are given on corn, equipment required per steer, costs, and expected returns. Similar data regarding hogs are also available.

Decisions on the number of hogs and steers must be made before crop yields and livestock prices are known. Investments made to expand livestock enterprises must be made from retained earnings. Production costs of corn and family living costs must be considered in determining profits.

The objectives are to maximize the net worth of the farm operator and to avoid short-run financial ruin.

The game is only one of the many possible farm simulations obtainable by varying the parameters and the starting assumptions.

II. Training Purpose

The authors list the following possible teaching objectives of the game:
1. To develop ability to determine income opportunities for different livestock enterprises
2. To understand sources of variability in returns and costs and uses of various strategies to maximize returns
3. To illustrate problems of growth under uncertain price and yield conditions and capital restraints
4. To evaluate and attain firm objectives under resources and personal constraints
5. To provide farm management experience

III. Decisions Made by Participants

1. Number of steers and numbers of hogs
2. New facilities for steers and for hogs

DECISIONS MADE BY ADMINISTRATOR

1. Initial conditions, parameters, and conditions

IV. ADMINISTRATION

The administrator should brief the participants with regard to objective, problem orientation, forms used, and evaluation. Calculations may be made by hand. Data and forms are provided.

V. SOURCE

Odell L. Walker and Wayman A. Halbrook, *Operational Gaming and Simulation as Research and Educational Tools in the Great Plains,* Ag Econ 325, 2 RVB 67 (Game is appendix of this article), Oklahoma State University, Stillwater, Oklahoma.

(M)

Oregon Farm Management Simulation

I. DESCRIPTION

In this farm management game participants make annual operational decisions that will optimize net farm income each year and net worth in the long run. Participants are required to make decisions such as crop choice, land purchases and use, machinery purchases, fertilizers and use, and irrigation. It is possible to produce as many as seven crops; the yield functions of nitrogen and phosphorus fertilizer are given for each crop along with costs. The original farm has eight fields of 80 acres each; additional acres of different soil grades can be purchased. Several alternatives are available for machinery purchase. Maximizing long run net worth requires careful allocation of resources so that costs and yields are optimized.

II. TRAINING PURPOSE

The game is designed to demonstrate the typical kinds of problems found in managing a farm. The relationship between economic principles and their use in managing a farm is clearly demonstrated.

III. DECISIONS MADE BY PARTICIPANTS

1. Land purchases (1-8 choices)
2. Crops to produce (1-7 choices) for each field
3. Pounds of nitrogen per acre for each field
4. Pounds of phosphorus per acre for each field
5. Type of irrigation system for each field
6. Machinery purchases
7. Borrowing

IV. ADMINISTRATION

The game is computer scored and programmed in FORTRAN.

V. SOURCE

Student's Manual, Fred J. Smith and Stanley D. Miles, *Oregon Farm Management Simulation,* 213 Extension Hall, Oregon State University, Corvallis, Oregon.

(C)

The N.E. Farm Management Game (FMG 4)

I. DESCRIPTION

The game may be played by individual players or teams. Each organizes and operates a Connecticut Valley cash crop and dairy farm on a year-to-year basis. Emphasis is on organizational (top management) decisions.

From a given starting position, organizational adjustments are possible which can specialize the operation toward either cash crops or dairying. Capital structures will consequently change as will the relative risk and uncertainty of operation. Random deviates generate weather, price, and yield uncertainties associated with farming.

The player is responsible for a matrix of up to 40 interrelated decisions per playing year. These include crops to grow and type and size (20 to 400 cows) of dairy operation (see Section III). The stated objective is to increase net worth through operating the farm.

II. Training Purpose

The game gives participants (agriculturists, college students, and farmers) an opportunity to relate managerial principles to a specific set of farm organizational decisions. In a series of plays, set in a man-against-nature environment of perfect price competition, the impact of trade-off strategies between income needs, security desires, and acceptance and recognition by one's fellow man is quantitatively related to a growth objective measured as increases in net worth.

III. Decisions Made by Participants

1. Acreage of five crops on three land types
2. Fertilizer level by crop and land type
3. Dairy cows to buy and sell
4. Replacement animals to keep
5. Type of dairy housing system
6. Tobacco program participation
7. Off-farm employment
8. Feeding system to follow
9. The preceding will affect building and machinery investments, credit position, and purchase or sale of foodstuffs automatically

Decisions Made by Administrator

1. Stochastic or deterministic prices and yields
2. Price and yield levels
3. Level of player information provided

4. Business analysis data available
5. Number of years of simulation per play
6. Changes in institutional environment (specific parameters of game)
7. Family structure and level of nonproductive costs
8. Offering of land partials
9. Starting position and objective (s)

IV. ADMINISTRATION

FMG 4 was compiled on the CDC 3600 using CDC FORTRAN IV. It has also been adapted to the IBM 360-50. Earlier versions exist for the IBM 1620. Manuals, papers, and course outlines are available.

V. SOURCE

Earl I. Fuller, Department of Agriculture and Food Economics, University of Massachusetts, Amherst, Massachusetts.

(*C*)

The Poultry Farm Management Game
(POULT 4)

I. DESCRIPTION

The game may be played by individuals or teams. Each player organizes and operates a New England brown egg poultry farm on a year-to-year basis. Emphasis is on organizational (top management) decisions.

From a typical floor layer (wholesale market at 6,000 birds) starting position, adjustments are possible for growth in floor capacity or transfer to either low or high mechanized cage operations. Eventual size of the farm may involve a million dollar capital investment with several hundred thousand birds. Random deviates generate death loss, price, and production rate uncertainties associated with poultry farming.

The player is responsible for selecting housing and marketing systems as well as replacement strategies. In addition, he has an opportunity to raise replacement birds and/or pullets for sale. An opportunity exists for growing three crops as additional enterprises (see Section III). Fertilizer response to crops shows diminishing marginal returns. The stated objective is to increase net worth through operating the farm.

II. Training Purpose

POULT 4 gives participants (agriculturists, college students, and farmers) an opportunity to relate managerial principles to a specific set of farm organizational decisions. In a series of plays, set in a man-against-nature environment of perfect price competition, the impact of trade-off strategies between income needs, security desires, and acceptance and recognition by one's fellow men is related to a growth objective measured as increases in net worth.

III. Decisions Made by Participants

1. Marketing system for eggs (retail, jobbing, wholesale, or contract)
2. Housing system for layers (floor or low or high mechanized cages)
3. Contract production of eggs
4. Raising of replacement pullets
5. Raising of pullets for sale
6. Choice of three crops to grow
7. Fertilizer level by crop
8. The preceding will affect building and machinery investments and credit position automatically

Decisions Made by Administrator

1. Stochastic or deterministic prices and yields
2. Price and yield levels
3. Level of player information provided
4. Business analysis data available
5. Number of years of simulation per play
6. Changes in institutional environment (specific parameters of game)
7. Family structure and level of nonproductive costs
8. Starting position and objective(s)

IV. Administration

POULT 4 is written for computation by the CDC 3600 using CDC FOR-TRAN (FORTRAN IV). Manuals and papers are available.

V. Source

Earl I. Fuller, Department of Agriculture and Food Economics, University of Massachusetts, Amherst, Massachusetts.

(C)

Purdue Dairy Management Game

I. Description

As many as four dairies compete in a local market. The product is half gallons of milk which are sold retail (through home delivery) and wholesale (through retail outlets). Each team attempts to increase its share of the market by skillful management of its dairy. Since the decisions made by one team affect the results of the others, each team must constantly respond to changing conditions. The total market sales are affected by the combined decisions of all teams and are subject to seasonal fluctuations.

Other dairies from surrounding areas will enter the market if local prices are too high. The magnitude of the price differential between wholesale and retail price determines the degree of shift in sales between the two types of outlets. Sales effectiveness is a function of such factors as price, advertising, promotion, delivery efficiency, and others. Decisions are made on a monthly basis and results are returned in the form of an operating statement and sales data. About 20 minutes are allowed for each set of decisions, with about seven sets suggested. Team size usually ranges from two to four persons.

II. Training Purpose

The purpose of this dairy game is to make the participant aware of the type of problems dairy managers must face, to stress the importance of fi-

nancial planning, and to emphasize the nature of competition and its influence on strategy formulation.

III. Decisions Made by Participants

1. Retail and wholesale prices
2. Training of personnel
3. Hiring and termination of personnel
4. Advertising and promotion
5. Commission rate

Decisions Made by Administrator

1. Initial monthly sales potential
2. Role of the competitor, if desired
3. Adjustment of the game coefficients—that is, price elasticity

IV. Administration

The game is programmed in FORTRAN II, requires limited memory
capacity, and takes about one minute of computer time to process. Standard
forms are provided for decisions, estimated results, and break-even analysis.

Copies of the computer program may be obtained by writing Program
Information Department, Program Distribution Center, International Business Machines Corp., 40 Saw Mill Road, Hawthorne, New York; the source
program is also listed in *Management Games for Teaching and Research*.

V. Source

Participant's Manual, Emerson M. Babb and Ludwig M. Eisgruber, Educational Methods, Inc., 20 East Huron Street, Chicago, Illinois. Emerson M.
Babb and Ludwig M. Eisgruber, *Management Games for Teaching and Research*, 1966.

(C, 14, 15, 16, 238)

Purdue Farm Management Game

I. DESCRIPTION

The individual, or management team, operates a farm in a pure competition situation. The goal for each team is to maximize net worth by the proper choice of products to produce, choice of methods of production, and adjustment to changing external conditions. The team is given a history of certain product prices in the local area as well as the last three years' operating data. The game may be conducted in either a deterministic or stochastic mode. If the administrator decides on the latter, random deviation may occur in crop yields, livestock, crop prices, livestock prices, and prices of young stock. The game may be played by individuals or by teams which usually average five or six members per team. Six to eight decision sets appear to be adequate; however, this can be determined by the administrator. The computer output lists assets, yields and prices received, labor days used, financial summary, and net worth.

II. TRAINING PURPOSE

The purpose of this game is to demonstrate the principles of farm management. More specifically, the game is designed to demonstrate the interrelationships between the important variables of products, production methods, and environmental conditions—all of which influence success.

III. DECISIONS MADE BY PARTICIPANTS

1. Crop rotation
2. Fertilization
3. Livestock program
4. Land purchases
5. Sale and purchase of breeding stock
6. Borrowing

Decisions Made by Administrator

1. May restrict the following:
   a. Land purchase
   b. Availability of labor
   c. Corn or hay purchase
   d. Borrowing
2. Government programs
3. Coefficient variation—that is, price elasticity
4. Mode of operation—deterministic or stochastic

IV. Administration

The program is written in FORTRAN II and takes about one minute to process.

Copies of the computer program may be obtained by writing Program Information Department, Program Distribution Center, International Business Machines Corporation, 40 Saw Mill Road, Hawthorne, New York; the source program is also listed in the *Management Games for Teaching and Research*.

V. Source

Participant's Manual, Emerson M. Babb and Ludwig M. Eisgruber, *Purdue Farm Management Game*, Educational Methods, Inc., 20 East Huron Street, Chicago, Illinois. Emerson M. Babb and Ludwig M. Eisgruber, *Management Games for Teaching and Research*, 1966.

(C, 15, 16)

Purdue Farm Supply Business Management Game

I. Description

Each management team of three to five members takes over a farm supply store where the financial position has been steadily deteriorating. The management team may be competing with as many as three other teams in a local market. The store carries four products—complete seed, concentrate seed, bag fertilizer, and bulk fertilizer—which are sold to farmers on a cash or credit basis. Future sales are primarily dependent on fluctuations in livestock raised, type and acreage of the crops grown (all of which are not under the control of the team managers), and the decisions made by the management teams. The goal of each management team is to increase the net worth of its business over those of other teams. This can be done by skillful management of the business in controlling costs, correctly reacting to the policies of competitors, and understanding the nature of the products and the market. Team size usually ranges from two to four persons. Computer output provides an income statement, a balance sheet, and a general information sheet.

II. TRAINING PURPOSE

The game is designed to teach business management principles, planning, and financial analysis. It also stresses the influence of the competitive environment on the selection of alternative courses of action.

III. DECISIONS MADE BY PARTICIPANTS

1. Price for all products
2. Inventory orders for all products
3. Credit policy
4. Storage capacity expansion
5. Truck purchases
6. Hiring and firing
7. Advertising
8. Borrowing
9. Investments

DECISIONS MADE BY ADMINISTRATOR

1. Market potential and size
2. Cost of orders
3. May act as competitor
4. May set competitor's prices

    5. Adjustment of game coefficients—that is, price elasticity and wage rates

IV. Administration

The game is programmed in FORTRAN II and takes about one minute to process in the computer. Standard forms are provided for decisions and estimated results.

Copies of the computer program may be obtained by writing Program Information Department, Program Distribution Center, International Business Machines Corporation, 40 Saw Mill Road, Hawthorne, New York; the source program is also listed in *Management Games for Teaching and Research.*

V. Source

Participant's Manual, Emerson M. Babb and Ludwig M. Eisgruber, *Purdue Farm Supply Business Management Game,* Educational Methods, Inc., 20 East Huron Street, Chicago, Illinois. Emerson M. Babb and Ludwig M. Eisgruber, *Management Games for Teaching and Research,* 1966.

(C, 15, 16)

SIMFARM

I. Description

This farm management game allows either individuals or teams the chance to operate a farm in a simulated environment. Beginning with cash and certain loan possibilities, the farmer must acquire land by renting or purchasing a farm with various use characteristics. The players must determine the crops grown, the level of technology used, and the rotation schedule. For livestock production, decisions are made as to the type of livestock raised and the livestock technology used. Specific ranges are given for that crop and livestock yield on each class of land with a specified level of technology. Each farmer tries to operate his farm to attain goals set forth by the game administrator.

SIMFARM is designed so that the administrator can easily concentrate on specific objectives while using the game. Slight changes in the costs and incomes will focus attention on different aspects of farm management.

II. Training Purpose

This game is designed to familiarize participants with the typical problems one must face in the operation of a farm and to give the participants experience in making management decisions under a variety of management conditions.

III. Decisions Made by Participants

1. Farm purchases and rentals
2. Crop technology
3. Crop rotation
4. Crops grown
5. Livestock technology
6. Livestock raised
7. Machinery used
8. Nonfarm investments

Decisions Made by Administrator

1. Deterministic or stochastic model used
2. Game objectives
3. Persons per team

IV. Administration

This computer-scored game is programmed in FORTRAN for use on the CDC 3600 and IBM 360 computers, requiring about 16K memory and two tape decks. The administrator has the option of choosing a deterministic or stochastic model. Each farm receives the following printouts: a summary of farm production, a net worth statement, and a loan statement. The administrator receives information about the status of the market.

V. SOURCE

Warren H. Vincent, *Simfarm,* Department of Agricultural Economics, Agriculture Hall, Michigan State University, East Lansing, Michigan.

(*C*)

BANKING

Banking

I. DESCRIPTION

Participants in this game represent competitive bankers. Groups of three are formed to represent a market consisting of three institutions. The administrator reads, from a prepared list, one possible transaction after another and each participant, acting as a banker in a market consisting of three competitive institutions, decides whether or not he wishes to be a party to the transaction. The profit of his bank as well as the number of useful activities occurring in his community depend on these decisions. Information on investment opportunities, new deposits, and interest rates is available along with the last period's balance sheets. Success is measured by bank profit and increase in loans made to customers.

II. TRAINING PURPOSE

This game seeks to emphasize the creation of money through credit expansion, the significance of credit to business activity, and the influence of the banking system on putting savings of people and businesses to productive use.

III. DECISIONS MADE BY PARTICIPANTS

1. Bank's interest rate
2. Rate, quantity, and risk combination at which loans are granted
3. Quantity of securities bought and/or sold

Decisions Made by Administrator

1. Reserve ratio
2. Volume of investment opportunities offered each period

IV. Administration

Worksheets for recording decisions and decision results are provided along with factor sheets which give detailed facts of the game. All computations are manual.

V. Source

Erwin Rausch. Direct inquiries to Science Research Associates, Inc., 259 East Erie Street, Chicago, Illinois.

(M)

Bankloan

I. Description

Bankloan is played between two sets of teams, one representing banks and the other representing companies attempting to secure loans. The object of the bank players is to obtain the maximum interest income from loans and to maintain deposits. The company players attempt to secure the most favorable borrowing terms and to give up the least in compensating balances. The bank players must analyze and evaluate loan applications of the companies, consider the risks involved, and then decide on proper loan restrictions in granting the loan. By placing restrictive covenants on the loans in such areas as collateral, debt/equity ratio, current ratio, expenses/sales ratio, and receivables turnover, the banks can reduce the chance that a loan will go bad. At the same time, if banks are too restrictive, they will lose loans to another bank. The bankers receive financial data about each company and interview company players. Interview information must be used to evaluate the capabilities of the companies to meet their loan obligations.

II. Training Purpose

The game provides participants with experience in evaluating loan applications, interviewing applicants, and analyzing differences in risk so as to tailor loan conditions to specific situations.

III. Decisions Made by Participants

A. Banks
  1. Interest rate
  2. Restrictive covenants
B. Companies
  1. Acceptance or rejection of loan from various banks

IV. Administration

The game may be played with six or more players. Actual play requires about one and one-half hours. A discussion period may follow. Decisions are made on a "Loan Agreement" form.

V. Source

Manual, *Bankloan*, Abt Associates, Inc., 55 Wheeler Street, Cambridge, Massachusetts.

(*M*)

Bank Management Simulation

I. Description

This general banking game allows teams of three to five members to operate a simulated $50 million commercial bank for several years in a single day. In order to operate the bank profitably, the teams must follow a balanced program of deposit solicitation, loans, and investments. Up to nine bank officers may be hired by the teams. They must determine the officers' salaries and allocate their time either in conservation of present accounts or solicitation of new accounts in any of three types of commercial accounts. While interest rates to depositors are fixed, the teams set the rates and service charges for each of the account sizes. Consumer and real estate loans are affected by the interest rates charged and the advertising and promotional expenditures. This last item also influences the amount of time deposits. The bank can invest in 90-day treasury bills and 2-year U.S. Government notes. Performance is measured by profits achieved and increases in capital growth through retained earnings.

II. TRAINING PURPOSE

This game was designed to teach overall asset management to bank officers. Through this simulation they can learn the interrelationships of the various banking activities.

III. DECISIONS MADE BY PARTICIPANTS

1. Officers hired and fired
2. Officer assignments
3. Rates on all loans
4. Service charges
5. Compensating deposit charges
6. Advertising and promotion

DECISION MADE BY ADMINISTRATOR

1. Periods of play

IV. ADMINISTRATION

The game is computer scored and programmed for IBM computers.

V. Source

Players' Instructions, *Bank Management Simulation,* IBM Technical Publications Department, 112 East Post Road, White Plains, New York.

(C, 291)

Credit Union Management Simulation

I. Description

In this game an unlimited number of teams, composed of five to eight members per team, act as management (board of directors) of simulated credit unions. The boards make decisions for six-month periods and may play up to six periods.

The teams begin play with reports from a hypothetical credit union. These reports include a balance sheet, income and expense statement, cash flow report, and financial industry and credit union forecast. The teams use these reports as a basis for decisions on rates charged and paid, promotions, and investments. After the reports are completed and evaluated for a six-month period, new reports are furnished the teams for another sequence.

II. Training Purpose

The purpose is to give the participants experience in making decisions in the essential areas of credit union financial management—specifically the allocation or management of resources.

III. Decisions Made by Participants

    1. Loans to members
       a. Maximum amount and rate for new personal loans
       b. Maximum amount and rate for auto loans
       c. Maximum amount and rate for mortgage loans
       d. Rates on loans covered by shares
    2. Investments

    a. Government securities and periods to maturity

    b. Certificates of deposit

    c. Securities to sell

3. Promotion expenses to increase shares purchased and loan demand
4. Funds loaned to other credit unions
5. Funds borrowed from banks or other credit unions
6. Semiannual dividend rate
7. Interest refund

IV. ADMINISTRATION

This game is computer scored on an IBM 360.

V. SOURCE

Player's Manual, H. E. Thompson, *Credit Union Management Simulation,* Graduate School of Business, University of Wisconsin, Madison, Wisconsin, 1968.

(C)

The Fiduciary Activity Simulation for Training

I. DESCRIPTION

The players in this game, acting as officers in a trust company, receive nine client profiles. After consultation with the game administrator, the players must submit "account decisions" on special forms giving their appraisal of a client's requirements and the communications which led them to these conclusions. After scoring of the account decisions by a controller, an experienced "arbitrator" leads the players into greater clarification of the client's needs, allowing the players to create detail concerning personal or corporate financial condition. After this, the arbitrator reveals all client background information and makes necessary changes in the player's appraisal. The players are then given the opportunity to make investment decisions in a hypothetical market for their clients. These investments are made by committees which give the players the chance to view many client positions and asset employment.

II. Training Purpose

This game was designed for the United States Trust Company of New York. It provides experience for trainees in interrelating three aspects of the Trust Company's operation: (1) the special situation of every client, (2) the investment market, and (3) the administrative machinery of the Trust Company. It allows the trainees to meet these factors in a simulated situation and to observe the interrelationships.

III. Decisions Made by Participants

1. Clients' investment requirements
2. Communications with the arbitrator
3. Investments purchased and sold

IV. Administration

This is a manually scored game in which the role of arbitrator is played by an officer of the Trust Company. He makes all decisions concerning the feedback to the trainees.

V. Source

The Fiduciary Activity Simulation for Training, Abt Associates, Inc., 55 Wheeler Street, Cambridge, Massachusetts.

(M)

Operation Federal Reserve

I. Description

This game places team members in the top management echelon of one of four national banks, each of which is a member of the Federal Reserve System. These teams interact with most of the external factors affecting banks, but not with each other; i.e. one bank does not get more loan applications because another refused to grant a loan.

The objective of each team is to optimize profits while maintaining adequate balances of reserves and other assets. Income is gained by interest earned on callable and noncallable loans and by securities.

II. TRAINING PURPOSE

Operation Federal Reserve is a general banking game designed to illustrate the economic effects of the decisions of the Federal Reserve Board. It also develops an understanding of money, credit, and banking, and clarifies the cause-effect relationships of the money market.

III. DECISIONS MADE BY PARTICIPANTS

1. Callable and noncallable loans granted
2. Callable loans called in
3. Purchases and sales of securities
4. Purchases and sales of treasury bonds
5. Changes in balance with Federal Reserve Board
6. Loans to be rediscounted

DECISIONS MADE BY ADMINISTRATOR

1. Reserve and margin requirements
2. Rediscount rate
3. Treasury bond rates
4. Open market committee actions
5. Callable and noncallable loan applications

IV. ADMINISTRATION

This game can be scored manually in a few minutes.

V. SOURCE

Allen A. Zoll, 3rd, *Dynamic Management Education,* United Business Supply, Seattle, Washington, 1966.

(*M*)

Stanford Bank Management Simulator

I. DESCRIPTION

This general banking game requires that the players manage a $500 million commercial bank. The economic model is designed so that decisions of one team do not affect the other teams. The model presents a generalized picture of banking conditions in the late 1950's and early 1960's.

Quarterly decisions are based on information from the previous quarters —economic and statistical information, the conditions of other teams, each team's own operating results, and a statement of condition.

This game can be played in short or long form. The short form allows the participants to concern themselves with general decisions of banking— the salary levels to pay, service charges, investments, interest rates, and the like. The long form of the game allows the players to make the periodic decisions—bank expansion, the issuance of capital notes and capital stock, and the payment of dividends. The long form of the game increases the number of computer cards needed from three to four.

II. TRAINING PURPOSE

This general banking game allows the participants to gain an overall view of banking. It allows them to look at the relationship between the decisions they make and the economy. They must concern themselves with both short- and long-term decisions.

III. DECISIONS MADE BY PARTICIPANTS

1. Salary levels
2. Interest rates on loans
3. Compensating balances
4. Service charges
5. Advertising and promotion
6. Business development
7. Maximum F.R.B. borrowing

8. Maximum public time deposits
9. Level of unpledged securities
10. Investment purchases and sales
11. Bank branch expansion
12. Issuance of capital notes and capital stock
13. Dividends

IV. ADMINISTRATION

This simulation is computer scored. At the end of each quarter the computer prints out a balance sheet, an income statement, and the loan and investment portfolios for each company. It also provides economic and statistical information and a summary of the operations of all the teams.

V. SOURCE

Participant's Manual, A. A. Robichek, C. W. Haley, and W. D. Wiebuhr, *Stanford Bank Management Simulator,* Graduate School of Business, Stanford University, Stanford, California, 1965.

(C)

FOREST PRODUCTS

Dynamic Forest Products Management Simulator

I. DESCRIPTION

This game is based on a simulated segment of the forest products industry. It consists of an interaction game of six teams—three distributors or wholesalers and three producers. The product mix is of two basic types, a high grade paneling product and a low grade sheathing product. New high grade paneling can be "created" by expenditure of research and development funds for product development. A second R&D expenditure for process improvement will tend to reduce manufacturing costs for both the paneling and sheathing grades.

The producers must compete against each other both for raw material (timber) and for markets (wholesalers). Each producer owns a small amount of timber but must rely primarily on public timber which becomes available in random quantities. Actual oral bidding among the producers takes place for timber. "Official" appraisal costs, grades, and quantities become available for bidding by the producers. The highest bid over the appraisal price determines the successful bidder for timber. Logging costs and transportation costs vary for each timber sale.

Producers must convert harvested timber into veneer using recovery ratio information for each of the two log grades. The supply of veneer is then manufactured into plywood and sold to wholesalers on a negotiated price and quantity basis.

Wholesalers must purchase their product mix from the three producers of plywood. The three wholesalers compete for sales in four marketing areas on a price basis. The demand for the sales areas is highly correlated to industrial and residential building indices. Individual company sales are weighted by the salary-commission structure and number of salesmen in the marketing area.

All decisions are made on a monthly basis with operating statements, inventory levels, sales levels, and production levels being reported at the end of each period. The accounting statements are based on a direct costing procedure as a method for better training.

Inventories are maintained for standing timber, logs by grade at the mill, veneer by grade, and plywood by grade for each producer. Wholesalers have inventories of each product (which are increased whenever a new product is manufactured) and grade of plywood manufactured by the producers.

At many points throughout the game, a stochastic process is used to suggest the realism of operating under risk conditions.

II. TRAINING PURPOSE

This forest products simulator has been designed to create a complex and realistic environment for management training. It provides a facility for making decisions and receiving feedback in production, marketing, and financial areas of a business concern. Participants may experiment with inventory rules, manufacturing processes, and marketing and price strategies.

III. DECISIONS MADE BY PARTICIPANTS

A. Manufacturing
   1. Acquisition of raw material
   2. Desirable log mix
   3. Inventory levels of:
      a. Standing timber
      b. Logs
      c. Veneer
      d. Plywood
   4. R&D expenditures for plant or process
   5. Borrowing and repayment
   6. Negotiations for price and quantity with wholesalers
B. Wholesalers
   1. Negotiations with producers for price and quantity
   2. Inventory levels of old and new products as they are manufactured
   3. Borrowing and repayment
   4. Marketing/price strategies
   5. Advertising strategies
   6. Market forecasts

IV. ADMINISTRATION

The role of the administrator in most instances is passive. His primary function is to conduct oral bidding for timber sales when sales are announced to the participants. Further, he will have to assist in communicating price and quantity decisions between wholesalers and producers. The indicators may be constructed or changed by the administrator. The simulator has been programmed in FORTRAN IV for use on an IBM 360/50 with disk and tape facilities.

V. SOURCE

Kenneth D. Ramsing, College of Business Administration, University of Oregon, Eugene, Oregon.

(C)

The Georgia-Pacific Management Game

I. DESCRIPTION

This is an interaction game involving five teams, two of which act as manufacturers that supply three wholesalers with two products. One product is a commodity item, such as Fir Plywood, and the other product is a high margin specialty item, such as paneling. The wholesalers compete with one another in the sales of these products. The teams make a wide range of decisions relating to the operation of their businesses in an attempt to increase their relative shares of the market and the rate of return. The manufacturing teams negotiate with the wholesalers as to sales price and quantity.

The total market is divided into four geographical areas. Each wholesaler has a home area in which he has the advantage in transportation costs. In the fourth area, all three teams compete on an equal basis. Each wholesaler has a sales team, whose individual backgrounds and personality characteristics are provided. The sales team may be assigned in any manner to the different geographical areas, and salesmen may be hired, fired, or trained.

Decisions are made on a monthly basis, and an operating statement including income, assets, market information, sales analysis, production costs, and inventory is provided before each set of decisions is made. Total market information, including income statements and balance sheets for the other teams, is distributed each quarter. Twenty minutes are allowed for making decisions.

II. TRAINING PURPOSE

The game provides participants with experience in making overall financial, marketing, and personnel decisions for the operation of manufacturing or wholesale businesses in a competitive environment. In a short training period, they can see the results that their decisions would have over a period of several months and get an insight into the consequences of different marketing strategies.

III. Decisions Made by Participants

Manufacturing Teams
    1. Borrowing and repayment
    2. Purchase of raw materials
    3. Research and development
    4. Plant investment
    5. Negotiations with wholesalers as to price and quantity

Wholesaling Teams
    1. Negotiations with manufacturers
    2. Borrowing and repayment
    3. Placement of sales force
    4. Hiring, firing, and training
    5. Marketing expenditures
    6. Prices
    7. Markets

Decisions Made by Administrator

    1. Production costs
    2. Transportation costs
    3. Raw materials price
    4. Price and marketing sensitivities
    5. New bulletins, forecasts, trends, indicators
    6. Starting values, objectives, local ground rules

IV. Administration

The game is scored on an IBM 1401 computer. Scoring takes from five to ten minutes.

V. Source

Jay L. Lammons, Manager—Marketing Services, Georgia-Pacific Corporation, Commonwealth Building, Portland, Oregon. This game has been developed by the Georgia-Pacific Corporation. It is not available to training directors.

(*C*)

Purdue University Forest Management Game

I. DESCRIPTION

Three teams are organized to manage three districts of an even-aged forest. Each district is divided into 60 compartments ranging in size from 230-590 acres, and each compartment is managed as a homogeneous unit of uniform site. Decisions concerning the preparation of the annual budget of expenditures and the annual schedule of management activities are required by each team. The objective of each team is to operate in the most efficient manner while supplying a mill with pulpwood on a sustained yield basis.

Each team is evaluated and compared with the other teams on the basis of its yearly performance as measured by net income before taxes and return on investment. Based on the relative performance of each district, a given amount of money is allotted to each of the three districts for the coming year. This money is then allotted to the various management activities available to each district.

II. TRAINING PURPOSE

This game is designed to provide students of forest management with an opportunity to experience budgeting, scheduling, and other decision-making problems associated with operational forest management. The game concentrates more on activities associated with operational management than it does on top-level policy decisions. Consequently, policy formulation is not emphasized as strongly as are the yearly decisions.

III. DECISIONS MADE BY PARTICIPANTS

1. Where and how much to harvest
2. Where and how much to thin
3. Residual basal areas for thinned compartments
4. Where to plant

5. Where and how much site to prepare
6. What type of site preparation
7. How much to spend on fire control
8. Desirability of an inventory
9. Where and how much timber to schedule for sale in two years (Necessary because harvest cuts are prepared for sale two years prior to actual harvesting)
10. How much to spend for property tax

DECISIONS MADE BY ADMINISTRATOR

1. Determination of yearly costs, market price, allowable cut, and allotted budget for each district
2. Running the game

IV. ADMINISTRATION

The game is written in FORTRAN IV for the CDC 6500. The program requires 32K words of core and one tape or disk drive.

V. SOURCE

B. Bruce Bare, Department of Forestry and Conservation, Purdue University, West Lafayette, Indiana.

(C)

INSURANCE

A Life Insurance Company Management Game

I. DESCRIPTION

A game model of a mutual life insurance company has been programmed to allow one to thirty teams to manage a mutual life insurance company for a period up to ten years.

Each team is responsible for making decisions in three general areas. The price of the product is determined by each team. There is no competition for sales, so each team acts independently in its pricing action. The elements of the pricing decision are the premium rate to be charged, the dividend percentage to be allowed to new policyholders as well as existing policyholders, and the degree of underwriting selection used in the classification of risks.

The teams control the expenses of their operations. Most of these expenses relate to the selling function. The teams can determine the commission rates to be paid in the first policy year as well as renewal policy years, the level of persistency bonus (which improves the lapse rate), and the amount spent in the training of new agents. Each team competes for new agencies. Their success is a function of the number of new agencies they request as well as the level of compensation that they pay to agents. The additional decisions by which the team can elect to increase expenses are in the advertising area and in the improvement of home office service.

The third major area of decisions is in the allocation of new investments. The participants have a choice of government bonds, corporate bonds, mortgages, preferred stocks, and common stocks.

Decisions are made on a six-month basis. After each decision period, a semiannual statement of operations is printed out showing each team's policy exhibit (amount of insurance in force, new business, decreases), balance sheet, and the summary of operations. In addition, there is a detailed listing of general expenses. At the end of every second six-month period, each team is provided with pertinent information on the operation of the other teams.

Each team is allowed to formulate its own objectives. The relative success of each team is measured in terms of those objectives.

II. TRAINING PURPOSE

This life insurance management game gives the participants experience in making top-management decisions. It also assists them in understanding the intricate operation of a life insurance company.

III. DECISIONS MADE BY PARTICIPANTS

1. Premium rate
2. Underwriting policy

3. Advertising budget
4. New agencies to be established
5. Agency training
6. Home office service improvement
7. Persistency bonus
8. First-year commission rate
9. Renewal commission rate
10. Dividends
11. Investment distribution of new funds

DECISIONS MADE BY ADMINISTRATOR

1. Scheduling of new money rates for investment purposes
2. Controlling the total number of new agencies available
3. Controlling industry mortality fluctuations
4. Controlling industry sales trends

IV. ADMINISTRATION

The IBM 360 has been used in running the game using FORTRAN IV. A tape unit has been incorporated to store the necessary data from period to period. This game is described in the *Transactions of the 18th International Congress of Actuaries* in a paper entitled "Simulation Models for Life Insurance," by Russell M. Collins, Jr. and J. S. Hill.

V. SOURCE

Minnesota Mutual Life Insurance Company, Actuarial Department, 345 Cedar Street, St. Paul, Minnesota.

(*C*)

Management Decision Game

I. DESCRIPTION

Four teams are formed (two to seven members per team), each to manage a casualty type of insurance company. The companies compete for sales and profit in a single line of insurance in a growing market. Decisions are made annually concerning allocation of funds both for investment (securities and operating assets) and for marketing effort. Each team establishes a level of underwriting control and specifies premium rates. Share of the market is determined by a competitive model involving rates, underwriting control, and marketing effort. Results are obtained annually and presented in a balance sheet and an income statement. Teams compete over a period of six to eight simulated years.

II. Training Purpose

This exercise contributes to the participants' understanding of the interaction among the ratemaking, underwriting, marketing, and investment functions as they determine share of the market and corporate profit in a highly competitive environment.

III. Decisions Made by Participants

1. Investment in securities
2. Investment in operating assets
3. Marketing expenditure
4. Rate level
5. Degree of underwriting control

IV. Administration

The game may be scored both by an RCA 501 computer and by hand.

V. Source

Bernard Shorr, Research Department, Travelers Insurance Company, One Tower Square, Hartford, Connecticut. The game is not available for distribution outside of the company.

(*M, C*)

Managerial Game for Insurance Companies

I. DESCRIPTION

The game is played with two to five companies being involved. Each company is represented by five to six players from middle management rank or higher. The game simulates a company insuring privately owned automobiles and residential property. The players must make basic decisions such as price, the amount of liability retained on each risk, and the amount of dividends to be paid out. The teams must budget the number of policies to be sold, considering the funds available and the rate of growth, so that the company does not suffer financial stress. All business is written up for one year, but decisions are based on quarter years. The companies are permitted to borrow funds, and they have control of the amount of dividends to be paid out or the amount of profits to be retained. Investments are not allowed. The beginning information given each team includes balance sheets, sales data, and income statements.

II. TRAINING PURPOSE

The game gives the participants an opportunity to practice making decisions concerning an insurance company in a realistic environment.

III. DECISIONS MADE BY PARTICIPANTS

1. Price
2. Marketing costs
3. Underwriting retention on an individual risk and the amount of reinsurance required
4. Policies sold and premium
5. Premium from other lines
6. Dividends

DECISIONS MADE BY ADMINISTRATOR

1. Cost of training new agent
2. Policies sold per agent

3. Renewal ratio
4. Cost of catastrophe reinsurance
5. Cost of marketing information
6. Commission rate

IV. ADMINISTRATION

The game is programmed for computer administration.

V. SOURCE

John S. McGuinness, Bankers Life and Casualty Company, 4444 Lawrence Avenue, Chicago, Illinois.

(C)

Nationwide Insurance Model

I. DESCRIPTION

This model simulates the casualty insurance industry with three to five insurance companies competing for policy sales. The newly appointed management team begins by studying the operating methods used by the previous management of their company. The main variables which influence strategy selection are insurance rate (price), sales effort, market and product research, underwriting standards, policyholder selectivity, staffing, competition, and economic climate. Participants attempt to maximize volume and financial strength. An umpire provides feedback on the results of decisions, the competitive environment, and the general economic climate. Participants are required to prepare worksheets and annual reports. The game is usually played for 15 to 20 quarters with each set of decisions requiring approximately 25 minutes to complete.

II. TRAINING PURPOSE

This insurance game is designed to demonstrate the relationships between the interacting variables which influence the insurance industry.

III. Decisions Made by Participants

1. Price or rate
2. Sales expense
3. Market and product research
4. Policyholder selectivity
5. Loss control expenditures
6. Policies in force forecast
7. Service capacity

IV. Administration

The game is manually scored.

V. Source

Participant's Manual, *Nationwide Insurance Model* (Executive Decision Model No. 2), Management Center, Nationwide Mutual Insurance Company, Columbus, Ohio, 1962.

(M)

OASIS: Office Administration Simulation Study

I. Description

Nine teams are formed (two to five participants per team), each to manage certain clerical functions in an insurance company field office. Four types of transactions are processed by the clerical staff: claims, new business, changes, and renewals. Transactions enter the office each quarter, and appropriate staffing levels to process them are to be determined. Overtime and outside contract services may be used. Turnover rates for the clerical staff are to be determined. The game extends over eight simulated quarters (two years). Each team is given eight quarters of prior history in the office before it makes its first decision. Budgets (based on a variable budgeting system) are to be prepared for each of the two simulated years. Results are scored on service provided (depends on percentage of transactions completed each quarter, or backlog) and on certain expense measures relative to budget requirements.

II. TRAINING PURPOSE

OASIS gives participants experience in variable budgeting and provides an opportunity to plan in the areas of number and salary level of personnel, use of overtime, and outside contract services. The focus is on developing appropriate means for satisfying various service and expense objectives.

III. DECISIONS MADE BY PARTICIPANTS

1. Number of employees to be added at each salary rate
2. Number of employees to be promoted
3. Overtime and outside contract services plan
4. Priorities for processing transactions
5. Provisional budgets

IV. ADMINISTRATION

Analysis and scoring are by a FORTRAN IV program written for the UNIVAC 494 computer. The game can be run at a remote location, with results transmitted over a telecommunications network to an IBM 1050 terminal.

V. SOURCE

Bernard Shorr, Research Department, Travelers Insurance Company, One Tower Square, Hartford, Connecticut. The game is not available for distribution outside of the company.

(C)

Simulation of Life Insurance Decisions
(SOLID)

I. Description

Management teams are given a life insurance company of reasonable size to manage. Each team makes decisions of both a technical and a competitive nature. All business sold is ordinary—no group, term, industrial, or health coverages are involved. Decision areas include agency management, premium/dividend, underwriting, and investments. Actual claims are simulated and it is possible to run the game assuming either that each team takes control over the same company or that teams operate different companies of the same size and historical background. Periods of play are half-year intervals, with a time lag from the analysis of results until the implementation of decisions based on those results.

Because of the unique long-term nature of the life insurance business, it is desirable to play this game for many more periods than other management games. Decisions are implemented on a realistic basis and may show their effect only after many years. A final static decision run over many periods is provided for. Results are presented in the form of a life insurance company annual statement with comparative summaries in alternate periods.

II. Training Purpose

SOLID is designed to provide a realistic administrative experience in life insurance management. It may be used as an educational device to define the technical terms of business during the course of play, or it may be used as a tool for training in management when the technical knowledge is presumed.

III. Decisions Made by Participants

1. Average premium level
2. Underwriting standards
3. Retention limit
4. Advertising

5. New agency goal
6. Agency training
7. Home office service improvements
8. Persistency bonuses
9. First-year commissions
10. Renewal commissions
11. Dividend level
12. Investment of new funds

DECISIONS MADE BY ADMINISTRATOR

1. Industrywide mortality fluctuations
2. Industrywide sales gains
3. Investment returns on new funds
4. Claims—numbers and amounts

IV. ADMINISTRATION

SOLID is written in its full form in FORTRAN 1130. An earlier version is available in FORTRAN 360.

V. SOURCE

David G. Halmstad, West Lane, P.O. Box 124, Ridgefield, Connecticut.

(C)

PETROLEUM

A Management Game for the Petroleum Industry

I. DESCRIPTION

The game presents a hypothetical marketing area in which as many as seven oil companies are competing. An eighth company is programmed internally to represent the effect of independent competition. Minimum quality of the products must be met. Each company is assigned an initial share of the product market which is divided into three retail, three wholesale, and three unbranded jobber markets. The national economy of 1947-1958 is simulated for the companies to operate in. In this context the petroleum is assigned a fixed share of the national economy. The products sold are gas—premium and regular—and distillate and residual fuel oil. The decision inputs are annual and quarterly, with the annual decisions being all financial and the quarterly decisions largely marketing.

Each company is assumed to be a net purchaser of crude oil. The largest producer influences the price that all have to pay. Improvements in refining are geared toward maximum gasoline production at market octane level. Joint drilling ventures, transfers, exchanges, and agreements on petroleum products are not allowed.

II. Training Purpose

The training purpose is to illustrate the dynamics of the petroleum industry as influenced by decisions based on long-range objectives (ten years or more). These decisions are made under time pressure with incomplete information in the context of an entire integrated company.

III. Decisions Made by Participants

A. Annual decisions
   1. Total company capital expenditures and operating budget
   2. Percentage allocation to administrative department
   3. Percentage allocation to production department
   4. Percentage allocation to refining department
   5. Percentage allocation to marketing department
   6. Dividends declared
   7. Stock issue requested
   8. Long-term loan requested
   9. Length of loan

B. Quarterly decisions
   1. Crude runs to refineries

2. Premium and regular gasoline manufacturing
3. Tank wagon price of premium
4. Tank wagon price of residual
5. Discounts on unbranded gasoline, commercial distillate, home consumer's distillate, unbranded distillate, and commercial residual
6. Commercial residual
7. Posted price of crude oil
8. Percentage allocation marketing budget to advertising
9. Transfer price of premium, regular, distillate, and residual

IV. ADMINISTRATION

The model is programmed for an 1103. Computing time is 3 minutes, with printout time about 15 minutes. The results of quarterly operations are given to the teams in the form of a balance sheet, statement of income, and a summary of operations.

V. SOURCE

Participant's Manual, Max H. Post and William Viavant, *A Management Game for the Petroleum Industry,* Texas Instruments Supply Co., Dallas, Texas.

(C)

The University of Oklahoma Petroleum Game

I. DESCRIPTION

This game simulates the petroleum industry in which as many as ten companies compete for sales of a premium and regular gasoline, distillate and residual fuel, and petrochemicals. The products are marketed through retailers, wholesalers, and unbranded jobber markets. It is assumed every company is a net purchaser of crude. The game stresses the importance of the four areas of marketing, production, refining, and administration. The computer output provides feedback from the decisions made in each of these areas.

II. Training Purpose

The game is designed to give management personnel in various divisions of an integrated oil company an appreciation for the problems, requirements, and limitations of the decision makers in the other functional units of the organization. The production man will see the value of advertising and the critical factors in pricing; the marketing man will recognize the need for research and capital expenditures for modernization; the refinery man will understand why a firm drilling and production posture is desirable. And all of them will watch their decisions influence the profitability of the company's operation.

III. Decisions Made by Participants

Annual
1. Total budgets—marketing, production, administration, and refining
2. Dividends
3. Capital stock
4. Borrowing
5. Research and development

Quarterly
1. Budget for development and exploratory drilling
2. Average depth for exploratory wells
3. Posted price of crude
4. Crude runs to refineries
5. Amounts of products to produce
6. Prices of products produced
7. Discounts in specific markets
8. Transfer prices
9. Advertising

IV. Administration

The game was coded in FORTRAN II for the IBM 7090. The program contains over 1,000 statements and uses 2,000 internal parameters, weighing factors, and time series coefficients.

V. Source

Player's Manual, B. Walton, E. Z. Million, and W. Viavant, *University of Oklahoma Petroleum Game,* Computer Laboratory, University of Oklahoma, Norman, Oklahoma, 1961. Direct inquiries to: E. Z. Million, School of Business, University of Oklahoma, Norman, Oklahoma.

(*C*)

TRANSPORTATION

Air Canada Management Game

I. Description

This is a total enterprise game in which two airlines compete for passenger service from a central station to four other stations. Although the two teams are given different historical records, they begin the game with identical equipment and must follow the same rules.

Each team must carry out all management functions of its firm in a very competitive situation. Teams must decide how many flights they should schedule on each of the four routes and the composition of each of the routes, i.e., the ratio of first-class to economy seating. The teams can increase their share of the market by advertising and giving better service, both in the terminal and on the plane. All regularly scheduled maintenance is done at the central station, but extraordinary repairs may be done at the other stations at a much higher cost. Although most financing is generally done with internal funds, short-term and emergency loans are available. Costs are assessed for flying time, advertising, passenger services, maintenance, overhead, and financing. These costs are compared with revenues received to evaluate performance.

II. Training Purpose

This game is designed to show the interrelationships among the various departments of the airline. Participants must try to balance the costs incurred in providing the services with the revenue received.

III. Decisions Made by Participants

1. Number of scheduled flights for each route
2. Advertising expenditures
3. Passenger service expenditures
4. Marketing research
5. Maintenance procedures
6. Means of financing

IV. Administration

This game is programmed for the IBM 1401 computer.

V. Source

Participant's Manual, *Air Canada Management Game,* Air Canada, Place Ville Marie, Montreal 2, Canada. Direct inquiries to A. A. Lackman, Manager, Programme Development and Coordination.

(*C*)

Appalachian Airlines Simulation Game

I. Description

The game provides participants with experience in making decisions similar to those made by top management in the airlines industry. The game, designed for from two to nine teams, is dynamic and noninteractive and contains both deterministic and probabilistic elements. The team members represent a new executive team which has just taken over a company operating at a loss. Their objective is to improve the profit position of the company. Feedback in the form of output includes income statement, balance sheet, flight loads, and umpire record.

II. Training Purpose

The training purpose is to improve the decision-making process, reactions, goal selection, and implementation in a decision-making environment similar to that faced by middle to top management in an airline industry.

III. Decisions Made by Participants

1. Scheduling type of aircraft, configuration, route, and arrival time
2. Advertising policy for each city
3. Market information to be purchased

Decisions Made by Administrator

1. Selection of game parameters
2. Selection of the initial set of operating conditions under which the players assume control of the airline

IV. Administration

The game may be scored manually or with an IBM 1620 or 7040 computer. Manuals for supervisor, administrator, and operator along with the FORTRAN II program for both computers are furnished.

V. Source

Participant's Manual, Frank L. Hendrix, *Appalachian Airlines Simulation Game,* Bureau of Business and Economic Research, College of Business Administration, The University of Tennessee, Knoxville, Tennessee, 1966.

(*M, C*)

The District Simulation Management Game

I. Description

In this competitive general management game the participants play the role of district managers for independent truck leasing firms. Three individuals manage the three firms located in the district. They offer trucks to two kinds of customers, lease and transient. Those customers who lease trucks are long-term users, generally keeping the same truck for five years. For this game all transient customers are assumed to use the trucks for one week. For each of these two kinds of customers, there are three types of trucks, defined by their original cost, their general characteristics, and their probable customer use. The players try to maximize profits by buying and maintaining a fleet of trucks and by marketing these trucks to transient and lease customers.

II. TRAINING PURPOSE

This game is designed to provide realistic experience for personnel in the vehicular leasing industry. It attempts to show the results of good and poor management decisions, decisions which will be applicable to the real world.

III. DECISIONS MADE BY PARTICIPANTS

1. Lease rates per mile and per year
2. Transient rates per mile and per week
3. Marketing expenditures
4. Trucks bought and sold
5. Maintenance and service expenditures
6. Plant improvement
7. Expenditures to decrease loans

IV. ADMINISTRATION

This game has been programmed in FORTRAN II for an IBM 1401 computer. About three minutes on the IBM 1401 are required to process one period for three teams. The computer prints out a general industry report and a confidential report with information for each player.

V. SOURCE

Terry Wayne Kennedy, "Application of Simulation and Management Gaming to Vehicular Leasing" (Thesis), University of Miami, Coral Gables, Florida.

(C)

Travel Industry Management Simulation
(TIMSIM)

I. Description

Any number of teams are formed (up to 999), each to manage a hotel. Each management team must make a series of decisions involving rooms, promotional expenditures, expansion, convention and tour business, financing, restaurant and bar operations, etc. The decisions of each team then interact with those of the other teams as well as with the simulated environment. The simulated environment is based upon the results of an intensive field study in which hotel operations of all sizes are studied. In addition, the instructor's manual provides modifications which can be made so that the game can be adapted to unique situations, such as resort areas, convention centers, and communities that receive no tour and convention business. The game is played on a quarterly basis and the results of decisions are reflected in the profit and loss statement and the balance sheet for each hotel.

II. Training Purpose

The game is designed to provide students of the travel industry management, be they academic or practitioner, with greater insights into the decision-making problems faced by the hotel manager.

III. Decisions Made by Participants

1. Number of rooms
2. Price of rooms
3. Convention and banquet facilities
4. Restaurant and bar facilities
5. Promotional expenditure for advertising
6. Promotional expenditure for sales force
7. Special promotion expenditure
8. Uniqueness expenditure
9. Extra services expenditure

10. Discounts for convention and tour business
11. Maintenance and housekeeping expenditure
12. Quantity of help
13. Quality of help
14. Manager's bonus
15. Expenditure for additional competitive information
16. Amount and rate of borrowing

DECISION MADE BY ADMINISTRATOR

1. Weighting for special cases

IV. ADMINISTRATION

The game is written in FORTRAN IV and can be run on any system employing the FORTRAN language.

V. SOURCE

Laurence Jacobs, College of Business Administration, University of Hawaii, Honolulu, Hawaii.

(*C*)

Transportation Management Simulation

I. DESCRIPTION

In this game the participants direct a firm which has motor freight terminals in four eastern cities. Each team analyzes the company's financial structure, competitive position, and market outlook; teams make decisions on sales efforts, advertising levels, number of personnel, and customer services. The results of decisions are influenced by market conditions and competitive action.

Ideally each team is composed of six members—a general manager, controller, and four terminal managers. However, as few as three participants may comprise a team.

II. TRAINING PURPOSE

The game is designed to give participants general management indoctrination, budgetary control appreciation, company policy determination, and management control experience.

III. DECISIONS MADE BY PARTICIPANTS

1. Number of salesmen
2. Advertising expense
3. Local pickup and delivery of less than trailer load shipments
4. Size of loading dock work crews
5. General management expense
6. Safety, insurance, and driver training expenditures
7. Maintenance expenditures
8. Hiring and termination of drivers
9. Borrowing

DECISIONS MADE BY ADMINISTRATOR

1. Control of parameters
2. Control of terminal potential
3. Economic climate

IV. ADMINISTRATION

The game is designed to be run on an IBM 1620 computer with the program in FORTRAN II. Scoring may, however, be done manually. One clerk can usually score period results for four companies in three hours. An operating manual includes necessary procedures and records as well as enough blanks and forms for a six-member team to go through 18 simulation periods.

V. Source

Participant's Manual, Ronald W. Boling, *Transportation Management Simulation*, Bureau of Business and Economic Research, College of Business Administration, University of Tennessee, Knoxville, Tennessee.

(C, M)

RETAILING AND WHOLESALING

ASCOT

I. Description

The game simulates the operation of a service station competing with as many as four other stations relatively close to each other, in a local trading area. Each manager, or management team, has the opportunity to make such decisions as would be required in an actual competitive service station situation. (To obtain decision data the game's developers actually ran a service station for two years.)

In addition to boothlike structures simulating the service station, background noises as sound effects are piped into the competition area. In the competition participants are free to "scout" the competing stations. Each station is assumed to be four or five years old and well established. The stations sell regular and premium gasoline as well as the other items normally sold in a service station.

II. Training Purpose

The purpose of this game is to give the participants experience in making management decisions in a competitive service station situation in such a manner as to increase market position, net assets, and general growth.

III. Decisions Made by Participants

1. Selling price of premium gasoline
2. Selling price of regular gasoline
3. Class of service (basic, medium, or high)
4. Weekday business hours
5. Sunday business hours
6. Markup on sales
7. Advertising and promotion

Decisions Made by Administrator

1. Introduction of periodic operating and business conditions into computer

Decisions Made by Participants and Administrator

1. Inventories
2. Wage policy, extra wages, and rent
3. Savings and loans
4. Station records

IV. Administration

The game is played on ASCOT, a special purpose computer, which calculates and indicates sales and profits resulting from all decisions. Several years of station operation are compressed into about two hours of playing time. Forms are included in the introduction to the participant's manual, but the mathematical model is not available from the source.

V. Source

M. A. Cayley, Imperial Oil Limited, 111 St. Clair Avenue West, Toronto, Ontario, Canada. Inquiries concerning the ASCOT computer should be directed to Arthur Porter, Head of Industrial Engineering, University of Toronto, Toronto, Ontario, Canada.

(C, 221)

Automobile Dealer Simulation

I. DESCRIPTION

The business is an automobile dealership; the game simulates the problems involved in automobile marketing. The participants form three management groups selling similar but different makes of cars.

Each decision period represents one-quarter of a year. Teams have 30 minutes for all decisions. The game may be continued for as many quarters as desired.

The companies may be organized in any manner desired. Each company sells a low priced car, has been in business for some time, and is in a reasonably good financial position but has no available information regarding past policies, procedures, or operating results. Each dealership has a new car department, a used car department, a service department, and a parts and accessories department. Four sets of decisions, one for each department, must be made for each quarter.

Umpires receive the decisions from the competing teams and calculate the results, using as data the decisions made, past records, and mathematical equations which provide the economic background. At the end of each year of operations an annual summary is published by the umpires and distributed to each company. At the conclusion of play the umpires evaluate the various strategies of the three companies, explain the results, and answer questions of the participants regarding the scoring and evaluation.

II. TRAINING PURPOSE

The purpose of this game is to provide practice in decision making. The game is planned to show the interrelationships of decisions and the problems in integrating plans into a unified course of action which will satisfy the persons who control a business organization. Participants have an opportunity to work with others, to weigh and evaluate data available, to determine data needed and their value, to make decisions, and to observe the interrelationships and the effects of their decisions.

III. Decisions Made by Participants

1. Prices for new and used cars
2. Number of new car salesmen and used car salesmen
3. Local advertising for new and used cars
4. Market research
5. Similar decisions for other departments

Decisions Made by Administrator

1. Evaluation of teams and their strategies
2. Computations of results
3. Critique of the final outcome

IV. Administration

The game is manually scored by the umpires. Each group is given an evaluation of its performance. The game is relatively simple.

V. Source

John J. Rath and Bruce E. DeSpelder, *Automobile Dealer Simulation,* Bureau of Business Research, School of Business Administration, Detroit, Michigan, 1960.

(*M*)

Business Management Decision Simulation
Orange Coast College

I. Description

Three teams are formed, each to operate a two-store department store chain. Three marketing areas exist, and there are two competing stores in each area. Each team prepares a sales budget for one quarter and decides expenditures for merchandising, product and methods research, and purchase of market information. The return on product and methods research depends on chance, but the probability of success increases with increased expenditures. Each team must order merchandise equivalent to expected sales and is penalized for failure to sell all merchandise budgeted for. If a team is very successful in operating one of its stores, a customer preference factor will increase for the store, the value of which will carry over to succeeding quarters. Performance is evaluated by a biannual report showing sales, net profit, and share of the total market. The game may be run as many times as desired, but usually eight quarters are sufficient.

II. Training Purpose

This game provides participants with experience in making major merchandising decisions in the operation of a retail department store chain.

III. Decisions Made by Participants

1. Preparing a budget from estimated sales
2. Advertising
3. Marketing research
4. Research and development—product and process

IV. Administration

Manual scoring requires about 30 minutes.

V. Source

Department of Business Administration, Orange Coast College, 2701 Fairview Road, Costa Mesa, California.

(*M*)

Note: This game is adapted from Paul S. Greenlaw, "The Kroger Company," *Supermarket Decision Simulation,* 1959.

Ford Dealership Simulation

I. Description

This proprietary management game is used by Ford Motor Company in its Ford Marketing Institute. Monthly decisions are made by teams composed of a dealer and several subordinate department managers. These teams are responsible for operating a large automobile dealership which sells both new and used cars, sells parts, and operates service and body shops. The facilities for all teams are the same at the beginning of the simulation but may be expanded if desired. The teams also make decisions concerning the purchase of new cars, the desired used car inventory, the financing of new and used car sales, advertising, and personnel matters. The objectives of the participants in this competitive simulation are to make profits, increase their share of the market and total sales, and maintain proper inventory and working capital levels.

II. Training Purpose

This simulation allows the participants to test various strategies for the operation of an auto dealership and to observe the results in a short time. It also lets the players share ideas and interact with each other.

III. Decisions Made by Participants

1. Vehicles purchased
2. Salesmen hired
3. Used cars needed
4. Advertising
5. Financing of sales
6. Personnel salaries

IV. Administration

This computer-scored game is conducted by experienced full-time instructors. Decisions are fed by the FMI teletype into Ford's computer in

Dearborn. The computer prints out monthly balance sheets, income statements, a diagnostic analysis, and a cash flow summary.

V. SOURCE

"Management by Computer," *NADA Magazine,* December 1967, pp. 64-67.

(C)

Kroger Supermarket Decision Simulation

I. DESCRIPTION

In this simulation, three supermarket chains operate two stores each. The market is divided into three regions; each chain has one store in two of these regions. For each team there is one region in which it has no store and no opportunity to build one. Separate decisions are made for each of the two stores run by the chain. The main variables which control the allocation of sales to each of the stores are advertising, special promotions, traffic leaders available, and product and methods research. Game managers are able to purchase market research concerning competitors and market trends. Management must carefully balance goods purchased with demand. The game administrator provides each chain with sales reports for each quarter and annual reports of sales, profit, and market shares every fourth quarter.

II. TRAINING PURPOSE

The game is designed to teach participants to synthesize and make decisions effectively as members of interacting business factors in a competitive situation.

III. DECISIONS MADE BY PARTICIPANTS

1. Merchandise purchases
2. Advertising
3. Special promotions

4. Traffic leaders
5. Product and methods research
6. Marketing research

DECISIONS MADE BY ADMINISTRATOR

1. Decision time available
2. Product and methods innovations

IV. ADMINISTRATION

This game is manually scored using prepared forms accompanying the game.

V. SOURCE

Player's Manual, Paul S. Greenlaw, *Kroger Supermarket Decision Simulation,* The Kroger Co., 35 E. 7th Street, Cincinnati, Ohio.

(*M*, 174)

Pitt Amstan Market Simulator

I. DESCRIPTION

This game has been specifically designed to duplicate the problems encountered by the branch managers of the Amstan Supply Division of the American Radiator and Standard Sanitary Corporation. Six competing distributors sell three product lines. Each of the six players is given a detailed list of the buying habits of some 300 possible customers to which he tries to sell three product lines. The list includes historical data about each customer, as well as the importance to each of them of factors like price, services, and advertising.

The player begins the game with six salesmen of different ability whom he can deploy in any way he sees fit; he may hire, fire, and train them. The game requires that the players decide how much time each salesman spends with each of the 300 customers—it may well be best to concentrate on the most important customers and let the others fall where they may. Profits are determined by the computer, which has more information than the players about each of the customers, as well as the outputs of the players.

II. TRAINING PURPOSE

The *Pitt Amstan Game* serves many purposes. Most importantly, it teaches the branch managers to balance revenue received with the costs incurred with each customer. It also gives the top executives a chance to view the problems of the branch managers. Finally, it is used to test the management capabilities of prospective branch managers.

III. DECISIONS MADE BY PARTICIPANTS

1. Allocate time of salesmen
2. Hire, terminate, and train salesmen
3. Set prices and terms

DECISIONS MADE BY ADMINISTRATOR

1. How each customer buys
2. From whom he buys

IV. ADMINISTRATION

This game is programmed for both the IBM 650 and the IBM 7070. The program runs an hour and a half on the IBM 650 and ten minutes on the IBM 7070.

V. SOURCE

American Radiator and Standard Sanitary Company, Amstan Supply Division, 100 Ross, Pittsburgh, Pennsylvania; or University of Pittsburgh, Computer Center Director, Pittsburgh, Pennsylvania.

(*C*, 7, 43, 127, 138, 174, 209, 239)

Purdue Supermarket Management Game

I. Description

In this game situation, the management team has just purchased a super-market that currently has a weak financial position. Each team has financial data for the past year, including the decisions made by the previous manager during the last week of his tenure. This includes data on profit margins, specials, advertising, and other information pertinent to supermarket operation. The team of three to five members is competing with two to five other supermarkets in a given area of a large city. Each of these stores has four departments—produce, meat, grocery, and dairy. The team, through decisions on marketing, personnel, and advertising strategy, is to improve the operation of the store while competing with the other teams.

The decision period is one week, and six to eight decision sets are suggested. The game is deterministic. Current decisions affect future as well as current results. The computer output includes an operating statement, a balance sheet, and general information.

II. Training Purpose

This business game provides a decision-making situation which demonstrates the interrelationships of the key factors which influence the profit margin in a supermarket. The simulation is designed to teach economic and accounting principles and the necessity of planning.

III. Decisions Made by Participants

1. Margin on products
2. Ordering of products
3. Specials
4. Stamp expenditure
5. Hiring and terminations
6. Advertising
7. Borrowing

Decisions Made by Administrator

1. Initial market potential
2. May act as one of the teams

IV. Administration

This is a computer game programmed in FORTRAN II and takes about one minute for computer processing. Forms are provided in the manual for decisions, cash budget, and decisions records.

Copies of the computer program may be obtained by writing to Program Information Department, Program Distribution Center, International Business Machines Corporation, 40 Saw Mill Road, Hawthorne, New York; the source program is also listed in *Management Games for Teaching and Research*.

V. Source

Participant's Manual, Emerson M. Babb and Ludwig M. Eisgruber, *Purdue Supermarket Management Game*, Educational Methods, Inc., 20 East Huron Street, Chicago, Illinois. Emerson M. Babb and Ludwig M. Eisgruber, *Management Games for Teaching and Research*, 1966.

(*C*, 15, 16)

Retail Management Game

I. Description

The players in this competitive retailing game operate a men's clothing store. The participants control such things as store size and layout, purchasing, marketing, financing, personnel, and price. The complex demand model includes 23 factors, many of which concern competitors' actions and other factors of the external environments.

The game is designed to allow the administrator to change the parameters to fit his own needs. The game administrator may vary the number of goods sold, the factors affecting demand, team size and composition, the effects of the different variables on demand, etc. Only the noncompetitive price index, which is based on empirical evidence wherever possible, is inflexible.

II. Training Purpose

This game is designed to give the players experience in retail management in a complex and realistic environment. It allows the participants to view the effects of the factors determining demand and consumer behavior.

III. Decisions Made by Participants

1. Price
2. Store labeling
3. Advertising
4. Personnel
5. Store layout and size
6. Financing
7. Union negotiation
8. Buying

Decisions Made by Administrator

1. Team composition
2. Number of products sold
3. Number of factors affecting demand
4. Importance of factors affecting demand

IV. Administration

Once the administrator has set up the game parameters to achieve his desired objectives, it is very easy to administer. Decisions are fed into a computer which prints out information such as net profits for each store.

V. Source

Robert E. Schellenberger, "A Computerized Multipurpose Management Game Applied to Retailing," *Journal of Retailing,* Vol. 41, No. 4, Winter 1965-66, pp. 10-20.

(C, 227)

Retailing Department Management Game

I. Description

Acting as the buyer for two departments of a large Midwestern department store, the participants in this game try to maximize the profit performance of their company. Each of these departments sells a single product line. These product lines (A and B) have different costs, sales prices, overhead costs, etc. Because there is a two-period lag time for ordering merchandise, the participant begins the game with specific quantities of his two products ordered for the first two periods. In these two periods the player must decide upon the number of clerks he will need and the prices he wishes to charge for each of his product lines. In the following periods, he must also order merchandise. Costs are assessed for sales clerks' salaries, overhead, carrying costs, and merchandise purchases. Revenues are received for sales of merchandise. These sales are limited by three factors—sales clerks available, merchandise available, and market demand. As stated before, the objective of each participant is to maximize profits.

II. Training Purpose

The purpose of this game is to expose the participant to the problems a retail store buyer faces in buying merchandise. It is designed to point out specifically the problems of forecasting demand, inventory, personnel requirements, and profitability of products.

III. Decisions Made by Participants

1. Merchandise ordered
2. Sales clerks hired
3. Price

Decisions Made by Administrator

1. Modifications of market trends
2. Time available for decisions

IV. Administration

This game can be scored manually in about three minutes. When more variables are added to create a more complex situation, computers are usually needed for scoring.

V. Source

Jay R. Greene and Roger L. Sisson, *Dynamic Management Decision Games,* John Wiley & Sons, Inc., New York, 1959, pp. 25-37.

(*M*, 108, 109)

Wholesale Building Material Simulation

I. Description

The Swedish corporation Inter Pares is made up of 30 wholesalers in the building material industry with total sales of over $100 million. Inter Pares is the first Swedish company to attempt to tailor a management simulation for its own educational purposes. Three teams (companies) are located in one geographical area. The demand for building materials is approximately $5 million per year in this area. The teams may sell three different types of products, two of which are carried as inventory. Product A represents building materials which have the possibility of product differentiation (floor covering, doors, etc.). Product B includes no possibilities for product differentiation (cement). Product C represents the bids building material firms make when they offer all material needed for construction of an apartment complex, a hospital, etc.

The simulation is primarily directed toward the marketing decision of pricing, credit, advertising, salesmen's salaries, and market analysis. The computer version is characterized by easy manipulation of the value on demand elasticities, quantity discounts, "import prices" from other areas, etc. When the teams take over, the periods January through March have already been completed. Teams have approximately equal positions on April 1. The decision period is one month.

II. TRAINING PURPOSE

The simulation is part of a large-scale education program for salesmen in member firms. The particular purposes of the simulation are to show the interdependence of variables, to teach quantitative decision-making analysis, and to discuss Pareto optimality and other types of objective functions.

III. DECISIONS MADE BY PARTICIPANTS

1. Ordering quantities of Products A, B, and C
2. Offered price for Products A, B, and C
3. Credit offers for Products A, B, and C
4. Marketing costs for Products A, B, and C
5. Purchase of market analysis or not
6. Salesmen's salaries

DECISIONS MADE BY ADMINISTRATOR

1. Direction of the "dynamics" of the game: direction of demand, cost developments, etc.

IV. ADMINISTRATION

The game can be run manually and by computer. The UNIVAC 1108 and IBM 360-65 versions are programmed in FORTRAN. The manual version requires three assistants and one administrator.

V. SOURCE

Sven Sundqvist, Handelshögskolan i Stockholm, Sveavägen 65, Stockholm Va. Sweden.

(C, M)

Selected Bibliography

1. Abt, Clark C., and Richard C. Scott, Jr., "Simulations and Training Programs," *Banking,* Vol. LIX, No. 49 (1966).
2. Acer, J. W., *Business Games: A Simulation Technique.* Iowa City, Iowa: State University of Iowa, 1960.
3. *Achievement Motivation and Risk-Taking in a Business Setting: A Study of the Relationship Between Achievement-Related Motives and Risk-Taking Behavior in a Simulated Business Situation.* New York: General Electric Company.
4. Ackoff, Russell L., "Games, Decisions, and Organizations," *General Systems: Yearbook of the Society of General Systems,* Vol. IV (1959), pp. 145-150.
5. Agersnap, T., and E. Johnson, "Decision Game of Managerial Strategy as a Research," *Proceedings 6th International Meeting of the Institute of Management Science* (1961).
6. Amos, J. M., "Educational Aspects of Business Games," *Journal of Business Education,* Vol. XL, No. 11 (1964).
7. "Amstan Supply's Business Game: P. & H. Wholesaling's Top Training Tool," *The Plumbing-Heating-Air Conditioning Wholesaler,* Vol. XV, No. 8 (1960), pp. 40-44.
8. Amstuz, Arnold E., "Management Games—A Potential Perverted," *Industrial Management Review,* Vol. V, No. 1 (1963), pp. 29-36.
9. Anderson, D. W., "A Game That Teaches Production Control Techniques," *Office,* Vol. LV, No. 5 (1962), p. 1324.
10. Andlinger, G. R., "Looking Around: What Can Business Games Do?" *Harvard Business Review,* Vol. XXXVI (July-August 1958), pp. 147-152 and "Business Games—Play One!" *Harvard Business Review,* Vol. XXXVI (March-April 1958), pp. 115-125.

11. Andrews, Robert B., and Thomas E. Vollman, "Uniproduct: A Pedagogical Device," *California Management Review,* Vol. X, No. 2 (1962), pp. 65-70.

12. Appley, L. A., "Executive Decision-Making: A New Strategy," *Think,* Vol. XXIII, No. 12 (1957), pp. 2-6.

13. "Are Management Games Just Games?" *Iron Age,* Vol. CXCVII, Pt. 3 (June 23, 1966), p. 53.

14. Babb, E. M., "Dairy Business Management Game Conducted by Purdue University," *American Milk Review,* Vol. XXV, No. 1 (1963), pp. 79-82.

15. ———, "Business Games as a Marketing Extension," *Journal of Farm Economics,* Vol. XLVI, No. 5 (December 1964), pp. 1024-1028.

16. ———, M. A. Leslie, and M. D. Van Slyke, "The Potential of Business Gaming Methods in Research," *The Journal of Business,* Vol. XLIX, No. 4 (1966), p. 465.

17. Barton, R. E., "Desiderata for a Flexible Management Game," *Bulletin of Operations Research Society of America,* Vol. XIV (1966), pp. 63-64.

18. ———, *The E & E Management Game.* St. Louis, Missouri: Ernst & Ernst, 1967.

19. ———, *The Imaginit Management Game.* Lawrence, Kansas: University of Kansas, 1965.

20. Bastable, C. W., "Business Games, Models, and Accounting," *The Journal of Accountancy* (1960), pp. 56-60.

21. Bechberger, G. W., W. F. Keleher, and F. L. Hunziker, "These Men Are Playing . . . Maintenance Management Games," *Factory* (1961), pp. 80-83.

22. Bellman, R., "Top Management Decisions and Simulation Processes," *The Journal of Industrial Engineering,* Vol. IX, No. 5 (September-October 1958), pp. 459-464.

23. ———, *et al.,* "On the Construction of a Multi-Stage, Multi-Person Business Game," *Operations Research* (August 1957), pp. 469-503.

24. Bernard, L., "Electronic Dry Run: Sylvania Admen Take a Whirl at Management, Prove Skilled Bosses," *Advertising Age* (May 1, 1961), p. 76.

25. Birnberg, Jacob G., and Raghu Nath, "Laboratory Experimentation in Accounting Research," *The Accounting Review,* Vol. XLIII, No. 1 (January 1968), pp. 38-45.

26. Boguslaw, R., and W. Pelton, "STEPS: A Management Game for Programming Supervisors," *Datamation* (November-December 1959), pp. 13-16.

27. Boocock, Sarane S., "Changing the Structure of Secondary Education," *Educational Technology,* Vol. VIII, No. 3 (1968), pp. 3-6.

28. ————, and E. O. Schild (eds.), *Simulation Games in Learning*. Beverly Hills, California: Sage Publications, 1968.

29. ————, "Simulation Games Today," *Educational Technology*, Vol. VIII (1968), pp. 7-10.

30. Bonini, C. P., *Simulation of Information and Decision Systems in the Firm*. Englewood Cliffs, New Jersey: Prentice-Hall, Inc., 1963.

31. Brown, R. G., "A General-Purpose Inventory-Control Simulation," D. G. Malcolm (ed.), *Report of System Simulation Symposium*. Baltimore, Maryland: Waverly Press, 1957.

32. ————, *An Inventory-Control Simulation*. Cambridge, Massachusetts: Arthur D. Little, Inc., 1958.

33. Buchin, Stanley I., "The Harbets Simulation Exercise and Management Control," Charles Bonini, *et al.* (eds.), *Management Controls: New Direction in Basic Research*. New York: McGraw-Hill Book Company, 1964, pp. 127-139.

34. Campbell, Forrest M., and E. Robert Ashworth, "Monopologs: Management Decision Making Game Applied to Tool Room Management," *The Journal of Industrial Engineering*, Vol. XI, No. 5 (September-October 1960), pp. 372-377.

35. ————, *et al.*, "The Maintenance Game," *The Journal of Industrial Engineering*, Vol. XV, No. 1 (January 1964), pp. 30-36.

36. Cangelosi, Vincent E., and William R. Dill, "Organizational Learning: Observations Toward a Theory," *Administrative Science Quarterly*, Vol. X, No. 2 (September 1965), pp. 175-203.

37. ————, "The Carnegie Tech Management Game: A Learning Experience in Production Management," *Academy of Management Journal*, Vol. VIII, No. 2 (June 1965), pp. 133-138.

38. Carson, John R., "Business Games: A Technique for Teaching Decision-Making," *Management Accounting* (October 1967), p. 31.

39. Carter, I. F., "Exercising the Executive Decision-Making Function in Large Systems," R. Glaser (ed.), *Training Research and Education*. New York: John Wiley & Sons, 1962, pp. 409-427.

40. Christian, William, "Don't Bet on Business Games," *Business Automation* (July 1961), pp. 22-25.

41. Churchill, Neil C., and Richard M. Cyert, "An Experiment in Auditing," *The Journal of Accountancy* (February 1966), pp. 39-43.

42. ————, Merton H. Miller, and R. M. Trueblood, *Auditing, Management Games, and Accounting Education*, Carnegie Institute of Technology Series on Contribution to Management Education. Homewood, Illinois: Richard D. Irwin, Inc., 1964.

43. Cincotti, Peter M., "A New Marketing Training Tool," *Journal of the American Society of Training Directors*, Vol. XIV (October 1960), pp. 7-10.

44. Clarkson, G. P. W., *Portfolio Selection: A Simulation of Trust Investment.* Englewood Cliffs, New Jersey: Prentice-Hall, Inc., 1961.

45. Cohen, Kalman J., *et al.,* "The Carnegie Tech Management Game," *The Journal of Business,* Vol. XXXIII, No. 4 (October 1960), pp. 303-321.

46. ———, *et al., The Carnegie Tech Management Game: An Experiment in Business Education.* Homewood, Illinois: Richard D. Irwin, Inc., 1964.

47. ———, *et al., The Carnegie Tech Management Game: A Progress Report on Mark III.* Pittsburgh: Carnegie Institute of Technology Graduate School of Industrial Administration, 1960.

48. ———, "The Educational Uses of Management Games," *Data Processing Yearbook, 1962-1963.* Detroit, Michigan: American Data Processing, Inc., 1963, pp. 135-142.

49. ———, and Merton H. Miller, "Management Games, Information Processing and Control," *Management International,* Vol. III, No. 3-4 (1963), pp. 159-177.

50. ———, *Trends in the Educational Uses of Management Games, Behavioral Theory of the Firm.* Pittsburgh: Carnegie Institute of Technology, 1962.

51. ———, "Simulation of the Firm," *American Economic Review,* Vol. L, No. 5 (1960), pp. 534-540.

52. ———, and Eric Rhenman, "The Role of Management Games in Education and Research," *Management Science,* Vol. VII, No. 2 (January 1961), pp. 131-166.

53. Coleman, J. S., "In Defense of Games," *American Behavioral Scientist,* Vol. X, No. 2 (October 1966), pp. 3-4.

54. Collett, Merril J., "Simulation as a Management Development Tool," *Personnel Administration,* Vol. XXV (March 1962), pp. 48-51.

55. Colley, J. L., Jr., "Simulation as a Production Aid," *The Journal of Industrial Engineering,* Vol. X, No. 4 (July-August 1959), pp. 296-298.

56. "Computers and Management Games," *Personnel Journal,* Vol. XL, No. 3 (July-August 1961), p. 123.

57. Conway, R. W., "Simulation in Profit Planning," D. G. Malcolm (ed.), *Report of System Simulation Symposium.* Baltimore, Maryland: Waverly Press, 1957.

58. Craft, C. J., and L. A. Stewart, "Competitive Management Simulation," *The Journal of Industrial Engineering,* Vol. X, No. 5 (September-October 1959), pp. 355-363.

59. ———, *Management Games Using Punched Cards and Computers.* New York: Peat, Marwick, Mitchell and Company, n.d.

60. ———, "Management Games Using Electronic Computers," *Management Controls,* Vol. VII, No. 10 (October 1960), pp. 196-202.

61. Craigin, S., and P. Fernalo, *Simulation Management Lab.* Boston: Harvard University Press, April 1959.

62. Cushen, Walter Edward, "Operational Gaming in Industry," Joseph F. McCloskey and John M. Coppinger (eds.), *Operations Research for Management, II.* Baltimore, Maryland: Johns Hopkins Press, 1956.

63. Cyert, R. M., D. C. Dearborn, and W. R. Dill, *The C. I. T. Management Game.* Pittsburgh: The Carnegie Institute of Technology, 1958.

64. Dale, A. G., and C. R. Klasson, *Business Gaming: A Survey of American Collegiate Schools of Business.* Austin, Texas: The University of Texas Bureau of Business Research, 1964.

65. ———, "Management Decision Tester: Computer Used to Simulate Operations of Small Business," *Computers and Automation,* Vol. IX (October 1962), pp. 47-49.

66. ———, *et al., Small Business Executive Decision Simulation.* Austin, Texas: University of Texas, 1963.

67. Daly, Andrew A., "In-Basket Games," *Journal of the American Society of Training Directors,* Vol. XIV, No. 8 (1960), pp. 8-15.

68. Datz, I. M., "Simulated Shipping," *Datamation,* Vol. XII, No. 2 (1966), pp. 61-63.

69. Day, Ralph, "The Noncomputer Decision Game as a Teaching Device for Business Courses," *Collegiate News and Views,* Vol. XIV (May 1961), pp. 17-19.

70. Deacon, A. R. L., Jr., *Selected References on Simulation and Games.* Saranac Lake: AMA Academy, April 1960.

71. "Decision-Making Simulation, Remington Rand UNIVAC's Simulation Program for Sales Management," *Imaginative Uses for the Computer,* Automatic Data Processing Policy Report 36, John Diebold and Associates, 1959, pp. 21-28.

72. Deep, S. D., B. M. Bass, and J. A. Vough, *Some Effects on Business Gaming of Previous Quasi-T Group Affiliation.* Pittsburgh: University of Pittsburgh Graduate School of Business, 1968.

73. Dennick, W. H., and F. X. Olanie, Jr., "Bank Management Game," *Bankers Monthly,* Vol. LXXVII (September 1960), pp. 56-60.

74. Dill, William R., *et al.,* "Experiences with a Complex Management Game," *California Management Review,* Vol. III, No. 3 (1961), pp. 38-51.

75. ———, J. R. Jackson, and J. W. Sweeney (eds.), *Proceedings of the Conference on Business Games.* New Orleans: Tulane University Press, 1962.

76. ———, ———, ——— (eds.), *Proceedings of the Conference on Busi-*

ness Games as Teaching Devices. New Orleans: Tulane University Press, 1962.

77. ———, et al., *Some Educational and Research Results of a Complex Management Game.* Pittsburgh: Carnegie Institute of Technology Graduate School of Industrial Administration, October 1960.

78. ———, and Neil Doppett, "The Acquisition of Experience in a Complex Management Game," *Management Science,* Vol. X, No. 1 (October 1963), pp. 30-46.

79. ———, "The Business Game," *Carnegie Alumnus,* Vol. XLV (November 1959), pp. 4-9.

80. ———, "What Management Games Do Best," *Business Horizons,* Vol. IV, No. 3 (Fall 1961), pp. 55-64.

81. Dobles, Robert W., and Robert F. Zimmerman, "Management Training Using Business Games," *Training and Development Journal,* Vol. XX (June 1966), pp. 28-34.

82. Dobrin, Saxe, "Let's Pretend—A Game for Marketing Men," *Industrial Marketing* (June 1958), pp. 49-51.

83. Dow, D. S., M. J. Kaitz, and H. A. Orenstein, *The Development of a System Training Method for Presentation of a Business Game.* Santa Monica, California: System Development Corporation, June 1959.

84. Drury, J., "A Business Management Game," *Computer Bulletin 6* (September 1962).

85. Eilon, S., "Management Games," *Operations Research Quarterly,* Vol. XIV (June 1963), pp. 137-149.

86. Emery, J. C., "Simulation Techniques in Inventory Control and Distribution," *Operations Research Reconsidered,* AMA Management Report 10 (1958).

87. "Executives Play Games," *Chemical and Engineering News,* Vol. XXXV, No. 17 (May 13, 1957), pp. 40-41.

88. "Exploring the Think in Plant Management," *Factory,* Vol. CXIX (December 1961), p. 130.

89. Feeney, G. J., "Simulating Marketing Strategy Problems," *Marketing Times,* Vol. II, No. 1 (January 1959).

90. Fessler, M. E., C. B. Saunders, and J. D. Steele, *Proceedings of the National Symposium on Management Games.* Kansas: University of Kansas Center for Research in Business, 1959.

91. Flood, M. M., "Some Experimental Games," *Management Science* (October 1958), pp. 5-26.

92. Focarino, J., and W. Wright, "A Sales Game You Can Play Too!" *The American Salesman,* Vol. V, No. 11 (July 1960), pp. 26-37.

93. "For Global Gamesmen: INTOP Bring International Touch to Training of Corporate Executives," *Business Week* (November 30, 1963), p. 70.

94. Frank, H. E., and S. J. Pringle, " 'In Tray' Training Exercises," *Journal of the American Society of Training Directors,* Vol. XVI (April 1962), pp. 27-30.

95. French, Wendell L., "A Collective Bargaining Game," *Journal of the American Society of Training Directors,* Vol. XV, No. 1 (January 1, 1961), pp. 10-13.

96. ———, "A Collective Bargaining Game at the University," *Journal of the American Society of Training Directors,* Vol. XVI, No. 1 (January 1962), pp. 12-17.

97. Fulmer, J. L., *Business Simulation Games.* Chicago: South-Western Publishing Company, 1963.

98. Gainen, L. R., R. A. Levine, and W. H. McGlothin, *Baselogs—A Base Logistics Management Game.* The RAND Corporation, 1958.

99. Gearon, J. D., "Labor vs. Management: A Simulation Game," *Social Education* (October 1966), pp. 421-422.

100. Geisler, M. A., *Determining Preferred Management Techniques in New Systems Through Game Simulation.* The RAND Corporation, 1962.

101. ———, and W. A. Steger, "How to Plan for Management in New Systems," *Harvard Business Review,* Vol. XL (September-October 1962), pp. 103-110.

102. Glass, A. J., "Columbia Firm Shows Big Deficit Selling Gismos in Business Games," *New York Herald Tribune* (March 26, 1960).

103. Goldschmidt, K., "Comments on Business Games," *OR JORSA,* Vol. VI, No. 1 (February 1958).

104. Gray, Clifford F., and Robert G. Graham, "Do Games Point to Managerial Success?" *Training in Business and Industry,* Vol. V, No. 6 (June 1968), pp. 36-38.

105. Gray, J., *et al.,* "Business Game for the Introductory Course in Accounting," *Accounting Review,* Vol. XXXVIII (April 1963), pp. 336-346.

106. Grayson, C. Jackson, *Decisions Under Uncertainty: Drilling Decisions by Oil and Gas Operators.* Boston: Harvard University School of Business, Division of Research, 1960.

107. Greene, Jay R., "Business Gaming and Marketing," *Marketing Keys to Profit in the 1960's.* Wenzil K. Dolva (ed.), Chicago: American Marketing Association, 1960, pp. 67-77.

108. ———, "Business Gaming for Marketing Decisions," *Journal of Marketing,* Vol. XXV, No. 1 (1960), pp. 21-25.

109. ———, and R. L. Sisson, *Dynamic Management Decisions Game, Including Seven Noncomputer Games.* New York: John Wiley & Sons, 1959.

110. Greenlaw, P. S., L. W. Herron, and R. H. Rawdon, *Business Simula-

tion in Industrial and University Education. New York: Prentice-Hall, Inc., 1962.

111. ———, "Dayton Tire Simulation—A Marketing Game," *Marketing Concepts in Changing Times,* Richard M. Hill (ed.). Chicago: American Marketing Association, 1960, pp. 316-327.

112. ———, "Designing Parametric Equations for Business Games," *Academy of Management Journal,* Vol. VI, No. 2 (June 1963), p. 150.

113. ———, "Marketing Simulations—Problems and Prospects," *Marketing: A Maturing Discipline,* Martin L. Bell (ed.). Chicago: American Marketing Association, 1961, pp. 68-74.

114. ———, and Stanford S. Knight, "The Human Factor in Business Games," *Business Horizons* (Fall 1960), pp. 55-61.

115. Greenwald, H., "Putting Reality into a Game," *Automatic Data Processing,* Vol. IV, No. 5 (May 1962).

116. Guetzkow, H., *Training for Policy-Making Roles Through Organizational Simulation* (Proceedings, 14th Annual Conference). Chicago: American Society of Training Directors, 1958.

117. Haines, G. H., "The Rote Marketer," *Behavioral Science,* Vol. VI, No. 4 (October 1961), p. 357.

118. Haldi, John, and Harvey M. Wagner, *Simulated Economic Models.* Homewood, Illinois: Richard D. Irwin, Inc., 1963.

119. Hamburger, W., *Monopologs, An Inventory Management Game,* The RAND Corporation, 1956.

120. Hammerton, M., "Measures for the Efficiency of Simulators as Training Devices," *Ergonomics,* Vol. X, No. 1, pp. 63-65.

121. Hanan, Mack, "Who Picks Up the Marketing Marbles?" *Industrial Marketing,* Vol. L, No. 5 (May 1965), pp. 108-124.

122. Harling, John, "Simulation Techniques in Operations Research—A Review," *Operations Research,* Vol. VI (1958), pp. 307-319.

123. Hawkes, R., "Computer Simulates Executives' Problems," *Aviation Week and Space Technology* (June 18, 1962).

124. Hellebrandt, E. T., and W. D. Fleishhacker, *General Business Management Simulation.* Athens, Ohio: Ohio University, 1959.

125. ———, and ———, *Ohio University Executive Development Program.* Athens, Ohio: Ohio University, 1959.

126. Herder, John H., "Do-It-Yourself Business Games (Noncomputer Simulation)," *Journal of the American Society of Training Directors,* Vol. XIV (September 1960), pp. 3-8.

127. "Here's a Realistic Way to Play Wholesaler," *Business Week* (September 3, 1960), pp. 108-112.

128. Herron, Lowell W., *Executive Action Simulation.* Englewood Cliffs, New Jersey: Prentice-Hall, Inc., 1960.

129. Hickok, W. H., *A Bibliography of Research Studies on Games and*

Simulations. Portland, Oregon: Northwest Regional Educational Laboratory, 1967.

130. Hoffman, T. R., "Programmed Heuristics and the Concept of Par in Business Games," *Behavioral Science,* Vol. X, No. 2 (1965), pp. 169-172.

131. Hoggatt, Austin C., "An Experimental Business Game," *Behavioral Science,* Vol. IV, No. 3 (1959), pp. 192-203.

132. ———, *Simulation of the Firm,* Research Paper RC-16, International Business Machines Corporation, 1957.

133. ———, and F. E. Balderston (eds.), *Symposium in Simulation Models: Methodology and Applications to the Behavioral Sciences.* Cincinnati, Ohio: South-Western Publishing Company, 1963.

134. Holland, Edward P., "Simulation of an Economy with Development and Trade Problems," *American Economic Review,* Vol. VII, No. 3 (1962), pp. 408-430.

135. Hunter, G. T., *Management Experience in Business Gaming,* International Business Machines Corporation, 1958.

136. Hutte, Herman, "Decision-Making in a Management Game," *Human Relations,* Vol. XVIII, No. 1 (1965), pp. 5-20.

137. "In Business Education, the Game's the Thing," *Business Week* (July 25, 1959), pp. 54-64.

138. "In the Pitt-Amstan Marketing Game," *Business Week* (September 3, 1960), pp. 108-112.

139. "Intercollegiate Business Games," *Business Week* (November 28, 1959), pp. 177-178.

140. "It's Almost Like Working," *Business Week* (August 4, 1962), pp. 94-95.

141. Jackson, James R., *Business Gaming in Management Science Education* (Proceedings of the Sixth International Meeting of the Institute of Management Sciences in Paris), 1961, pp. 250-262.

142. ———, "Learning from Experience in Business Decision Games," *California Management Review,* Vol. I, No. 2 (1959), pp. 92-107.

143. ———, *UCLA Management Game No. 1: Instructions for Players* (Management Sciences Project Discussion Paper No. 64). Los Angeles: University of California at Los Angeles, 1958.

144. ———, and Kendall R. Wright, *UCLA Executive Game No. 2: Mathematical Model and Computer Code* (Management Sciences Project, Discussion Paper No. 70). Los Angeles: University of California at Los Angeles, 1958.

145. ———, "Simulation Research on Job Shop Production," *Naval Research Logistics Quarterly,* Vol. IV, No. 4 (December 1957).

146. Jensen, B. T., "Business Games for Executive Training," *Advanced Management Office Executive,* Vol. II (June 1963), pp. 13-14.

147. Johnston, Donald R., "An Evaluation of the Business Decision Game," *Journal of the American Society of Training Directors,* Vol. XV (May 1961), pp. 33-41.

148. Kennedy, M., "A Business Game for Accountants," *Journal of Accounting* (March 1962).

149. Kepner, Charles H., and Benjamin B. Tregoe, "Developing Decision Makers," *Harvard Business Review,* Vol. XXXVIII (September-October 1960), pp. 115-124.

150. Keyes, Raymond F., *A Survey of Business Simulation.* Boston: Boston College Graduate School of Business, 1960.

151. Khemakhem, Abdellatif, "A Simulation of Management-Decision Behavior," *The Accounting Review,* Vol. XLIII, No. 3 (July 1968), pp. 522-534.

152. Kibbee, Joel M., "Dress Rehearsal for Decision-Making: The Growing Use of Business Games," *Management Review,* Vol. XLVIII (February 1959), pp. 4-8, 71-73.

153. ———, "Management Control Simulation," Donald G. Malcolm and Alan J. Rowe (eds.), *Management Control Systems.* New York: John Wiley & Sons, 1960.

154. ———, et al., *Management Games.* New York: Reinhold Book Corporation, 1961.

155. ———, "Management Games and Computers," *Proceedings of the Western Joint Computer Conference.* Papers presented at the Joint IRE-AIEE-ACM Computer Conference, Los Angeles, May 9-11, 1961.

156. King, Peter S., *et al.,* "The M.I.T. Marketing Game," Martin L. Bell (ed.), *Marketing: A Maturing Discipline.* Chicago: American Marketing Association, 1961, pp. 85-102.

157. Klasson, Charles R., "Business Gaming: A Progress Report," *Academy of Management Journal,* Vol. VII, No. 3 (September 1964), pp. 175-188.

158. Klingensmith, V. Terry, "Hospitals Have In-Baskets, Too!" *Training Directors Journal,* Vol. XVII (August 1963), pp. 13-17.

159. Kniffin, Fred W., "Opportunities for Management Games," Richard Hill (ed.), *Marketing Concepts in Changing Times.* Chicago: American Marketing Association, 1960, pp. 328-336.

160. Kuehn, Alfred A., and Doyle L. Weiss, "Marketing Analysis Training Exercise," *Behavioral Science,* Vol. X, No. 1 (1965), pp. 51-67.

161. ———, and R. L. Day, "Simulation and Operational Gaming," W. Alderson and S. Shapiro (eds.), *Marketing and the Computer.* Englewood Cliffs, New Jersey: Prentice-Hall, Inc., 1962.

162. "Learning Can Be Fun—Even for Busy Executives," *Business Week* (May 4, 1957), pp. 164-170.

163. Lett, H. V., *Simulation of an Industry for Use as a Management*

Training Game, M.I.T., School of Industrial Management (B.S. thesis), 1961.

164. Lubin, John Francis, "Simplified Management Decisions Games," Wharton School of Finance and Commerce, University of Pennsylvania (April 23, 1959).

165. MacCrimmon, K. R., and James R. Jackson, *A Hand-Computed Version of UCLA Executive Game No. 2,* Management Sciences Research Project, Research Report 59. University of California at Los Angeles, May 1959.

166. McDonald, John, and Franc Ricciardi, "The Business-Decision Game," *Fortune,* Vol. LVII, No. 3 (March 1958).

167. McGehee, William, "Business Games: Where They Fit into Training," *Textile World* (January 1966), pp. 68-71.

168. McGill, Don, "Decisions, Decisions, Decisions," *Industrial Distribution* (June 1960), pp. 115-130.

169. McGuinness, John S., "A Managerial Game for an Insurance Company," *Operations Research,* Vol. VIII (March-April 1960), pp. 196-209.

170. McKenney, James L., "An Evaluation of Business Games as a Learning Experience," *Journal of Business,* Vol. XXXV (1962), pp. 278-286.

171. ———, and W. R. Dill, "Influences on Learning in Simulation Games," *American Behavioral Scientist,* Vol. X, No. 2 (October 1966), pp. 28-32.

172. ———, *Simulation Gaming for Management Development.* Boston: Division of Research, Graduate School of Business Administration, Harvard University, 1967.

173. McManus, G. J., "New League for Business Games," *Iron Age,* Vol. CLXXV (February 4, 1960), p. 49.

174. McRaith, J. F., and C. R. Goeldner, "A Survey of Marketing Games," *Journal of Marketing,* Vol. XXVI, No. 3 (1962), pp. 69-72.

175. Maffei, R. B., "Simulation Sensitivity and Management Decision Rules," *Journal of Business,* Vol. XXXI, No. 3 (July 1958), pp. 177-186.

176. Malcolm, Donald G., "Bibliography on the Use of Simulation in Management Analysis," *Operations Research,* Vol. VIII (1960), pp. 169-177.

177. ———, *et al.,* "CREMEX—A Research and Development Management Simulation Exercise," *Management Technology,* Vol. III, No. 2 (December 1963).

178. "Management on Maneuvers: Business Games and Human Relations Labs Are New Trends in Training," *Chemical Week,* Vol. VC (October 17, 1964), pp. 71-74.

179. "Management Society Plays Economic War on Univac Battlefield," *Advertising Age,* Vol. XXXI (March 28, 1960), p. 28.

180. *Mantrap: Management Training Program. The Player's Manual.* Houston, Texas: University of Houston Press, College of Business Administration, Center for Research in Business and Economics, 1963.

181. Martin, E. W., Jr., *Management Decision Simulation.* Homewood, Illinois: Richard D. Irwin, Inc., 1960.

182. ———, "Teaching Executives via Simulation," *Business Horizons,* Vol. II (Summer 1959), pp. 100-109.

183. Massy, William F., Peter S. King, and C. Davis Fogg, "The Place of a Business Game in the Marketing Curriculum," *Industrial Management Review,* Vol. II (May 1961), pp. 43-58.

184. Mattessich, Richard, *Simulation of the Firm Through a Budget Computer Program.* Homewood, Illinois: Richard D. Irwin, Inc., 1964.

185. Mayer, C. S., and F. C. Herringer, "When Management Plays Games," *Credit and Financial Management,* Vol. LXVII (June 1965), pp. 16-17+.

186. Meier, Robert C., "Decision Making Versus Strategy Determination: A Gaming and Heuristic Approach," *University of Washington Business Review,* Vol. XXV, No. 4 (April-June 1966), pp. 34-41.

187. Mellor, P., and K. D. Tocher, "Steel Works Production Game," *Operational Research Quarterly,* Vol. XIV (June 1963), pp. 131-135.

188. Merrill, Harwood F., "Running a Company—By Simulation," *Management News* (September 1959).

189. Mikula, A., "Academic Games," *Pennsylvania Schools Journal,* Vol. CXVI (1968), p. 538.

190. Million, E. Z., "The Production Model of a Petroleum Management Game," *Journal of Petroleum Technology* (September 1962).

191. ———, *The University of Oklahoma Petroleum Game,* Oklahoma University Research Institute (April 1962).

192. Moore, L. B., "Experiencing Reality in Management Education," *Journal of the Academy of Management* (October 1958), pp. 7-14.

193. Moravec, A. F., "Using Simulation to Design a Management Information System," *Management Services,* Vol. III, No. 3 (1966), pp. 50-58.

194. Nanus, Burt, "Management Games: An Answer to the Critics," *Journal of Industrial Engineering,* Vol. XIII, No. 6 (November-December 1962), pp. 467-469.

195. ———, "Univac Games for Marketing Education," Martin L. Bell (ed.), *Marketing: A Maturing Discipline.* Chicago: American Marketing Association (1961), pp. 57-67.

196. Nicholson, B., "Sales Management Plays the Game," *Sales Management,* Vol. LXXXVIII (January 19, 1962), pp. 43-47.

197. "Oil Industry Makes a Big Move into Business Games," *Petroleum Week,* Vol. XII (February 17, 1961), pp. 68-69.

198. "120 Businessmen Play Mass Management Game," *Computers and Automation,* Vol. X (July 1961), pp. 11B-12B.

199. Pelaez, Jose Gil, "Un Laboratorio do Decisiones: El Business Game," *Arbor,* Vol. CLXIII, No. 4 (July-August 1959), pp. 365-371.

200. "Pick a Problem: Build a Business Game," *Sales Management,* Vol. LXXXVIII (April 20, 1962), pp. 81-82.

201. Porter, George, "Learning Through the Use of Small Games and Puzzles," *Journal of the American Society of Training Directors,* Vol. XV (March 1961), pp. 13-21.

202. "Price Agreements: An Experiment with a Complex Business Game," *The Quarterly Review of Economics and Business,* Vol. VI, No. 3 (Autumn 1966), pp. 53-62.

203. *Proceedings of the National Symposium on Management Games.* Lawrence, Kansas: The University of Kansas (May 1959).

204. *Production-Manpower Decision Game, General Description (Processed).* New Orleans: Tulane University Computer Center, n.d.

205. "Profits Set Score at B-School Tournament," *Business Week* (March 18, 1968), pp. 156-158.

206. "Putting Executives in the Goldfish Bowl: With Closed Circuit TV and Group Analysis, Top Men at RCA Are Observed as They React to Simulated Problems," *Business Week* (September 2, 1961), pp. 162-164.

207. Raia, Anthony P., "A Study of the Educational Value of Management Games," *The Journal of Business,* Vol. XXXIX, No. 3 (July 1966), pp. 339-352.

208. Rankin, James F., "The Game that Leaves Nothing to Chance," *Food Business* (November 1959), pp. 15-18.

209. Rawdon, R. H., *Learning Management Skills from Simulation Gaming.* Ann Arbor, Michigan: University of Michigan, Bureau of Industrial Relations, 1960.

210. Ray, C., "Play the Game," *The Director,* Vol. XI, No. 8 (February 1959), p. 283.

211. Redfield, C. E., "Should Business Men Play Management Games?" *Office,* Vol. LIII (June 1961), pp. 14-15+.

212. Reed, L. R., *A Study of the Feasibility of Using Operational Simulation Techniques for Evaluating Administrative Skills Possessed by Instructional Communications Specialist.* (Unpublished Ph.D. dissertation.) Syracuse, New York: Syracuse University, 1966.

213. Renshaw, Jean Rehkop, and Annette Heuston, *The Game Monopologs.* The RAND Corporation, RM-1917-1 (July 17, 1957) revised March 31, 1960.

214. Ricciardi, Franc M., "Business War Games for Executives: A New Concept in Management Training," *Management Review,* Vol. XLVI, No. 5 (May 1957), pp. 45-56.

215. ———, "Top Management Decision-Making Simulation," *Report of System Simulation Symposium, American Institute of Industrial Engineers* (1958), pp. 42-46.

216. ———, *et al., Top Management Decision-Making Simulation: The AMA Approach.* New York: American Management Association, Inc. (1957).

217. ———, "Training in Decision-Making," *Paper Trade Journal* (June 23, 1958), pp. 36-37.

218. Richards, Max D., and Fred W. Kniffin, "Business Decision Games—A New Management Tool," *Pennsylvania Business Survey,* Vol. I (June 1960), pp. 4-9, and Vol. I (July 1960), pp. 7-10.

219. Robbins, Robert M., "Decision-Making Simulation Through Business Games," *Journal of the American Society of Training Directors,* Vol. XIII (September 1959), pp. 12-19.

220. Roberts, Arthur L., "What's Wrong with Business Games?" *The Journal of Industrial Engineering,* Vol. XIII, No. 6 (November-December 1962), pp. 465-467.

221. Robinson, Patrick J., "Cases in Simulation: A Research Aid as a Management 'Demonstration Piece,' " *Report of System Simulation Symposium, American Institute· of Industrial Engineers.* Baltimore, Maryland: Waverly Press (1958), pp. 47-58.

222. Roelofs, T. B., and A. D. Tholen, "A Simulation and Gaming System, SIGMALOG: General Description," *Research Analysis Corporation* (August 1967).

223. Rowe, A. J., and R. R. Smith, "Now Training for Production Is a Play-It-to-Win Game," *Factory Management and Maintenance,* Vol. CXVI, No. 3 (March 1958), pp. 146-148.

224. "Sales Game," *Sales Management,* Vol. C, No. 6, Part I (March 15, 1968), pp. 59-70.

225. "Sales Game," *Sales Management,* Vol. C, No. 7, Part II (April 1, 1968), pp. 45-56.

226. "Sales Strategy Game," *Sales Management,* Vol. C, No. 6, Part II (March 15, 1968), pp. 63-78.

227. Schellenberger, R. E., "Computerized, Multipurpose Management Game Applied to Retailing," *Journal of Retailing,* Vol. XL (Winter 1965-1966), pp. 10-20.

228. Schelling, T. C., "Experimental Games and Bargaining Theory," *World Politics,* Vol. XIV (October 1961), pp. 47-68.

229. Schrieber, A. N., "Gaming—A Way to Teach Business Decision-Mak-

ing," *University of Washington Business Review,* Vol. XVII, No. 7 (April 1958), pp. 18-29.

230. ———, "The Theory and Application of the Management Game Approach to Teaching Business Policy," *Journal of the Academy of Management,* Vol. I (August 1958), pp. 51-57.

231. Shubik, Martin, *A Short Bibliography on Simulation, Gaming, and Allied Topics.* New York: Operations Research and Synthesis Consultation Service, General Electric Company (May 1959).

232. ———, *Business Gaming.* Expository and Development Paper No. 5. New York: General Electric Company (June 9, 1958).

233. ———, "Games, Decisions and Industrial Organization," *Management Science,* Vol. VI, No. 4 (July 1960), pp. 455-474.

234. ———, *Simulation, Its Uses and Potential.* Expository and Development Paper No. 2, Parts I/II. New York: General Electric Company (June 1958).

235. ———, "Simulation of the Firm," *The Journal of Industrial Engineering* (September-October 1958), pp. 390-391.

236. ———, "Simulation of the Industry and the Firm," *American Economic Review,* Vol. L, No. 5, pp. 908-919.

237. Shure, Gerald H., and Robert J. Meaker, *Bargaining and Negotiation Behavior,* Technical Memorandum No. TM-2304/100/00. Santa Monica, California: System Development Corporation (February 1967).

238. "Simplifying Management Games for Extension Programs," *Journal of Farm Economics,* Vol. XLVIII, No. 4, Part I (November 1966), pp. 1026-1027.

239. *Simulation and Gaming: A Symposium,* AMA Management Report 55 (1961).

240. "Simulation Film Now Available," *Industrial Distribution,* Vol. C (August 1960), pp. 84-85.

241. Sisson, R. L., "Games," *Systems and Procedures Journal,* Vol. XII (May 1961), pp. 32-36.

242. Six TATHAM-LAIRD Marketing Teams Match Wits, Skill with IBM 650 Unit," *Advertising Age,* Vol. XXXI (May 23, 1960), p. 134.

243. *The Small Business Executive Decision Simulation: Operating Manual.* Austin, Texas: University of Texas, Bureau of Business Research, 1963.

244. Smith, Adair, *et al.,* "General Motors Institute Experiences with Business Gaming," *Journal of the American Society of Training Directors,* Vol. XV (April 1961), pp. 27-32.

245. Smith, Charles, "What's in the Box, Doc?" *Journal of the American Society of Training Directors,* Vol. XV (January 1961), pp. 27-31.

246. Smith, R. M., "AMA Introduces 'War-Game' Principle to Train Ex-

ecutives in Decision-Making," *Office Management and Equipment,*
Vol. XVIII, No. 6 (June 1957), pp. 28-31.

247. Smith, Robert M., "Management Games Toy or Trend?" *Office Management and American Business* (September 1960), p. 15.

248. *Some Educational Games Designed by Abt Associates, Inc.,* Cambridge, Massachusetts: Abt Associates (December 1967).

249. Spooner, Peter, "A Game of Managers," *Business* (February 1959), pp. 77-79.

250. Sprowls, R. Clay, and M. Asimow, "A Computer Simulated Business Firm," D. G. Malcolm, *et al.* (eds.), *Management Control System.* New York: John Wiley & Sons (1960), pp. 321-322.

251. Stanley, J. D., "Management Games: Education or Entertainment?" *Personnel Journal,* Vol. XLI (January 1962), pp. 15-17+.

252. Starbuck, W. H., and E. Kobrow, "The Effects of Advisors on Business Game Teams," *American Behavioral Science,* Vol. X, No. 3, Part II (1966), pp. 28-30.

253. Steele, J. C., "Simulated Management Experience: Some Comments on Business Games," *Kansas Business Review* (October 1958).

254. Steger, Joseph A., "A Simple but Effective Business Game for Undergraduates," *Journal of Business Education,* Vol. XLIII, No. 5 (1968), pp. 202-205.

255. Steger, Wilbur A., *The Use of Gaming and Simulation Devices in Business.* Santa Monica, California: The RAND Corporation, 1957, p. 1219.

256. Steinmetz, Lawrence L., "Management Games—Computer Versus Non-Computer," *Journal of the American Society of Training Directors,* Vol. XVI, No. 9 (September 1962), pp. 38-45.

257. Stenberg, V. A., "The Business Game of the American Management Association," *Encyclopaedia Britannica Library Research Service.*

258. Stephens, Warren S., "A Business Game in Orientation," *Journal of the Society of Training Directors,* Vol. XVI, No. 11 (October 1962), pp. 55-57.

259. Stern, M. E., "Catalytic Power of Business-Decision Gaming in Teaching Management Science," *Computers and Automation,* Vol. XI, No. 11 (November 1962), pp. 12-14+.

260. Stessin, Lawrence, "Managing Your Manpower," *Dun's Review and Modern Industry,* Vol. LXXV (April 1960), p. 83.

261. Stone, M. M., *Supermarket Battle Maneuvers, A Management Game,* Burroughs Corporation, Electro Data Division.

262. "Sylvania's Sugar-Coated Training Pill," *Sales Management,* Vol. LXXXIV (January 15, 1960), pp. 38-39.

263. Symonds, Clifford H., "A Study of Management Behavior by Use of

Competitive Business Games," *Management Science,* Vol. II, No. 1 (September 1964), pp. 135-153.

264. Teaching Research, *Instructional Uses of Simulation: A Selected Bibliography.* Monmouth, Oregon: Oregon State System of Higher Education, 1969.

265. Thompson, D. L., "Next Sales Meeting, Try a Game," *Journal of Marketing,* Vol. XXVII, No. 1 (January 1963), pp. 71-74.

266. Thorelli, Hans B., "Integrated Use of Simulations in Management Education," *Personnel Journal,* Vol. XL, No. 2 (1964), pp. 67-71.

267. ———, "An International Business Operations Game," *Data Processing,* Vol. IV, No. 10 (1962), pp. 22-27.

268. ———, "Game Simulation of Administrative Systems," Wroe Alderson and Stanley J. Shapiro (eds.), *Marketing and the Computer.* Englewood Cliffs, New Jersey: Prentice-Hall, Inc., 1963, pp. 334-348.

269. ———, Robert L. Graves, and Lloyd Howells, "The International Operations Simulation at the University of Chicago," *The Journal of Business,* Vol. XXXV, No. 3 (July 1962), pp. 287-297.

270. ———, and Robert L. Graves, *International Operations Simulation: With Comments on Design and Use of Management Games.* New York: The Free Press, 1964.

271. *Top Management Decision Simulation.* New York: American Management Association, 1957.

272. Torgersen, P. E., and G. B. Thomas, "Simulating an Acceptance Sampling Plan," *Industrial Quality Control,* Vol. XX, No. 6 (1963), pp. 27-29, 32.

273. Tracey, W. R., E. B. Flynn, Jr., and C. L. Legere, "Systems Approach Gets Results," *Training in Business and Industry,* Vol. IV, No. 6 (June 1967), pp. 17-21.

274. "200 Play in Five-City Business Game," *Steel,* Vol. CXLVI (March 14, 1960), pp. 52-53.

275. University Council for Education Administration, *Simulation in Administrative Trainees.* Columbus, Ohio, 1960.

276. "Use of Simulation Procedures," *Journal of Farm Economics,* Vol. XLV, No. 4 (November 1963), pp. 876-877.

277. Vance, Stanley C., *Management Decision Simulation.* New York: McGraw-Hill Book Company, 1960.

278. ———, and Clifford F. Gray, *Management Decision Simulation: A Computer Manual.* Eugene, Oregon: University of Oregon, Graduate School of Business, 1965.

279. ———, "Management Simulation Games," *Chicago Sales and Marketing News* (July 1965), pp. 5-6.

280. ———, and Clifford F. Gray, "Use of a Performance Evaluation Model

for Research in Business Gaming," *Academy of Management Journal,* Vol. X, No. 1 (March 1967), pp. 27-37.

281. "War Games for Business Men from a Correspondent Who Plays Them," *The Economist* (June 29, 1957), p. 1161.

282. Ward, Lewis B., "The Use of Simulation of Business Problems," *Management Record,* Vol. XXII, No. 6 (1960), pp. 30-33.

283. Watkins, H. F., "Business Games in Business," *Operational Research Quarterly,* Vol. X, No. 4 (December 1959), pp. 228-244.

284. "What Three Men Learned by Playing the Sales Game," *The American Salesman,* Vol. V, No. 12 (August 1960), pp. 61-65.

285. Wikstrom, W. S., "The Serious Business of Business Games," *Management Record,* Vol. XXII, No. 2 (February 1960), pp. 6-8.

286. Wilkinson, R. K., and G. Mills, "The Use of a Business Game in Management Training," *Journal of Industrial Engineering,* Vol. XVI, No. 4 (1965), pp. 282-285.

287. Williams, E. H., "Business Games: Their Use for the Training of Managers," *Personnel Management,* Vol. XLIII (December 1961), pp. 239-244.

288. Wollaston, Justin G. F., "The Name of the Game Is Gaming," *Systems and Procedures Journal,* Vol. XIX, No. 1, Issue 87 (January-February 1968), pp. 24-26.

289. Wright, K. R., *et al., U.C.L.A. Executive Game No. 2 Computing Instructions.* Discussion Paper No. 69. Los Angeles, California: University of California at Los Angeles, April, 1958.

290. Yokoyama, T., Y. Osawa, and K. Yamaoka, *Business Game.* Tokyo, Japan: Nippon Keizai Shinbun Sha, 1960, p. 303.

291. "Your Wits Versus the Computer's: Bank Simulation Game Is Officer Training Gimmick," *Banking,* Vol. LIII, No. 2 (August 1960), p. 54+.

292. Zimmerman, John W., "Business Gaming" (Abstract of Speech), *Journal of the American Society of Training Directors,* Vol. XIV, No. 7 (July 1960), pp. 25-27.

293. ———, and Seymour Levy, "Decision Simulation for Top Management Training," *Journal of the American Society of Training Directors,* Vol. XIV, No. 5 (May 1960), pp. 3-11.

294. ———, "Non-Mathematical Simulation—Dynamic Development Guide," *Journal of the American Society of Training Directors,* Vol. XVI, No. 6 (June 1962), pp. 30-35.

295. Zoll, A. A., *Business Games in Management Training at the Boeing Airplane Company.* Seattle: Boeing Airplane Company, n.d.

Index of Sources